What Reviewers Say About Walton's Books

"The best portrait we have of Norman Rockwell. A delightful glimpse into his private and public life. Like his work, this book about him is warm, homey, unpretentious and frequently amusing." **St. Louis Globe-Democrat**

"Rockwell is fortunate in this admiring biography written by a good friend and associate. Donald Walton has done a careful job of documenting his hero's life." **New York Times**

"One of the 100 best books of the year" **Philadelphia Inquirer**

"A superb portrait in words. This book has an easy style, as if the author were having a casual conversation. Walton has done a superb job of giving us an insight into a very special person." **Chatanooga Times**

"This book is highly readable with a pleasantly anecdotal text. Should become a winner with the general public." **Library Journal**

"Donald Walton's biography is an exceptionally well-written book. A biography to be read and treasured." **Roanoke Times**

"This is a lovely biography. Welcome for its insight into a man who can accurately be called one of the most popular artists of his time." **Mineapolis Times**

More Reviews of Donald Walton's Books

ABOUT " ARE YOU COMMUNICATING"

"Are You Communicating is a well-researched and well-presented book with plenty of quotes, quizzes and quips to allow for a 10-minute skim or a cover-to-cover plunge. The author is practical and entertaining. For a fun read with some worthwhile advice, this book will be a welcome addition to anyone's library." **Wyoming State Tribune**

"One of the best business books of the year." **Library Journal**

"Provides valuable tips on improving comunication. The advice Walton offers is easy to swallow because it is engagingly organized and written." **The Kansas City Times**

"This book is a shot in the arm for all of us who communicate." **Communication Briefings**

"Managers seeking to improve their ability to communicate will benefit from the advice Walton offers. The fact that he offers that advice in a visually-appealing, fun-to-read format is all the better." **Chicago Tribune**

"Walton's book is loaded with tips on the do's and dont's of verbal and non-verbal communication. It's an excellent guide to help you examine and streamline the way you interact with others at work and play." **Waterbury Ct. Daily**

Our Weird Wonderful Ancestors

Soap - Opera Stories of Life and Love in 1776

Donald Walton

ARCHER &
WILLIAMS

Publisher's Cataloging-in-Publication
(Provided by Quality Books, Inc.)

Walton, Donald (Donald W.)
    Our weird wonderful ancestors: intimate tales of their
lives and loves in 1776 / Donald Walton. -- 1st ed.
    p. cm.
    Bibliography: p.
    Includes index.
    Preassigned LCCN: 98-70123
    ISBN: 0-9662625-4-9

    1. United States-- Social life and customs-- 1775-1783. 2.
United States-- History-- Revolution, 1775-1783--Anecdotes.
1. Title.

E163.W35 1998   973.3
                           QBI98-199

First Edition - 1998
Manufactured in the United States of America.
098765432

Book design and jacket/cover by Dennis Atkinson - Icon Studios.
Type computer set in New Times Roman 12-point.
Printed by Thomson-Shore in Dexter, Michigan.

To EDITH
a kindly critic
my support in times of stress
the light of my life

ALSO BY DONALD WALTON

Are You Communicating?

A Rockwell Portrait

Art Is To Enjoy

Contents

Why This Book Was Written

Everyone knows about the glorious achievements of the patriots who began their fight for America's independence in 1776. They were magnificent people whose names and deeds are written large in thousands of history books.

But heroes and heroines are human too. Truth is that the great ones who founded our nation were tough, ornery, lusty people-- often stranger than the characters in a modern-day soap opera. Wilder too! Don't be surprised at that. Timid, mousy, predictable folks are not the ones who perform incredible deeds and change the course of history.

Don't be suprised either if you discover that many things the heroes and heroines of 1776 did in their struggle for independence were far different from the myths that have grown up around them. History is often truth prettied up and varnished over with the soft patina of time. You can take the words of a couple of experts for that.

"What is history but a lie agreed upon?"
Napoleon Bonaparte
"It's just one damned thing after another."
Harry S. Truman

If you sometimes ask *"What's the world coming to?"* you can be assured it's not coming to anything new. The hijinks of high society that titillate us today are often reruns of escapades that took place a couple of centuries ago, for newspapers then were as packed with the antics and amorous adventures of celebrities and their spouses and mistresses as tabloids and television shows are today.

Life was rough and raw back in 1776 and the years following. Politics was nasty, rife with name-calling that often led to shooting. Families, including the most prestigious, had their hidden scandals. Alcoholism, adultery, bigamy, sexual abuse, slandering, swindling-- any perfidies you care to name-- were present then as now.

Lifestyles of the Famous
Of the approximately two and a half millions who lived in America during the War for Independence, most led dull existences filled with laboring from dawn to dusk. Their stories shed little light on the times except to confirm that life was hard.

That's why the intimate portraits in this book focus mostly on famous people of that era, both in America and the mother countries of England and Europe. They were the movers and shakers who spearheaded the changes which took place. And besides being more illuminating, let's face it-- their stories are more fun!

Among them you'll find virtuous heroes and heroines. Others were rogues of the wickedest sort. But you'll discover that *many were both,* for human nature is seldom totally pure or totally bad.

"No one of us, no, not one, is perfect."
Thomas Jefferson

What Your Teachers Never Told You
In these intimate portraits, you'll discover things you never imagined about what life was really like in 1776, both in the royal palaces of Europe and in humble colonial homes.

America was a frontier land where you'd find many strange people, customs and activities. For example-- bundling and bigamous brides, tarts and transvestites, boozing and bear-baiting, gambling and gamboling.

Does that sound like the activities of a rowdy crowd? It was. Not so surprising, since many of our ancestors came from the lowest and most unruly levels of society in the Old World. Those trouble-makers were packed aboard ships, sometimes in chains, for the wild shores of America where they faced a long term of often killing labor.

The toughest ones lived. And begot us.

An Intimate View

Some years ago when I lived in the Philadelphia area, about midway between Valley Forge and the bloody battlefield of the Brandywine, I began to search out many true stories of those involved in our War for Independence. The more surprising things I discovered about the men, women and children of that time, and the way they lived, the more fascinated I became.

That led me to believe that all Americans ought to know more about our diverse ancestors-- the royalists as well as the rebels, the swingers as well as the steadfast citizens. Here I've tried my best to present a fresh unvarnished view of how they lived, loved and survived in a time of fierce civil war.

They were truly great people. But they were also *human* as they stumbled along through the soap-opera aspects of their lives. Like us, you might say.

It's time you got to know them better... *time to learn the secrets of their lives and loves.*

D. W.

Mr. and Mrs. John Hancock (the former Dorothy Quincy) painted by Edward Savage. Known as the "financier of the Revolution, he later served as the Governor of Massachusetts for nine terms.

1
The Fairy-Tale Life
of John Hancock

If you have the common misconception that all of our illustrious forefathers were prim and proper fuddy-duddies, learning the truth about Hancock's private life should quickly dispel that myth. The most eligible bachelor in New England, John was the 1700s equivalent of a media star. Rich and fun-loving, he was the sort of off-beat celebrity who'd be the darling of our paparazzi and TV talk show hosts today.

A flamboyant character who loved attention, he looked and acted like a royal prince. He was called *The Merchant Prince,* a title justified not only by his regal airs, but also his great wealth. John's life story is truly like a fairy tale... or a soap opera.

Traveling in Style
Maybe a good way to introduce you to the fabulous life of John Hancock is to imagine you could come face-to-face with him. Perhaps some evening in 1776 at the City Tavern in Philadelphia (still operating today) when he arrived with his entourage after a hard day at the nearby State House where he'd been presiding as head of the Second Continental Congress.

You couldn't miss his arrival. Hancock traveled in style-- in a huge yellow coach drawn by a matched team of six beautiful bay horses, and with four footmen in fancy purple velvet livery perched atop it. John certainly knew how to make an entrance.

He himself was just as colorful as his transportation. Even in his day, when wealthy men often affected fancy frilly clothing, Hancock was regarded as something of a peacock. He loved to wear gaudily-colored velvet suits embellished with oodles of lace and gold or silver embroidery. Wherever he appeared, his apparel made a fashion statement that attracted attention.

> **"John Hancock came in wearing a red velvet cap, a**
> **blue damask cape lined with velvet, a white lace stock,**
> **a white satin gold-embroidered waistcoat, black satin**
> **small clothes (knee-britches), red Morocco slippers**
> **and white silk stockings."**   Newspaper Report, 1776

Although John's wardrobe included a rainbow of colors, purple was by far his favorite. In fact, one biography of Hancock is titled, *"The Purple Patriot"*.

Called Many Names

As often happens with the rich and famous, Hancock had his share of critics who winced at his fancy airs. If anyone in Boston referred to the young *Merchant Prince,* perhaps with the raise of an eyebrow, you knew whom he meant.

Many thought John's fondness for purple, the royal color, and his ostentatious travel trappings were out of place for an anti-royalist. They sneered that Hancock fancied the style of the British king they disliked.

There may have been some truth to that charge. When he was 23, impressionable young John was sent to London on company business. There he witnessed the coronation of George III, an event that opened his eyes to the glamor of royal living. A line from his letter home attests to the impression it made.

> **"The coronation was the grandest thing that**
> **I shall ever meet with."**   John Hancock

When he had enough money of his own to emulate King George, Hancock did, and prided himself on the stir he made among the spectators.

Other detractors took issue with another facet of Hancock's life. They observed that some of the methods he used to augment the profits of his shipping firm were decidedly illegal. As a result, they called him *King of the Smugglers.*

From Orphan to Tycoon

It may be that many of his critics were motivated by jealousy, because Hancock's success story rivaled that of Cinderella's. He began life in a poor family, but lucked into a fortune.

When only nine years old, his clergyman father died, leaving the family penniless. His mother married another minister of modest means who'd have a hard time supporting her and her three children. She and her new husband decided that everyone would be better off if only her two youngest-- a boy and a girl-- stayed with her.

Nine-year-old John could go to live with his Aunt Lydia and Uncle Thomas, a childless couple who were willing to take the lad in.

Lydia and Thomas Hancock were rich, very rich. The elderly couple doted on their young nephew, and determined to give him every advantage. After sending the lucky boy to Harvard, where he graduated at 17, Uncle Thomas took him into the family business. That was a mercantile trading company which Uncle Thomas operated with a special twist that vastly increased its profitability.

Beating the Tax Collectors

Uncle Thomas had perfected a variety of techniques for evading the taxes which the British imposed on tea, wine and other commodities. This saved him a great deal of money.

One method he used was to hide expensive, heavily-taxed tea in large hogsheads that presumably contained cheap molasses for the rum distilleries. He also bribed the tax collectors, so they didn't go nosing around his ships' holds for undeclared taxables. The collectors were generally amenable to looking the other way. Poorly paid, they habitually received more income under the table than they did from their meager salaries.

Beating the British import duties any way you could was not considered a great crime by the Colonials, but Uncle Thomas did it exceedingly well. In fact, his tax shenanigans paid off so handsomely that he was able to keep four large merchant ships constantly moving between England and America. *As a result, he accumulated the largest fortune in New England.* When Uncle died, Nephew John was only 27 and the lucky heir to the whole money machine.

The Happy Bachelor

Some said that the heir to the smuggler's empire was not as astute as the founder of the firm had been. But he did alright, following in his uncle's footsteps in evading import duties.

Q: How often did John break the smuggling laws?

A: By the time war was imminent, he'd accumulated 500 citations for smuggling, but hadn't yet been hauled into court to pay any fines. If he'd paid all the penalties, they'd have been 100,000 pounds, or twice his net worth. Of course, after the fighting started, Hancock never did settle up. The war was a lifesaver for his business.

John worked hard, and played hard too. As you'd expect, the rich young Merchant Prince who was fond of partying never lacked for friends among the young ladies of Boston. Never robust as a child, he was slight of build, but had elegant manners, a gorgeous wardrobe, a happy likable personality...and all that money!

Mothers of marriageable daughters naturally eyed the most eligible bachelor, though they despaired of his ever settling down.

In an age when young men of means ordinarily married young, Hancock continued to lead an unfettered life all the way through his 30s. He was beginning to show some wear from his love of fine wines and rich food, however. The Gout, curse of the privileged class, caused John considerable pain at times.

In later years, his gout became so servere that it frequently kept him in bed. A note that appeared in the minutes of the Continental Congress in 1775 confirms that John was often bothered by this complaint.

> **"Mr. Hancock, having a touch of the gout,**
> **there was no President in the chair today."**
> Minutes of the Continental Congress

16

During his early bachelor days, however, his infirmities didn't seem to keep socialite John from many parties or slow him down very much.

Friend of the Merry Widow

During his bachelor days, there'd been lively gossip for years to the effect that Hancock evaded matrimony because he found adequate comfort in the cozy bed of the widow, Dorcas Griffith. That may or may not be true. Many of the stories that come down to us about famous historical characters present more than one version.

Some reports say that Dorcas Griffith operated a grocery store located in a building owned by Hancock, and that the Widow Dorcas and Bachelor John developed an affiliation more intimate than simply that of tenant and landlord. Supposedly, Hancock visited the little grocery store with surprising frequency and consulted Dorcas in the back room for long periods.

The Other Version

As is common with stories from the distant past, many historians dispute that any such romance could have existed. They maintain that Dorcas was not a grocer's widow, but the proprietress of a raunchy tavern near the Boston waterfront where you could purchase not only rum but also female companionship. So if John ever had anything to do with Dorcas, they say, it couldn't have been an exclusive involvement, because she shared her favors with a multitude of visitors.

So you can take your pick-- did the footloose bachelor have an affair with one of his tenants, or didn't he?

The Patient Girlfriend

Regardless of whether or not Hancock had an affair with a widowed grocer named Griffith, it is certain that he maintained a lengthy and peculiar courtship with a young lady more suitable to his station.

She was Dorothy Quincy. There seemed to be an implicit understanding that John and Dorothy would marry, at some time or other. This situation dragged on for more than four years. The peculiar aspect of their relationship was that during that lengthy period Dorothy lived at the Beacon Hill mansion occupied by John Hancock and his Aunt Lydia. In essence, she was part of the family before John ever got around to announcing any sort of formal bond.

Bankroller of the Revolution

Despite the fun-loving aspects of his bachelor days, John was far from just a playboy. He tended faithfully to the business affairs of the House of Hancock. He also became intensely interested in politics, through his membership in several clubs which prominent men joined for social camaraderie and discussion of current affairs.

In the early 1700s, Hancock and some of his fellow club members became increasingly vocal about the injustices they felt Americans, and especially merchants, were suffering from the British. Hancock was looked to as a leader of these rebels who hated British taxes and evaded them whenever they could.

When their rebellious talk finally progressed to the point of armed resistance to the Crown, creating a need for cash support, Hancock became the chief financial backer. Like any war, the revolt against the King cost money. Lots of money! Fortunately for our ancestors struggling to exert their independence, Hancock had deep pockets, and he was not reluctant to dig into them for the Patriot cause.

Along with his other titles, he was often known as the *Bankroller of the Revolution.* Luckily for us, Hancock earned that title, for without his liberal support, the War for Independence could have been derailed before it really got underway.

Off to Philadelphia

In 1775, after a band of drunken British soldiers rioted in the posh Beacon Hill section of Boston and threw rocks at the Hancock Mansion, John decided the situation was getting dangerous. He was sure of that when ardent rebel Paul Revere rode by his house one night to warn that a troop of British soldiers was on its way to arrest him. Hurriedly, Hancock packed up Aunt Lydia and dear friend Dorothy to hustle them out of town to safety.

They started off for nearby Lexington. Enroute, his fellow plotter, Samuel Adams, joined the trio as they evaded the unfriendly soldiers and travelled southward. Both John and Sam had been chosen to represent Massachusetts at the Second Continental Congress due to convene in Philadelphia, so that's where they headed.

Soon after arriving there, delegate Hancock was chosen to be President of the Continental Congress. That was the start of a long and distinguished career in our young nation's service.

Q: How much did Hancock's job pay?
A: Not a cent! Congressmen were presumed to be prosperous gentlemen who neither needed nor wanted any payment for serving their country.

After a few months of deliberation, the delegates to the Congress recessed for a month to escape the summer heat. John Hancock had a surprise for them when they reconvened in September of 1775. At the age of 40, he announced that he'd finally married patient Dorothy Quincy.

A Jolly Gentleman
Even before he showed up at the Second Continental Congress, in May of 1775, Hancock had already established himself as a political power. After all, he controlled most of the purse strings for the rebel cause in New England. However, he was chosen President of the Congress not only because of his financial clout, but also because of personal qualities.

There was much distrust among the delegates from the various colonies, most of whom had never travelled outside their home territories. They didn't like strangers, and feared that others might pass resolutions unfavorable to their particular interests. As a result of this mistrust, they had a hard time agreeing on anyone to preside over the Congress.

Hancock, however, was a very likeable person who made friends on all sides. He was finally chosen as someone who could unite the delegates from North and South.

As a prominent Boston merchant, he merited the respect of his fellow Yankees. And the Southerners, to their surprise, found that

John Hancock was an affable jolly fellow, far different from many of his dour New England colleagues they distrusted. In fact, it was a Southerner, Benjamin Harrison, who settled an impasse between the two regional groups by engineering Hancock's election.

Harrison managed to persuade his persnickety Southern friends that Hancock was a most unusual Yankee, *almost* as good as they were.

> **"A most convivial companion, *for a New Englander.***
> **Without his Boston accent, he (Hancock) might pass**
> **for a gentleman."** Benjamin Harrison

Like the ladies and gentlemen of Southern plantations, Hancock believed that hard work should be balanced by an ample enjoyment of life. He was the life of the party. Any party.

Hancock showed up at every rout, an elaborate type of dinner party favored by the wealthy set. He loved card parties, dancing and music concerts.

There were plenty of all those affairs for him to enjoy. By the late 1700s the moneyed merchants and their ladies, who comprised the high society of cosmopolitan Boston, had moved a long way from the Spartan dictates of Cotton Mather.

Beginning of a Presidential Tradition?

It's true that a United States government had not yet been established when Hancock presided over the Second Continental Congress. But that gathering was the first time that all of the 13 colonies came together in a common cause, so we could stretch a point and perhaps say that John Hancock was *"America's First President"*. (The First Continental Congress, which took place a year earlier, was not an all-American meeting. That session wasn't so all-encompassing; it didn't include any delegate from Georgia.)

In his presidential-type role, John Hancock could be viewed as showing some characteristics that many of his successors also exhibited.

For example, like many later chief executives of our country, Hancock showed a proclivity for being flamboyant, bigger-than-life, and proud of it. He titillated the country's gossips with his freely-expressed libido and unconventional social habits. His personal charm was a powerful asset

His most important characteristics, however, were that he rose to the challenges of his time, and accomplished a great deal.

John Hancock's three-story house in Boston was
one of the most imposing mansions in the area.

A Fortune Down the Drain

Although Hancock started his career as the very wealthy young man-- heir to the largest fortune in New England-- he didn't end up that way. Toward the end of John's life, most of Uncle Thomas' fortune had disappeared. Sometimes he's criticized for that, and called a poor business man and a wastrel who wasted money.

Those who maintain such a belief miss the whole point of John Hancock's life.

Despite his flamboyant and expensive tastes, money was not the most important thing to Hancock. Neither was being a successful merchant. What he wanted most of all in life was a distinguished career as a public official, and he was prepared to sacrifice anything to achieve that.

In addition to his well-known career as a leader in the early efforts to unite America's colonies, Hancock served long and well in the government of his home state. He was chosen to become the first governor of the Commonwealth of Massachusetts. After a hiatus, he was elected again and served *nine terms* in that office before he died at the age of 56.

Tiffs With Washington Finally Resolved
Hancock's relationship with George Washington was not always entirely warm and friendly. When the Second Continental Congress picked a commander in chief for its army, as you'll read later, Hamilton thought he'd get that prestigious post. After Washington was appointed to the job instead, Hancock's nose was out of joint for quite a while.

The strained feelings lasted for many years. Even after the War, when Washington became president and made his triumphal tour of the major cities, he received a rather cool reception in one of them, Boston, where Hancock resided as governor of the Colony of Massachusetts. George expected to be invited to stay at the Governor's mansion (there were few decent living accomodations in the inns of those days, so it was customary to welcome visiting celebrities as personal house guests.) When no such invitation was forthcoming immediately, George took this as an affront.

Later in life, however, John eventually got over his envy. The best indication of this is the fact that he named one of his sons George Washington Hancock.

Always a Public Benefactor
Fortunately for us, his successors, John Hancock dug into his deep pockets time after time to help with the many costs of starting a revolution. And for other civic needs as well.

He became treasurer of Harvard, and gave so liberally to his alma mater that the college accorded him special honors. His home town of Boston was the first American city to enjoy street lights because Hancock paid for them. He also bought a fire engine for the city, bells and a steeple for his church.

So liberally did he spend his assets and time, for government and civic needs, that his fortune shrank considerably. Most politicians today might consider it asinine to work at one job after another without pay, and to contribute funds besides.

Hancock, bless him, had loftier goals.

Q: Where is John Hancock's hand?

A: Along with other notables of the Revolutionary War era, he was interred at the Granary Burying Ground in downtown Boston. However, it's possible that all of him may not still remain there! A widely circulated rumor maintained that grave robbers exhumed Governor Hancock the night after his burial, and hacked off his right hand. If this story is true, did some ghoulish collector want a trophy of the famous fingers that signed the Declaration of Independence in boldest of script?

George Washington, the Father of Our Country, was never a father.
But he doted on, and spoiled, his wife's children and grandchildren.

2
George Washington's Family

Along with our flag, George Washington is a premier symbol of America. Not a mere man, but a legend, whom we Americans are proud to regard as one of our wonderful ancestors. Even though that's not technically true for any of us, since George left no progeny.

We all know him as Commanding General of the Colonial military forces in the Revolutionary War and as the imposing First President of the United States. His glorious achievements and military struggles have been comprehensively covered over the centuries in a multitude of articles and books. It has been estimated that more than 500 Washington biographies have been published, though many are merely small pamphlets that repeat the same major points of his career (and inaccurate myths) over and over again.

But what about the *private life* of George Washington-- not the bigger-than-life image, but the human being?

What about his family background, his siblings, his romances? What sort of childhood did he have? (Forgetting the silly stories about chopping down cherry trees and throwing dollars, which he didn't have, across a wide river.) How did the taciturn childless gentleman get along with his wife Martha, her children and grandchildren? How was his health? What did he eat and drink? How did he spend his private hours?

No Aristocratic Background
Washington grew to be the closest thing to royalty we've ever had in this country. Believe it or not, as you'll read later, many citizens actually wanted to make him *King of America* after the war! Yet his

Washington's first job, as a surveyor, started him in acquiring land.

ancestors were far from royalty, in fact, they were not even anywhere near the top layer of English society.

Washington's rather plebeian background bothered some people when he became head of the Continental army. In British tradition which was strong in America, only the sons of noble families could ever become senior officers in the army or navy. And George's ancestors were neither rich nor noblemen.

Washington would be amazed at the amount of time and energy that's been expended since his death to trace his ancestry and establish a distinguished background for him. Repeatedly, he told inquirers that he knew practically nothing about his ancestors. And cared less.

He once wrote that he'd heard as a child that his forebears came from some place in the north of England, but he had no idea where. After Washington became President, England's Garter King of Arms, whose job was to keep track of family histories of heads of state, sent him a genealogical table and asked him to fill in the gaps. George couldn't do so. His reply shows how little importance the Father of Our Country placed on family pedigree.

> **" My genealogy is a subject to which I must confess I have paid very little attention."**
> President Washington

George's ancestors were squires in Northhampton. In other words, they were what we'd term an upper-middle-class family. Probably that's the most appropriate background for the premier hero of our democracy-- a rise from a modest beginning to greatness.

A Few Black Sheep in the Family

Most every family includes some dubious characters whose names are seldom mentioned. In that respect, the Washington clan was typically American.

The first of George's ancestors indisputably listed in the record books was a poor (unemployed) minister. He was the Reverend Lawrence Washington. The Reverend's reputation was not the best. Government records show he was driven from his parish because he was overly fond of the bottle.

Like other historical gossip, these accusations about George's cleric ancestor are believed by some researchers and questioned by others. But here's what they said about Reverend Washington in an official document of 1643, listing "Scandalous and Malignant Priests."

> **"He is a common frequenter of Ale houses, not only himselfe sitting daily tippling there, but also encouraging others in that beastly vice, and hath been oft drunk."**

Alcoholism was not an unusual failing of men of the cloth. However, this accusation may have been trumped-up, because at that time Cromwell was driving Anglican clergymen from their posts. The persecution of ministers certainly must have played a part in Reverend Lawrence Washington's losing his job. At any rate, that misfortune prompted his two sons to emigrate to America. One of them was John, George's great-grandfather.

Off to America

John Washington was known as a business man of limited resources and scruples. One of his claims to fame was the unusual background of his second and third wives. After his first wife (George's great-grandmother) died, John successively married two women of wide reputation in the colony. One had been accused of running a bawdy house. Her successor, her sister, had been popularly labeled as the Governor's whore.

At any rate, John and his brother Lawrence who emigrated to America with him (and who also had several wives) created a generous scattering of progeny throughout Virginia.

Whatever his marital problems, John Washington became a famous Indian fighter. Like his great-grandson George, he was made a Colonel of Militia and a member of Virginia's House of Burgesses.

Colonel John did well financially too, leaving large landholdings. He also owned many black slaves and indentured white servants. They added to his estate for they both were considered "property".

There were several more Johns and Lawrence's in the family. The names become confusing. Colonel John's eldest son (George's grandfather) was named Lawrence. That Lawrence had two sons, John and Augustine (George's father). Augustine's eldest son (George's beloved step-brother) was another Lawrence. One of George's younger brothers was named John Augustine. Got that straight?

A Hard-working Entrepreneur Father

George's father, Augustine Washington, was an extremely ambitious man who must have instilled in his young son many of his strong character traits. Augustine exemplifies the sort of hard-driving individual who, like many Americans afterward, tried a variety of vocations until he found one that worked. That would have been impossible in England where mobility was extremely limited.

Augustine first had an unspectacular career as a sea captain. Following that, he opened a small manufactory for iron, a product much needed in the farm country of Virginia. Finally, he left that business and bought a thousand acres of good farm land in Westmoreland County, about half way up the Potomac River.

Q: What's the proper name of George's birthplace?
A: You can take your choice. His parents' plantation was called "Wakefield" and was bordered by "Bridge's Creek" and "Pope's Creek". As a result, you may find his birthplace described by any of those three names.

The house where George was born burned down, but its site has been marked by a small marble miniature of the tall monument in our nation's capitol. (Trivia: One of George's best biographers, Rupert Hughes, claims an error was made in locating the little obelisk, and that it's placed not where the President was born, but over what was an *outhouse*. If this is true, George would not have appreciated such carelessness.)

A Limited Education
Although the son of a prosperous rural family in his early years, George, like many other lads of his time, received but a rudimentary formal education. This showed up later in his atrocious spelling, which he himself jested about. However, like many of his contemporaries, he churned out prodigious amounts of correspondence.

His makeshift schooling was due to the fact that George was the *second* son, and therefore not expected to become the chief heir and head of the family. Elder step-brother, Lawrence, the favored heir, was sent to England for a superior and costly education.

A Convict Schoolmaster Right At Home
George's first schooling came from an indentured servant in his home. When George was five, his father, still trading as a sea captain at times, traveled to England and brought back a cargo of

convicts. He sold most all of them, of course. But one was an educated man, so Captain Augustine kept him at the farm for a couple of years to tutor his younger son.

The family moved to the Fredericsburg area when George was seven. There he received a couple of more years of schooling from two other teachers. They taught him the rudiments of reading, writing, ciphering, geography and bookkeeping.

In the backwoods area of Virginia where he spent his early years, George was a reasonably educated young man. He could read and write and was a whiz at figures. But he was not in a league with the wealthy multi-lingual and widely-read Jeffersons and Randolphs who later became his colleagues.

The End of Prosperity

When George was 11 years old, Augustine died of "gout of the stomach" (probably cancer) at the age of 49. That was the end of the prosperous life for George and his mother.

Because of the Laws of Primogeniture, followed in the Colonies and originating in England to keep large estates intact, the eldest son got essentially *all* of the inheritance. Following the law, Augustine willed the bulk of his property to Lawrence, who was the senior of his two sons by a previous marriage. Lawrence inherited a 2,500-acre plantation and most of Augustine's other assets, making him a fairly wealthy man.

George, as eldest of Augustine's children by his second marriage, was willed the scraggly 250-acre Ferry farm. But with an important restriction. His mother, widow Mary Ball Washington, was to have control of it until George came of age. Actually, Ma Washington never did turn the farm over to George, and he never made any effort to get possession of it.

So, practically speaking, George's inheritance amounted to just about nothing at all!

Of course, Mary and her whole brood had a rough time after Augustine died. Suddenly she was reduced to raising her five living young children, ranging in age from 5 to 11, with the scant resources she could wring out of a small farm in the backwoods. No wonder she became a hard and bitter woman.

Tough, Pipe-smoking Momma

Not a great deal is known for sure about the lineage or girlhood of Mary Ball, although some eager genealogists have given her a variety of impressive ancestors. We know for certain that she was orphaned at 11, and then lived under the guardianship of a Major George Eskridge, after whom she named her first son.

Mary Ball married Augustine Washington when she was 21. He was a widower with two children. Together they had six more. Here's the list of her progeny:

George	1732 - 1799
Betty	1733 - 1781
Samuel	1734 - 1781
John Augustine	1735 - 1787
Charles	1738 - 1799
Mildred	1739 - 1740

Note that Mary bore her six children in just seven years-- *one every year* except for the brief gap after her fourth child. Note also that her last child died as an infant. That sort of birth record was typical for the times, and obviously not easy on the women.

Mary was only 35 when Augustine died. Unlike many widows, she never remarried. Widow Washington had a rough time raising her brood of youngsters. Like the vicissitudes of her early life, she survived this new struggle, but it did nothing to soften a basically tough personality. Even after her eldest son became very famous and very rich, she posed as a poor widow from the back country. She flaunted that image, often to his embarrassment.

For one thing, Ma Washington smoked a pipe incessantly. (George never smoked.) As you can imagine, Mary's habit was not regarded as lady-like behavior by the First Families of Virginia. Or by the satin-gowned matrons of Philadelphia and New York where her son became the leading citizen. Or, for that matter, by Martha, the wealthy wife George eventually married. Ornery Ma Washington didn't care a damn about any of those fine ladies, including Martha.

Mary Ball Washington was undeniably an ornery, cranky woman. But we can't overlook the fact that, under extremely difficult conditions, Widow Washington kept her family together and raised a wonderful son. What more can we ask?

A Hard Woman to Please
Even while Augustine was alive, Mary was reputed to be the disciplinarian in the family. She followed the prevalent wisdom of that time: namely, that to spare the rod was to spoil the child. Switches cut from the branches of a peach tree were the rods she preferred to use when she applied punishment to the legs and bottoms of George and his younger siblings. So formidable a woman was Mrs. Washington that one of George's young friends said he was more afraid of her than of his own parents.

Q: How proud was Ma Washington of her son George?
A: Incredible as it may seem to us, Ma Washington never once congratulated her son publicly, or otherwise expressed any pride in his accomplishments. Not when he was appointed to command the Continental forces. Not when he won great victories in the War for Independence. Not even when her famous son was elected President of his country by a unanimous vote.

Even after George was grown up and famous, Ma Washington still remained an unrelenting critic of her eldest son. She never approved of his military career, which she seemed to regard as just an excuse to run away from home and her. She told George repeatedly that it was his duty to stay at home and attend to his farming instead of traipsing off to wars.

Far from being supportive of any of George's activities, his mother seemed to go out of her way to humiliate him publicly. During the war, son George had to undergo constant criticism because of his mother. She remained an avowed and outspoken Loyalist to the King of England. *She was one of those people who wanted the American army, led by her son, to lose the War!*

If she'd gotten that wish, George, who was at the top of the King's "most-wanted" list, would have faced a decidedly unpleasant end. He'd have been not just hanged like ordinary wrong-doers, but *drawn and quartered* as well. That was a gory procedure reserved for only the vilest of criminals.

"George Has Abandoned Me"

When Washington was Commander-in-Chief of the Continental Army, he had to to refute charges that he and his siblings had abandoned his widowed mother. Mary applied to the Virginia legislature for public assistance. *She claimed she was a pauper and needed to go on welfare!*.

You can imagine the gossip that scandal stirred up. General George had to send a letter to the Virginia Legislature where he himself had been a member. George had to persuade his wealthy friends in the Legislature that his mother was well cared for. In fact, he had bought her "an elegant little house in Fredericksburg" so she could avoid the stress of running the old Ferry Farm. Far from being a pauper, she had servants and ample funds to live comfortably.

After the war, Mary continued to complain of lack of money. Harassed constantly, George reportedly suggested she sell her house and go to live with his brother, John, who'd invited her to do so. Ma would have none of that. Nor would she go to live at the presidential mansion. That must have been a relief to George, and especially to his wife Martha, for Ma Washington never showed the slightest approval of the daughter-in-law who brought wealth and social standing to her son.

Q: How often did Ma visit George and Martha?
A: Not once in all the years her son and daughter-in-law lived at Mount Vernon did Mother Washington come to visit them.

Mary stayed alone to the end, puffing away at her pipe, and complaining of everything. She battled daily with her servants who had to force the old lady to take her medicine. Tough to the end, the old lady battled her last illness.

Cancer finally conquered Ma, in the first year of her son's presidency, when she was 83 years old.

Strong and Gangly as a Youth

At a bit more than six feet two inches, George was a head taller than most of his contemporaries. Those who wrote about him said he had the largest hands and feet they'd ever seen. At an early age, he became noted for unusual strength and athletic ability-- qualities which gained admiration in the rough pioneer society of his youth, and later in military life.

He excelled at all sports that required muscle: wrestling, weight-lifting, hurling a heavy iron bar. He could also outrun other boys, and was good at games like quoits, and one that involved jumping with a long pole, evidently related to our present pole vaulting.

His special love was riding horses. George's skill in the saddle became evident, even while he was still a young man. One of his fellow Virginians, an excellent horseman himself, was impressed by that talent.

> "He (Washington) is the finest horseman of his age. The most graceful figure that could be seen on horseback."
> Thomas Jefferson

His skill as an equestrian made Washington outstanding at the popular Virginia sport of fox hunting, an activity pursued with almost religious fervor throughout that colony. That proved to be of great importance to the young man's career. It brought him hunting invitations from some the wealthiest and most influential men in Virginia, who spent every available hour riding to hounds.

Q: What did Washington name his foxhounds?
A: Sportsman Washington gave them affectionate names. Among his packs were dogs named Truelove and Sweetlips. Countess and Lady were two other favorites. Music was the name of a hound that must have bayed in melodious tones.

Riding with Lord Fairfax

One of the most avid huntsmen was the largest landowner in the Colony, Lord Fairfax, who occasionally came from England to check on his *millions* of acres in the New World. Fairfax took such a liking to George that the penniless young man became a constant riding companion and guest at the Lord's manor house. That friendship opened wonderful new opportunities.

Fairfax gave his young friend his first job, as part of a surveying party. He was to divide into lots an area of the Lord's vast holdings in the Shendoah Valley. That was George's start in the land business and of a life-long desire to acquire large landholdings himself.

To the dismay of strict religionists, throughout his life fox hunting occupied Washington more often than did theological activities. His diaries record that he attended church services only 15 times in one year (although, legally, church attendance was mandatory in Virginia). But he rode to the foxhounds 49 days in the same period.

Squire Washington, returning from hunting, honors two young visitors with a prize. It's "the brush", a bloody tail he's cut from an unlucky fox.

One of the most painful curses of old age for Washington was that he hurt his back at 63, and could no longer endure the bone-jarring action of chasing the fox.

Fond of the Ladies at an Early Age

Strapping young George developed a penchant for parties and an eye for pretty women at an early age. At 16, a tall husky lad who was already shaving, he became very conscious of his clothes. And of the young ladies in the neighborhod. In a letter to Lady Fairfax, Washington's patron commented on this.

> **"The lad is beginning to feel the sap rising, being in**
> **the spring of life, and is getting ready to be the prey**
> **of your sex, wherefore may the Lord help him."**
> Lord Fairfax

At that time-- and throughout his life, many biographers believe-- the young lady Washington admired most was Sarah Fairfax, usually called Sally. It was an unfortunate choice, for vivacious Sally had just married George's best friend, George William Fairfax.

Washington was only 16 at the time; Sally was two years older; George Fairfax was 23. The two men had just come back from the surveying expedition to the Shenandoah. Fairfax was the grandson of the great Lord Fairfax, and the son of Colonel William Fairfax who managed the family estates in Virginia.

Since Washington stayed at the Fairfax estate, Belvoir, more than he did at Ma Washington's Ferry Farm, he and George Fairfax became almost like brothers. They were actually related, since George's step-brother, Lawrence had married one of the Fairfax girls.

The newly-married couple and Washington comprised a strange trio. Fairfax was much different from the other George. He's been described as timid, an adjective certainly never applied to Washington. Raised in England by relatives, he was a sallow-complected man with big dark eyes, who'd been taunted as a child by innuendoes that he was a mulatto. Sally was a lively young lady whose only portrait shows a brunette who had a strong chin and nose and a determined mouth. She's usually described as pretty and high-spirited.

Teen-ager Washington, living under the same roof much of the time, was obviously fascinated by scintillating Sally and the gay life in the wealthy household. There was never any hint of hanky-panky between the two. Long after he married, however, George wrote affectionate letters to Sally and otherwise expressed his admiration.

With Sally not available, the young man was forced to aim his amorous pursuits in other directions.

Unlucky in Love

It may seem to us that George Washington, destined to achieve unequaled prestige and considerable wealth, would be a marvelous catch for some young girl. But he didn't look too good to the nubile maidens of Virginia. Or, more importantly, to their daddies.

The dashing young dandy pursued many, but failed to catch any as a marriage partner. Despite his manly charm, he was but an orphan boy with no property. And surveying was not a princely job. That didn't thrill the wealthy Virginia planters whose daughters George eyed covetously.

But George kept trying. He wrote love letters and very bad poems addressed to "the Lowland Beauty." His voluminous diaries, in which he kept a record of everything, never disclosed who she was. Understandably, half the socialite families in Virginia now claim that haughty beauty who turned the future president away was an ancestress of theirs.

Who Was the Lowland Beauty?

One young lady who might have been the Lowland Beauty was Betsy Fauntleroy whose father owned a huge estate on the Rappahannock. Betsy would have been an ideal wife, beautiful and rich, but she kept many suitors dangling. She was only 15 when George met her, and he kept up the pursuit for three years. Coquettish Betsy finally gave him a conclusive "get lost" and he took the hint.

At the same time he was hoping to win elusive Betsy and perhaps also writing to an unnamed Lowland Beauty, fickle George also had his eye on a third young woman. She was Sally Fairfax's younger sister.

George met Mary Cary when she was only 14, and had come to visit Sally at Belvoir. George, you'll recall, was also staying at that mansion, so he saw a lot of Mary. If romance blossomed then or in the years to follow, the fact that they both were very young would not have meant much. Girls as young as 12 became brides.

In letters to friends, he described Mary as "the very agreeable Young Lady who lives in the same house." Whether George ever proposed to Mary is disputed. One account claims he asked her father for her hand, and that Colonel Cary crankily told him to leave because "my daughter is accustomed to ride in her own coach."

Ambitious Young Man
In his twenties, George began his career-- two careers, in fact, which helped his financial situation.

First, with his connections to step-brother Lawrence and the Fairfax family, he became official surveyor of Culpepper County. This gave him a foothold into acquiring land in the West. By the time he was 21, he'd acquired 1,400 acres. That was not super big in the Virginia plantation country, but still a substantial holding.

At the same young age, he was appointed a major in the Virginia militia, which brought a salary of 100 pounds annually. That was a substantial income befitting a young gentleman, but it didn't make him rich as many of his hunting companions were. He later rose a step higher to the rank of Colonel with another boost in pay.

The main increase in George's fortunes, however, came from an unexpected inheritance that resulted from a painful personal tragedy

Loss of a Brother/Father
George's beloved step-brother, Lawrence, who'd been plagued for years with Tuberculosis, died in 1754.

No one had more influence in shaping George's character and life. Ever since Augustine Washington's death, Lawrence had been a father figure to young George, who was 14 years his junior.

George had accompanied his step-brother to Barbados when Lawrence spent a year in that tropical climate in a vain effort to help his lungs. Certainly George's fascination for military life was inspired by the brief career as a British naval officer of the big brother he idolized. And George's important entre into the upper levels of society was made possible by Lawrence's marriage into the Fairfax clan.

Soon after his step-brother's death, George became involved in the 2,500-acre farm Lawrence had named Mount Vernon. Lawrence's widow remarried in six months, so she moved to her new husband's home and rented the Mount Vernon farm to George. When she died seven years later, with no Washington progeny, the plantation became George's, as stipulated in his father's will. That made him a fairly prosperous planter. But he was destined to take a huge step up the financial ladder soon.

Enter the Rich Widow
George really hit the big-time financially when he married Martha Custis, the richest widow in Virginia.

Their courtship was brief, and there's no indication of any great romance that prompted it. Sally Fairfax is generally conceded to be the love of George's life. But the marriage of George and Martha was advantageous both to the ambitious young bachelor who wanted to settle down and to the widow who needed help in managing her children and her substantial estates. As some of his writings indicate, Washington's practical nature extended to his views on marriage. Here's advice he gave to his step-granddaughter.

> **"A good marriage partner should possess good sense, a good disposition, a good reputation and financial means."**
> George Washington

Martha had all those sensible qualities. Though theirs was not a wild, romantic union, the Washingtons were always an affectionate couple who complimented each other. George usually referred to his wife as "my dear Patsy", a nickname for Martha.

Martha, 27 at the time of her marriage, was a year older than her second husband. She was a quiet, gentle, motherly type of woman who doted on George. Like most women of her time, she'd had scarcely any formal education, but was well versed in domestic skills needed to run a household and care for her family.

"I'm an old-fashioned Virginia housekeeper."
Martha Washington
"She (Martha) is one of those unassuming characters which create love and esteem. A most becoming pleasantness sits upon her countenance."
Abigail Adams

Martha was only about five feet tall, scarcely coming to Colonel Washington's shoulder. Also a bit plump, she's often described as having a softly rounded figure. She was pretty, with large hazel eyes, dark hair and a high forehead.

Born on a modest plantation near Williamsburg, at 18 she married Daniel Parke Custis, a dozen years her senior. Her wealthy husband owned both city and country homes. One was a mansion in Williamsburg so large it was known as the Six Chimney House.

Colonel Washington (27) wed wealthy widow Martha Dandridge Custis (28) in a resplendent ceremony held at the bride's home.

The other was a magnificent estate on the York River. (Strangely, that home was generally referred to as the "White House".) Life there was on a grand scale, with Martha enjoying such luxuries as the choice of a sedan chair or a coach when she traveled.

A Good Estate Manager

Mr. Custis died young, of a "bilious fever", leaving his widow with two young children. They'd had two others who did not survive.

Custis also left Martha one of the wealthiest women in Virginia. Her estate included more than 17,000 acres of prime land, plus miscellaneous valuable assets such as cash, stock investments, farm animals and 300 slaves who were considered a form of livestock.

One third of this estate went to Martha, which her new husband automatically controlled. The other two thirds went to her two children, but George was named executor of their estates, giving him control over their property until they reached their majority.

New husband George proved to be a good family manager. In addition to Martha's holdings, he bought extra land to expand his own plantation on the Rapahannock. Over the years, he added a third story to the farmhouse and also a wing on each side of it to create the stately mansion on a hill we recognize as Mount Vernon.

Life of the Party

Ordinarily, we may regard Washington as a taciturn, forbidding figure. He could be that, and his often stern appearance certainly added to the commanding presence he had to maintain in running the war and the government. But he had an altogether different side, too.

As a part of a tolerant, fun-loving Virginia society, he enjoyed many of the hedonistic pursuits which straight-laced citizens in Northern Colonies still abhorred.

George was always first on the floor to dance with a pretty woman, anywhere, anytime. Even on a Sunday, which made it worse! In fact, he was invariably the last one to leave a dance, and therefore regarded as the life of the party.

Gambling was another of his favorite activities. Unfortunately, the card table was not a place where he generally excelled. Avid bookkeepeer that he was, Washington kept a precise record of his winnings and losses. Jotting down these records must have been painful to him, for as with most gamblers, they showed the cards were against him more often than not.

Q: What pleasure really riled the "religious right"?
A: Dancing was still viewed by many Americans as the Devil's temptation. Especially if it was "Mixt", often called "Gyrecandrical" dancing, after the Greek word referring to women. Curiously, a group of men leaping about to music to show their endurance and strength was okay.

Father of Our Country, but Never a Father
George Washington's inability to have any children proved to be an embarrassing source of speculation in a day when families of a dozen offspring, or more, were the norm.

Medical experts are unanimous in concluding that it must have been George, not Martha, who was unable to conceive in their marriage. When they met, Martha was a widow who certainly was not barren. In eight years with her first husband, she'd borne four children.

The most vicious gossips-- and they were possibly more vicious in the 18th Century than they are now-- speculated that George's infertility was due to youthful indiscretion. They said he'd contracted Syphilis as a teen-ager when he'd traveled to Barbados with brother Lawrence. There is no evidence whatever to support this slanderous charge against Washington.

A Doting Step-Father and Grandfather
With no children of his own, Washington doted on Martha's. They were little tots at the time of her remarriage. Tiny Patsy (a nickname for Martha) was only three; Jackie was five.

Ordinarily firm and stern, George proved to be a permissive pappa. Too lenient, some said. Perhaps he felt reticent about disciplining Martha's children. It's no doubt they were spoiled.Each child had a personal slave, dressed in livery, whose sole duty was to watch over and serve them. Of course, they had the finest imported toys, clothes, etc. that money could buy.

In Patsy's case, the pampering may have had some justification. She was a sickly child, and in her early teens it became apparent that the cause was Epilepsy. She suffered frequent seizures from which the doctors could give no relief. When only 17, Patsy fell down after dinner and died in just a few minutes. Even though she'd been ill for years, this sudden catastrophe devastated George and Martha.

After this loss, Jackie seemed to receive more pampering than ever. He was the kind of spoiled brat who'd be bounced out of prep school today. The master of the school he attended in his teens indicated, in a letter to step-father Washington, that Jackie was the worst student he'd ever tried to educate.

> **"He is exceedingly indolent and surprisingly voluptuous, with a propensity to the other sex I'm at a loss to describe. One would suppose Nature had intended him for some Asiatic Prince."**
> Schoolmaster Rev. Boucher

Despite the scant amount of learning Jackie accumulated at Boucher's little school, Pappa George enrolled him at King's College (later to become Columbia University). Before arriving there, however, impetuous Jackie continued his propensity to pursue the other sex. He shocked the folks at home by advising them he'd become engaged to a young lady in Maryland named Nelly Calvert.

Engagements without consulting parents were no-nos! George hurriedly gathered up the young swain and deposited him at King's College. Then he wrote to Nelly's father (an illegitimate son of Lord Baltimore, the founder of Maryland) decreeing that Jackie would be completing his schooling before any marriage could be contemplated.

Freshman Jackie continued to live high when he returned to college. Unlike Columbia students today, he had his own three-room suite, necessitated by the fact that had a personal valet. He also brought a horse and groom with him, though presumably they lodged in other quarters.

A Disappointing Heir

Jackie never amounted to much of anything. The things on which he concentrated most were his fancy clothes, his horses and hunting dogs.

He never worked at anything, perhaps because he never had to. Step-father Washington didn't dare lay a hand on him with Martha around, and he couldn't control the young man by cutting off an allowance because the millionaire Custis heir had more money than George.

When the Revolutionary War got underway, Jackie wanted no part of that. He changed his mind, though, when his step-father began adding titled Frenchmen to his staff. Noblemen from Paris intrigued Jackie. He thought it would be fun to hob-nob with them.

Always permissive, George arranged to have Jackie join him, not as a soldier but as a civilian aide to the General. That was a decision he soon regretted. Jackie stayed far from the bullets, but the worst hazard of camp life finished him. He contracted the common illness known only as "camp fever". At the age of 27, Jackie Custis died.

He left four children-- three daughters and a son. The two eldest girls stayed with their mother, who remarried. The youngest girl and her little brother, both infants, came to Mount Vernon to live with grandmother Martha Washington and her famous husband.

House Full of Children

Even though he fathered no children of his own, Washington became the patriarch of a large clan. Toward the end of his life, his home at Mount Vernon was always full of youngsters. He not only reared the second generation of Martha's offspring there, but also housed and fed 18 nephews and nieces for whom he served either as guardian or as a source of support.

George's father, Augustine Washington, had sired a total of eight children, and George outlived all the others. As his siblings died, he assumed varying degrees of responsibility for their children. Various nephews and nieces moved in and out of Mount Vernon. Sometimes when the house got too crowded, they boarded with friends of Washington's while he paid the bills.

When his brother Samuel died in 1781, shortly after marrying his *fifth* wife, George became the legal guardian of three of his small children. They became a close part of the family.

Grandchildren to Indulge

Of course, Martha's two grandchildren were the pair she and George doted on the most in their later years. Eleanor Parke Custis, called "Nelly" like her mother, was only two years old when her father Jackie died and she came to Mount Vernon. Her little brother, George Washington Parke Custis, was a tiny infant when he came to live with Grandma and the doting Step-Grandpa after whom he'd been named. To avoid confusion. Little George was usually called "Young Custis".

Unfortunately, the little boy, heir to a chunk of the Custis wealth and spoiled as his father before him had been, grew up to be a charming but indolent chip off the old block. He bounced successively through three colleges-- Pennsylvania University, the College of New Jersey (later called Princeton) and St. John's College. And he frequently frustrated Grandpa who tried constantly, but unsuccessfully to instill his responsible traits in the young lad.

> **"It would seem as if nothing I can say to you
> makes more than a momentary impression!"**
> George Washington

Fortunately, little George Washington Parke Custis straightened out later in life. After Big George's death, he married well, settled down on an estate opposite the new capital city of Washington, D.C. It's a place that's well-known today; in fact, it attracts thousands of visitors each year.

Later in life, George Washington Parke Custis frequently gave laudatory speeches about his grandmother's second husband. He even wrote a play which enjoyed a favorable run in Philadelphia. This literary effort was titled *Pocahontas, or the Settlers of Virginia.* Too bad Big George couldn't have seen how well Little George finally turned out.

Q: Where did the name "Arlington" come from?
A: When George Washington Parke Custis built a mansion and
estate across from the Capitol City, he named it Arlington".
When his only child married, he gave it to her and her
husband, a U.S. Army officer named Robert E. Lee, destined
to play a major role in a later war. Today Arlington is the
site of a special cemetery for heroes and heroines, an Army
fort and an odd-shaped military headquarters called the
Pentagon.

Beautiful Nelly

In sharp contrast to her little brother, Nelly grew up to be a dutiful and adorable young lady. She helped to entertain distinguished guests who came to see her Grandpa. And she delighted the old man by singing his favorite songs.

Nelly's marriage also pleased Washington. She fell in love with his sister's son, who lived at Mount Vernon. Her intended was Lawrence Lewis, an energetic young man whom George had just appointed as a major in the reorganized army.

The young couple picked a great date for their wedding. They decided to marry on February 22, Washington's birthday. When the newlyweds indicated they'd like to live somewhere near him, he hired Lawrence to run three of his properties. They included one of his farms and a mill. The third operation was a basic enterprise found in many early American communities-- it was *a distillery*. Generous George further promised that he'd will these three properties to the young couple when he died.

Sadly, that occurred soon afterward. Washington's happy birthday, coinciding with their wedding in 1799, was the last he ever celebrated.

3
A Nation of Gamblers

From its very beginnings, America has been a land for hustlers and gamblers. That's a characteristic we still see today when gambling is the fastest-growing industry in these United States. It was a characteristic of the people of 1776, a puny little group who dared to take a chance at infuriating the mightiest monarch in the world and defying his powerful army and navy.

When King James I decided to colonize an area on our southern shores, did he pay for this uncertain venture with money from the royal treasury? No way! The shrewd king decided that proceeds from a gambling operation could pay the bills.

Q: What financed the first American colony?

A: Lottery tickets. Way back In 1612, King James I set up a lottery, and raked in enough money from it to form the Virginia Company and provide it with the ships and supplies needed to transport settlers across the ocean. Appropriately, it was a gambling venture that provided the seed money for the adventurers who settled America's premier colony.

The first people who boarded ships to America were certainly gamblers. They risked everything they had, including their lives, for a fresh start in a strange land thousands of miles away, populated by strange savage tribes.

But they were betting on a chance to achieve a standard of living far beyond their reach in England. Their gambling habits persisted after they arrived in the New World.

Bet on Anything

Visitors from Europe remarked on the mania for gambling they saw in the New World. Colonial men were the most passionate gamblers. As do our countrymen today, they loved to bet on all sorts of sports. But they'd also bet on anything else with a debatable outcome.

They'd wager on whether it would rain or shine. On the arrival date of a ship. On the outcome of an election. On which side of the room a fly would alight. On which of two topers at the tavern would drink the other under the table.

Our rough ancestors especially liked to wager on rough sports-- the bloodier the better. These included many types of contests that are outlawed today.

Vicious Sports the Gamblers Loved

Bear baiting was big in the 1700s. In frontier communities, it was a natural outgrowth of the bitter battles settlers fought with the most fearsome of the forest denizens.

In this vicious sport, a bear that had been trapped was shackled to a tree. After the spectators placed their bets as to how long the animal would last, or if it would be victorious, a pack of dogs was unleased at it. In the snarling, roaring melee that followed, dogs and blood flew all over the place, to the delight of the excited gamblers.

To add a bit of humor and audience participation to this grisly game, the bear's eyes were sometimes put out beforehand. This enabled bolder members of the crowd to prod it with sharp sticks for a while before the dogs were turned loose on the animal. Not being able to see its tormentors, the bear would lash out wildly in all directions. The spectators considered this great fun to watch, and it added to the excitement for sometimes the blinded bear would get lucky and connect with a careless tormentor.

The factor that limited bear baiting was the rarity of capturing one of the ferocious creatures alive. So substitutes had to be found. Wolves were more often caught in pits or traps. Therefore, it became common to use them for sport and gambling. Like the bears, they'd be chained to a stake and set upon by a pack of dogs.

As in England, cock-fighting was a popular sport in the Colonies.

Sports That Persist Today

Domestic animals were raised for sport as well. Cock fighting, though rare today because it's illegal now, was a popular activity throughout the Colonies. In 1776, you'd see many posters and newspaper advertisements for it. For those who preferred something on a larger scale, bull baiting was another entertainment sometimes available. An especially ferocious bull would be corralled in a small enclosure where several bulldogs, bred for this sport, were turned loose on the infuriated animal.

Boxing was another bloody form of entertainment. There were no gloves to cushion the blows. The bouts were simple warfare that lasted until one man could no longer pick himself up to continue.

Fighting rules (if any) allowed for the most vicious tactics. Favorite methods of attack, used to supplement punching, were designed to maim the opponent. At these battles and other sporting events, the betting was almost as fierce as the action that inspired it.

Q: What did "bite, bullock and gouge" mean?

A: A gladiator would clamp his teeth on the nose or ears of his opponent, biting as hard as possible. He'd simultaneously grab the enemy by the genitals and twist hard (bullock is the term for a castrated bull). If he had a thumb free, he'd stick that into his opponent's eye, trying to flip it out of its socket. If these tactics worked to perfection, the bout would be finished... and so would the sorry loser, some of whose vital parts were out of operation, possibly forever.

Out to the Track

Early Americans loved horses, especially fast ones. In frontier communities, all that was needed was an open meadow and a few men proud of their speedy steeds to stir up boasts and bets.

Quarter horses, the favorite riding horses in Revolutionary days, were fast starters and unexcelled on a quarter of a mile straightway. They were raced and bet on throughout the colonies.

Where there was more money and leisure, as in the prospering lands of Virginia, wealthy gentlemen began to copy old-country customs. They imported thoroughbreds from England, and built large oval tracks. Long races called "course" races were run on these tracks. Some course races were as long as four miles. Outside Williamsburg, a major series of course races was held every Spring and Fall. Enthusiasts traveled from great distances to place their bets and cheer on their favorites at these major races.

The Devil's Playthings

Cards, dice, dominoes, cribbage boards-- devices used at a gaming table-- were called the devil's playthings by those early Americans who railed against gambling fever. Their sermonizing did little good. Even in the northern colonies where religious traditions remained stronger, games of chance became more and more popular.

George Washington was fond of cards. .Here he entertains friends at Mount Vernon. His journals, in which he recorded all expenses, show that George was an unlucky gambler.

At tea parties in wealthy homes, ladies whiled away their afternoons with games of *Whist,* precursor of present-day bridge. Or they played *Lanterloo,* often called simply *Loo,* which resembled poker. Hundreds of dollars might change hands at these friendly parties.

Invitations to parties were often written on the backs of playing cards, indicating the type of entertainment to be expected. Franklin's printshop in Philadelphia was a major producer of playing cards, and Postmaster Ben sold them in the postoffice.

Children played with their ivory "bones" or Dominoes. Decks of playing cards for children sometimes had brief moral precepts printed on the backs-- a sop to the critics who maintained that the little ones should devote their time to learning uplifting things.

Checkers or draughts was a universal game. And in upper class families, every young gentleman was taught the intricacies of Chess, the ancient game of combat between kings, queens, knights, bishops, and their retainers.

The Big Action
When serious gamblers got together, and there were many of them, the wagering became serious business. Some wealthy gentlemen in the South, where gambling seemed to be in the blood, ruined themselves with their big bets.

They'd gamble away all the cash they had. Then wager part of their land. Or their indentured servants or slaves, which were standard units of commerce with established values.

Perhaps the rich gentlemen of the South were trying to emulate the habits of the aristocrats of England. There big spenders such as Gentleman Johnny Burgoyne, who was to become the most bloodthirsty of British generals in battle against Colonial troops, were known to drop as much as 50,000 pounds in a single night at the gaming tables.

Beware of the Sharpers
A society where gambling was prevalent was bound to develop a skilled professional group adept at plucking the pigeons.

Larger taverns often had a backroom with a billiard table. If you fancied you were pretty good with a cue, some slick hustler would soon sidle up to admire your skill and encourage you to place a few bets on it. Starting with a modest amount that would soon double and quadruple.

Dice and card games, of course, were staples of the pros. A card game called *Put* was popular, as was another called *All Fours*. A gambler's favorite was *Faro*, much like the modern game, in which players pitted their skill against a dealer. *Brag* was a popular game similar to today's *Poker*.

Professional sharpers at fairs conned the yokels with *Thimblerig*. It was rigged all right. A type of shell game in which the sucker was sure he could spot the location of the pea. Only he always guessed wrong.

Everyone Loved a Lottery

Lotteries are an American tradition. Long after King James' initial lottery to pay the bill for Jamestown, they persisted as a major fund-raising source for worthy (and shady) projects of all descriptions.

The esteemed colleges of Harvard and Yale relied on them before the days of big alumni drives. When Faneuil Hall in Boston burned, proceeds from a lottery paid to rebuild it.

Before the days of Bingo, churches and parsonages were erected or furnished with funds from lotteries. In a nation of gamblers, it was easier to persuade people to buy a ticket that promised them a chance to win a prize, than it was to get them to put an extra coin in the collection plate.

Inevitably, the sharpers zeroed in on lotteries, as they had on other games of chance. Prizes became smaller and the sponsor's takes became all-consuming. To keep from alienating all the customers, respected sponsors such as churches had to guarantee exactly what the split would be. Fifteen percent was considered to be a fair share for the sponsor.

Sums involved were substantial for the 1700s. One lottery, co-sponsored by two churches and the College of New Jersey, was a $100,000 venture-- a fortune in those days. Tickets for that lottery weren't cheap either. They cost five dollars apiece. That was more than a skilled tradesman earned in a week, so it would be equivalent to at least five hundred dollars today. That's gambling fever!

4
Those Crazy British Kings and Queens

If you lived in America in 1776, the most important person and the one whose private life you'd hear the most about would not be Jefferson, Adams or even Washington. They were relative unknowns outside their home territories when the 13 colonies first began to act in unison. The number-one celebrity was the King, the most powerful monarch in the world and the big boss of America whose every move made waves that affected the inhabitants on these shores.

Unfortunately for both George III and his subjects, he was a weak but obstinate monarch often inadequate to the decisions he faced. Because his short-sighted policies drove the Americans reluctantly to rebellion, he's reviled in our history books, but not in British histories which tend to regard him tolerantly. They maintain that compared to other rulers of his day, with all his shortcomings and even occasional bouts of insanity, he was not such a bad guy.

Q: How English was George III?
A: He had only the faintest touch of English blood. That came from a great-great-etc. grandmother six generations back, descended from the Stuart line.

Granted, George III had his peculiarities. But if you or I were saddled with his strange genetic background and continual governing problems, we might be a trifle off our rockers too.

Consider where King George was coming from, and all the problems our illustrious ancestors threw at him.

German Princes Become English Kings

If you think the twentieth-century shenanigans of Di, Charlie, Fergie, Andrew, Anne and the rest of the Buckingham Palace crowd resemble a soap opera, you should compare them to what went on in the early 1700s when George's ancestors ruled England.

Before that clan took over, the 18th Century began sedately while Queen Anne, the last of the English Protestant Stuarts, occupied the throne. Shy, pudgy, homely Anne was a conscientious ruler who strove valiantly to perpetuate her line. When her grossly-fat Danish consort was not stuffing himself with victuals or hitting the bottle, he managed to impregnate her 17 times. Sadly, 16 of their offspring died as babies, and the remaining prince lasted only till he was 11.

When Anne died later, childless, the door was open to the claims of her closest male relative, who would have become James III. However, James was a Catholic, a fact which greatly bothered the power structure of predominantly Protestant England. The great Whig families who could make and break kings wanted no part of a "Catholic Pretender". Instead they looked for some Protestant prince who could take over the job.

The Right Religion

The choice for England's king was George Louis the Elector of Hanover. From the convoluted intermarriages of European royalty, there were other potential candidates who possessed closer blood claims, as well as more intelligence and better character. But George Louis won out because he professed the right religion.

That decision of the Protestant noblemen brought to England the Hanoverian kings and a long string of Georges.

The Hanoverians could speak almost no English. The first German-born King of England could converse only with those of his ministers who spoke French, a widely-used language. Although this difficulty in communicating was certainly awkward, it was not necessarily considered to be a handicap.

It diminished the role of the monarchs and shifted true power to a prime minister, which is what Parliament preferred. That governing body was happiest when kings stayed out of politics and concentrated on amusing themselves, one aptitude at which most of the King Georges excelled.

George I -- First of the Swingers

While still but a prince in his native Hanover, the first George married his cousin, 16-year-old Princess Sophia Dorothea of Zell (or Celle). This marriage of convenience to unite their two duchies proved unfortunate for Sophia Dorothea. While George was a libertine himself, he watched his wife jealously.

It seems that the pretty Princess, lonely and neglected while her randy husband slept around, succumbed to the handsome Count of Konigsmark who came to visit the Hanoverian castle. When Prince George learned of this indiscretion, the Count vanished .

His whereabouts remained a mystery for decades until George's son and successor visited the family castle at Hanover and ordered some rebuilding of that old structure. The renovators discovered the remains of Count Konigsmark under the floor of what had been the Princess's dressing room.

No Queen at the Coronation

Sophie Dorothea's fate was not a lot better than her lover's had been. Her husband kept her locked away at Hanover for the rest of her life. She had to remain in seclusion in Germany even after her husband moved to London to assume the English throne.

That's not to say the King lacked for female companionship. He brought with him two German mistresses. They were a strange pair-- one obscenely fat and the other skinny and tall.

His subjects made fun of this peculiar harem, but George liked the two ladies. He bestowed noble titles on both of them, making one a countess and the other a duchess.

A Belated Funeral

Neglected in life, Princess Sophia Dorothea was also neglected in death. For more than six months, George didn't bother to arrange for a funeral, so the Princess remained unburied in Hanover while

George remained in London. This unprecedented state of affairs created nasty comments in both countries, and doubtless nasty odors in the German palace.

Eventually George had to take time out from his diversions to do something about dead Sophie. He set out for Germany to arrange for a funeral. That's when he got his come-uppance.

While traveling by coach to Hanover belatedly to bury his wife, George I suffered a massive stroke. He died soon after in his former home, in the very room where he'd been born.

George II-- More of the Same

The Second King George carried on the Hanover tradition of disappointing his subjects. As a result, he was no more popular with them than the First George had been. The creators of popular rhymes circulated in the taverns observed that fact.

> **"George the First was always reckoned vile,**
> **but viler still was George the Second.**
> From an English ditty

That verse may be unfair, however. Although the Second George amused himself with mistresses, as his father had done, he didn't mistreat his Queen. She was a good German girl, Caroline of Anspach. Every evidence is that he loved Caroline very much and bedded her diligently. His mistresses, a kingly prerogative that everyone expected, were merely an *addition* to the happy conjugal life he enjoyed.

An Understanding Wife

Queen Caroline was extremely tolerant of the way of Kings. She figured that if her husband didn't amuse himself with one mistress, it would be with another, so she established an understanding with his long-time favorite girl friend. That was Lady Suffolk with whom the Queen maintained a polite relationship, if not an enthusiastic one, for many years..

However, things changed at the palace when George became a bit tired of Lady Suffolk. Caroline had cause to become perturbed when her husband ditched his old amorata for a beautiful and much younger number. She didn't object to the change of mistresses, but to the fact that he began staying in Hanover *permanently* to be near this new chick, the Countess Von Walmoden.

To get her straying spouse back home, Caroline finally wrote to him, suggesting he bring the Countess to England, rather than staying away so long in Germany with her. That seemed like an excellent idea to George. Only too happy to take his wife's practical suggestion, he promptly installed his cute German import as an addition to the palace extended family.

Bitter Quarrels with Sons and Heirs

There was one thing on which the King and Queen heartily agreed. That was their mutual dislike of their eldest son and heir, Frederick, the Prince of Wales.

> **"Our first-born is the greatest ass, the greatest liar, the greatest canaille and the greatest beast in the world, and we heartily wish he were out of it."**
> George II

So much did both parents detest their troublesome heir that when Caroline was on her deathbed, George wouldn't allow Frederick to say good-bye to her. And she was said to be grateful to be spared that visit.

Queen Caroline's final hours were marked with another unusual twist. While she breathed her last, devoted Caroline's chief concern was for the future happiness of her philandering spouse. Knowing that age had not dulled his strong need for sexual pleasures, Caroline urged him to marry again when she was gone. But the King refused to think of marriage; he vowed to depend on another solution, which was common to monarchs of that time.

> **"No, no, I shall have mistresses!"**
> George II's pledge to his dying Queen

Remaining faithful to his pledge, George never remarried. However, he was not one to remain celebate. He kept his bed warm, as he'd promised his wife, with an ample supply of compliant women.

The Untimely End of Frederick

The dread that George II and his Queen had of the Prince of Wales'
taking over the throne of England was misplaced. That day never
came to pass. Fred died before Daddy.

It was one of the few active occupations of the lethargic prince
that did him in. He liked to play Cricket, but evidently not very
skillfully. During a game, the inept prince got whacked solidly on
the head by a cricket ball and never waked up.

Fred's unexpected demise was not mourned by the populace. A
scurrilous verse that passed around London indicates that their
sorrow was only because the son and not the father was gone.

**"Here lies Fred, who was alive and is dead.
Had it been his father, I had much rather.
But since tis only Fred, there's no more to be said."**

Although Fred bowed out of the picture prematurely, the
Hanover succesion was secure. The Prince left an 11-year-old son
and heir. It was that boy, the Second George's grandchild, who
inherited the scepter and crown.

Enter George III

George Wilhelm Frederick, grandson of the Second George,
became King of Great Britain and Ireland when he was 22 years
old. He also ruled his ancestral homeland as Elector of Hanover,
where his Germanic name was spelled Georg Wilhelm Friedrich.

His new job as head of the British Empire was perhaps the most
prestigious in the world, but the Third George acquired it at a bad
time. The year was 1760 when England was embroiled in the long
and costly Seven Year's War with its several European enemies.
Other fracases lay ahead.

Soon after the Seven Year's War wound down, leaving the
English treasury in anemic shape, the crazy American Patriots
would be acting up. The even crazier Irish would continue their
defiance of English dominance. (So what's new?) In less than two
decades into George III's long reign, General Washington would be
walloping British troops and foretelling the beginning of the end of

Round of figure and face, with bulbous eyes, King George III
is shown here in court regalia, but on his country estates he
dressed so simply the press called him " Farmer George."

valuable colonies. Next would come a bloody showdown at
Waterloo with the Corsican conqueror, Napoleon.

The Third George's troubles would never end. And they began at
an early age.

A Difficult Childhood

In everything he undertook, well-meaning George III tried
diligently to do his best. Unfortunately, his best efforts usually
turned out to be not very good.

Young George didn't learn to read until he was eleven. Even with the best of tutoring, he never learned to write coherently with any semblance of grammar or identifiable spelling. Fortunately for him, he inherited a job where underlings could write down what he told them. Even that wasn't easy because his verbal communication tended to get garbled. Like many of his clan, the Third George was a lethargic clumsy clod, indifferent to learning.

> **"The cleverest tutors in the world could have done little to expand his small intellect."** Thackeray

There were a few things which interested the future King, mostly related to the details and trappings of royalty or the military. These he was capable of memorizing.

He could recite the intricate genealogies of his clan, and he knew the histories of important English families. He liked maps, which showed the fiefdoms of his and other royal families. He was well-versed in court etiquette. As a result of this fascination with the panoply of monarchies, when George assumed the throne of England, he became a stickler for the observance of correct procedures and rituals at his court.

Inept, timid young George needed someone to guide him in the intricacies of being a monarch.. He found such a companion and role model on whom he leaned for many years. That helpful guide was John Stuart, the Earl of Bute. The handsome Earl was a close friend of the boy's mother... some hinted *too close a friend.* The Earl, a polished courtier with all the graces awkward Georgie lacked, became the lad's tutor and later his prime minister.

Another German Princess
Inevitably, young George fell in love. He was far from a dashing figure. George was of medium height with sandy-colored hair, thick lips, a ruddy complexion. Even at an early age, the dumpy, potbellied Hanoverian physique was apparent, as were the bulbous eyes of that clan.

The girl who dazzled the shy clumsy lad was charming 15-year-old Lady Sarah Lennox. Lovely Sarah, however, was a non-royal and therefore unsuitable for marriage to a monarch. At least, that's what George's mother and the Earl of Bute decreed.

The Earl drew up a list of available princesses, all German Protestants, of course. The selection was small. Repeated interbreeding had scrambled the genes of so many royal families that one had to beware of madness in their offspring. Grandfather, George II, had worried about this when he chose a wife for George's father, Prince Frederick. Grandpa rejected many applicants, figuring that Freddie was nutty enough without compounding the genetic odds. He made this comment about one of the prospective brides that he turned away.

"I didn't think that grafting my half-witted coxcomb with a madwoman would serve to mend the breed." George II

Careful as Grandpa George was, he didn't chose too wisely when he finally chose Augusta of Saxe-Gothe for Freddie. Many of her children and grandchildren were severely mentally and physically handicapped. Some were congenital idiots.

At any rate, Augusta and her confidante, the Earl of Bute, made better marriage arrangements for her and Freddie's son, the Third King George. For the young monarch who was to become the arch-enemy of his American colonists, they zeroed in on a good sane German girl. She was unglamorous but sturdy Charlotte Sophia, Princess of Mecklenburg-Strelitz. Dutiful young George acquiesced in the choice.

Unlike his forebears, George III was decidedly moral in his marriage, a rarity among monarchs of his day. (Or of any day?)

By remaining ever faithful to Queen Charlotte, he disappointed many of his subjects. Generally leading dull lives themselves, they relished hearing a bit of scandal about royal mistresses, just as the tabloid-addicted English do today.

Like a Simple Country Squire

George III enjoyed time on his farms, and more resembled a rural squire than a mighty monarch. He was often called *"Farmer George."*

He loved hunting, fishing and picnicking with his family. On quiet evenings, he enjoyed listening to his Queen play the spinet. On Sundays and feast days, he never missed attendance at church. Surprisingly for royalty, the King and Queen were incredibly frugal in their private lives-- so much so that the newspapers, in impertinent cartoons, brazenly satirized their stinginess.

George III loved to dance, and never tired of his favorite songs. At parties where a few select couples joined him and his queen, if he especially liked what the orchestra played, he'd command the musicians to repeat the tune over and over ,while he comtinued to dance on for hours.

Like a good squire, George Wilhelm Frederick doted on his family. There was a lot to dote upon. He was especially possessive of his daughters-- all six of them. So closely did Daddy watch the girls, even after they were grown, that they called their group "the nunnery." They married late or not at all.

George had more difficulty in trying to smother his nine sons. As they grew to legal age, all of the boys scorned their Father's favorite haunts-- moldering Windsor castle out in the countryside, or the seashore at Weymouth where the King could play captain on his yacht, the Royal George. His nine boys were a sorry lot who did nothing to help the King or to win respect from their people.

> **"The damnedest millstones around the neck
> of any government that can be imagined."**
> Duke of Wellington

63

Like Wellington, other powerful noblemen of the Empire were also outspoken in their disgust of the Princes. But they had to put up with them. And their irritations with the heirs to the throne were nowhere near as vexing to them as his no-good sons were to their parents, the King and Queen.

Again, a No-Good Prince of Wales

As happened with the Windsor kings generation after generation, George III suffered big trouble with his son and heir. This Prince of Wales was an especially bad one.

None of George's sons amounted to anything. But if any of them contributed to their father's madness, it was the Prince of Wales who drove him to distraction. As in past generations, this prince reveled in the attention of those ever-present contrary politicians who set him up as a figurehead for their opposition to the King. And it was not just the predictable moves of a royal heir, impatient to inherit the power of the throne, that made young Freddie so obnoxious.

Fond of Wine and Women

The Prince's escapades began at an early age. When only 17, he himself said that he'd become "rather too fond of wine and women." The first failing helped to make him a pudgy boozy-looking man. The second led him into troublesome affairs and an illegal marriage.

When he was still 17, the Prince became enamored of a 21-year-old actress, Mary Robinson. He promised her 20,000 pounds, when he got some money of his own. The lady never collected on this promise though, because young Prince Georgie ditched her long before he became solvent.

His second liaison was more dangerous. Young Freddie fell madly in love with Mrs. Maria Fitzherbert, a stunning widow. Since that lady was a Catholic, there was no way the heir-apparent could marry her. To make matters worse, members of the royal family under age 25 were forbidden to marry without the King's consent. Prince Freddie did it anyway, secretly and illegally. The couple stayed married for ten years, though their secret soon became public knowledge.

Debts, Debts, Debts
One of the Prince's other passions, his overriding one, brought the end to his decade of illegal matrimony. Even more than women, George Augustus Frederich loved to gamble and spend money lavishly. In fact, he set records with his squandering, a failing especially galling to the penurious King who had to settle his son's debts.

The most costly folly the Prince became involved in was his building of an architectural monstrosity at Brighton. Erecting that huge oriental pavilion of many sumptuously furnished rooms sucked up more than half a million pounds. That infuriated frugal daddy George, and didn't go well either with the keepers of the purse strings in Parliament.

The only way Freddie could persuade Parliament to pay off his debts was to get rid of Maria Fitzherbert and marry a proper princess. He agreed to the deal and married his cousin, but that arrangement didn't last very long-- only until the birth of their first and only child.

While all those shenanigans were going on, George Augustus Frederick was acting as the Prince Regent, because his father was undergoing more seizures of insanity.

Madness Will Out
Not long after George III ascended the throne and married Charlotte, he suffered his first bout of madness. There were several to follow, and they became longer-lasting and more severe.

After his first illness, George developed an extremely nervous manner. His gestures became agitated. When he spoke, he rattled along frenziedly in a hoarse voice. He developed a habit of answering his own questions, or ending with his staccato trademark, *"What, what, what?"*

During his bouts of insanity, George was in great pain. Of course, his baffled doctors added to his discomfort with their standard procedures of bleeding, blistering, purging, etc. to "get out the bad blood." At times they tied him up in a straitjacket.

Q: What caused George III's madness?

A: Medical authorities can't accurately diagnose illnesses that occurred more than two centuries ago, but most believe George's trouble was Porphyria. In that rare hereditary disease, deficiencies of enzymes in the blood create an excess of porphyrins, which causes many problems. They include psychiatric disturbances, delirium, severe abdominal pains, muscle cramps and weaknesses as well as other nasty symptoms.

One personality change which occurred during these bouts made George more like his ancestors. When out of his normal mind, prudish George forgot his devotion to Queen Charlotte. At those times, he was likely to pounce licentiously upon any pretty lady of the court careless enough to come within his reach.

A Succession of Prime Ministers

Even the Americans tended to blame George's prime ministers and Parliament for their troubles more than they blamed him. At least they did in the early years of the War.

Q: Who was "Champagne Charley" Townshend?

A: The Chancellor of the Exchequer whom King George put in charge of the Colonies, i.e. in charge of squeezing more money from the Americans. He earned his nickname because of the huge quantities he quaffed of his favorite bubbly drink. Charley would turn up at Parliament so drunk he could scarcely stand, yet speak brilliantly on business of the day. Lord Townshend is also forever associated with another beverage-- tea. The Townshend revenue acts he devised, which placed import duties on the Colonists' beloved cup of tea, led to the Boston Tea Party and the first open rebellion against royal taxes.

Of course, the series of ministers who bungled relations with the Colonists were his choices and responsibility. There were many brilliant men George III could have selected, but his warped personality prevented the right decisions.

His boyhood tutor, the Earl of Bute was his first prime minister, and an inept one. So unpopular did the Earl become that he had to have a bodyguard when he travelled. Bute realized his weaknesses and repeatedly begged George to let him resign. The King finally acceded, but ministers he selected later, such as bumbling Lord North, made a mess of relations with America.

One of King George III's biggest mistakes was his miscalculation at the beginning of the Revolution. He simply couldn't comprehend that anything really important was happening in those fledgling American colonies which were located nearly 4,000 miles away. Even by the time of the Declaration of Independence, he still didn't realize the gravity of the situation. Here's what he wrote in his diary on that fateful day.

July 4, 1776: "Nothing of importance this day."
King George III

Several of England's leading members of government recognized the validity of many of the American Colonists' gripes. They favored working out some sort of compromise, as did the Americans. But George and the ministers he kept because they agreed with him, wouldn't give an inch. Instead, they lost what could have become their choicest chunk of empire.

As much as any other person, it was George III with his strange personality who was responsible for the outbreak of the American War for Independence. And for its outcome.

5
Alexander Hamilton
Genius and Philanderer

If you think the escapades of today's politicians are wild, you should read the stories about Alexander Hamilton that appeared in early-day newspapers. In those racy tabloids, Alexander was accused of being, among other things, an adulterer, a swindler, a forger and a liar.

It's true that Hamilton's life was weirder than a soap opera. He was certainly a volatile character who came from a rough beginning to a bad end, with many racy episodes in between.

"That fellow Aaron Burr shot and killed in a duel" is the way he's remembered by many. He was also one of the towering figures in American history, with a truly brilliant mind and a hunger for fame that brought him to great accomplishments.

After distinguishing himself in battle with the New York Artillery, Colonel Hamilton became General Washington's military secretary for more than four years. When Washington assumed the presidency, he picked Hamilton to be part of our first cabinet as Secretary of the Treasury, where he performed admirably in straightening out the country's finances..

But in addition to the many skills that made him a giant in public life, he had giant-size problems in his personal life.

Tough Laws
The scandals which Alexander's enemies delighted in publicizing in later years, started even before his birth.

His mother Rachel, a redheaded beauty, married at 16 but soon ran away from her husband. She and her mother, also separated from a husband, skipped about the islands of the West Indies. When

Rachel finally returned to home port, her husband had her arrested, charged with "whoring" and sentenced to jail.

After her stint in the pokey, Rachel departed permanently from her husband and their young son, Peter. She moved in with James Hamilton, a handsome neer-do-well from a prominent family. They had two sons, James Junior and Alexander.

Rachel's estranged husband, embarrassed at having his wandering wife referred to as "that Hamilton woman", sued for divorce. She was charged with bearing two illegitimate children, abandoning her legal son and "giving herself to whoring with everyone." As a convicted adulteress, Rachel was barred by the harsh laws of that time and place from ever remarrying. Therefore, Alexander and his older brother could never be legitimized.

> **"A bastard brat, and a man not to be trusted."**
> John Adams

Court records verifying all the sad details of Alexander's birth were exhumed and gleefully broadcast in later years when Alexander was at the peak of his political career. His political opponents, such as John Adams who bitterly opposed Hamilton's Federalist policies, delighted in referring to his illegitimacy.

Q: What made Adams so spiteful to Hamilton?
A: When Adams ran for the presidency, Hamilton opposed his candidacy. That split the Whig party in which both were powerful leaders. Adams didn't appreciate that.

A Rough Childhood

When Alexander was only 11 or 13 (records of his birth vary) his mother died of a fever, which he narrowly survived. Long before that, Papa Hamilton had wandered off, so the two young Hamilton boys were on their own.

For a few years, Alexander scraped out a dreary living as a clerk in an export-import firm. He seems to have developed his writing during those years. Not by penning lofty tomes that resembled his

His wife outlived Alexander by 50 years, She died holding a love letter that he'd written to her before marriage.

historic Federalist Papers, which were to play a big part in promoting the ratification of our country's Constitution, but by publishing a few poems in a popular gazette.

Shortly after his literary career began, teen-age Alexander left the Indies. A kindly Presbyterian minister recognized the young lad's rare intelligence, and raised funds to send him to the mainland to study for the law at King's College, now Columbia.

Off to the Wars and Fame

At college, Alexander soon became an enthusiast for rebellion against the King. He joined the revolutionary army in 1775, and became a staff officer just two years later. Distinguishing himself at the Battle of Princeton, he was promoted to Lieutenant Colonel by George Washington's and served as the General's aide-de-camp and personal secretary for four years.

Growing up on the island of Nevis, he'd spoken French, which enabled him to serve as Washington's interpreter to the French officers who joined the Colonial army. As a result, he developed a close friendship with the Marquis de Lafayette, about whom you'll read more in a later chapter.

Colonel Hamilton, war hero, married rich Betsy Schuyler in a lavish wedding attended by his friend and boss, Gen. Washington.

Toward the end of the War, getting back again to a field command, Hamilton once more proved himself to be an outstanding warrior in one of the attacks at the crucial battle of Yorktown.

Popular with the Ladies

As you might imagine, the handsome young red-headed war hero never lacked for female friends. Although he enjoyed his bachelor days, he realized that a wife could be an important asset to his political ambitions, if she met his strict standards. He took a practical approach to matrimony.

In a letter to a friend, Hamilton confided some of the many requirements he'd insist on in a prospective bride. Besides being beautiful, shapely, etc., the fortunate young lady would have to possess many qualities to satisfy the finicky Alexander.

> **"She must be young and handsome (I lay more stress upon a good shape). Sensible. A little learning will do. Well-bred, chaste and tender. As to her fortune, the larger the stock of that the better, for money is an essential ingredient to happiness in this world."**
>
> Alexander Hamilton

You'll note that the future lawyer, banker and treasurer of the United States was not one to overlook the importance of money, preferably in abundance. He found it too.

In 1780 (when he was 25 and still an officer just before the end of the war) the young lady he married was Elizabeth "Betsy" Schuyler. Her daddy, General Philip Schuyler, was a wealthy Dutch patroon, reigning over thousands of acres of rich land in upper New York. He was also a power in New York politics, which fit in pefectly with Alexander's ambitions.

Young Colonel Hamilton's friend and patron, General George Washington, held a reception for the newly-wedded couple. The poor outcast boy from the islands had snared it all -- money, social standing, military honors, a strong political base and a beautiful dutiful wife.

Fun on the Side

Hamilton showed considerable affection for his wife, after his fashion. He wrote many expressive love letters to his "beloved Betsy" when still with his army command. Of course, that was when they were newly married. The couple had eight children, if that proves anything in the days before birth control. His first flirtations, however, occured even before the marriage.

Elizabeth Schuyler had two sisters: Angelica, who was a year older, and Peggy, a year younger. Alexander was fond of all three of the Schuyler girls. From some of his letters, it's sometimes hard to figure out which one he liked best.

There was certainly exceptional rapport-- some people thought an unseemly amount of it-- with Angelica, who'd developed a crush on Alexander at first sight. Openly displayed fondness between the two in-laws never waned. In fact, family as well as outsiders were known to remark on their behaviour, and question whether it went beyond the proper bounds of brother-sister friendliness, or whether Alexander had married the right sister.

For example, after Angelica was married, Hamilton evidently paid some of her bills, and was a close companion during a period when her husband was away. This occurred after Angelica and her husband had lived for several years in England. Throughout those years, she and Alexander continued an affectionate correspondence.

While her husband remained in England as a new member of Parliament, Angelica came home to America for a lengthy visit without him. She had a brief get-together with her folks in upstate New York; then quickly headed for the city to see her sister and brother-in-law. However, she did not follow the usual custom of that day and stay at their home. Instead she roomed alone at a boarding house. Alexander paid the bill for her lodgings.

In letters after her departure back to England, both Alexander and Angelica expressed their extreme grief at having to part from each other.

Ambitious Alexander Launches Triple Careers

With the help of father-in-law Schuyler, Alexander launched his political career. He was elected a delegate from New York to the Continental Congress. That marked the start of an active and successful political life.

At about the same time, he also decided he wanted to be a lawyer. After three months of cramming, he passed his bar exams and opened an office at 57 Wall Street. His practice prospered, and he became one of New York's leading attorneys.

Just a few months after starting his law practice, Hamilton also decided that New York needed a sound banking system, and that he was the one to get it underway. So he became the founder and a director of the Bank of New York.

All three of these careers-- politics, the law and finance-- combined to make Alexander a very busy and successful leader. After the weak Articles of Confederation were replaced by our Constitution, with considerable help from promoter and writer Hamilton, his friend and admirer George Washington again called him to be a secretary. Not a personal military secretary this time, but a member of his cabinet. As expected, Hamilton did a superb job as Secretary of the Treasury, and succeeded in putting our struggling country, bankrupt from the war, on a sound financial basis.

Other Amorous Connections Cause Trouble

Besides keeping busy professionally, Hamilton seems to have been exceptionally active in his personal affairs as well. Whether or not

Alexander's relations with his sister-in-law were scandalous, as the gossips implied, he openly admitted to other pecadillos.

When he became Secretary of the Treasury at the end of the War, his political enemies accused him of speculating in Veteran's certificates, the pitiful bonuses the government promised to pay soldiers when the treasury finally had enough money to do so. Hamilton and other were implicated in taking advantage of the veterans by secretly buying up their bonus certificates for pennies on the dollar in order to hold them for an eventual full pay-off. You'll read more about those bonuses in a later chapter.

Thomas Jefferson wanted to have Hamilton impeached for improper conduct in office. Hamilton denied the charges of speculation. However, he both surprised and delighted his foes by the defense he chose.

Opening himself and his family to scandal, Hamilton said the speculator who accused him of being a partner in a scheme to defraud verterans was really a *jealous husband*. Alexander claimed the money involved was really a blackmail payoff to the husband of the woman with whom Hamilton had been having an adulterous affair. Here's what Hamilton wrote in a pamphlet he published to explain his innocence.

> "The charge against me is a connection with one James Reynolds for purposes of improper pecuniary speculation. My real crime is an amorous connection with his wife for a considerable time, with his privity and connivance, if not originally brought on by a combination between husband and wife with the design to extort money from me."
> Alexander Hamilton

A Long-lasting Scandal

Hamilton was surprised when there was much reaction to this public statement about a long-standing affair with the wife of a sleazy speculator, whom he implied was also her pimp. He had expected, perhaps like some politicians today, that his factual acknowledgement of a bit of hanky-panky would be viewed as no big deal.

Perhaps he was right that, in the long run, such pecadillos tend to be forgotten by the voting public. Another prominent man of the time, predicted sadly but philosophically that such would be the eventual outcome of the case.

> **"Hamilton is fallen for the present, but if he fornicates**
> **with every female in the cities of New York and Philadelphia,**
> **he will rise again, for purity of character, after a period**
> **of political existence is not necessary for public patronage.**
>
> General David Cobb

There's no record of how Alexander's disclosure was received at home, although the straying hsuband professed to be greatly concerned about the "extreme pain" his disclosures might cause to his "excellent wife."

As details of Hamilton's affair with Maria Reynolds unfolded, it became apparent that he'd paid a total of $1,200 to her husband. Many letters from all the parties involved showed up in the newspapers. Hamilton was accused by his detractors of forging some of them. They seemed to show that Hamilton had not shelled out the money to join in any financial scheme with Mr. Reynolds, but rather to keep him quiet about the affair with Maria. There's considerable logic to this, since the Reynolds couple lived well with no evident source of income.

The Maria affair was never definitely cleared up, but Hamilton escaped being tossed out of office over it. Nevertheless, his political opponents kept the gossip alive as long as they could and were vicious in their comments. His bitter-tongued enemy Adams was, as usual, at the forefront.

> **"Hamilton's ambitions come from a superabundance**
> **of secretions that he cannot find whores enough to**
> **draw off"**
> John Adams

The leading muckraking journalist of that time, James Callendar had a field day with the Hamilton-Maria Reynolds affair. Although he accused Hamilton of just about every wrongdoing-- speculation, lying, adultery, forgery, etc.-- he did exclude one possible misdeed. He doubted that the Secretary of the Treasury would have paid hush money to keep his extra-marital affairs a secret.

"Hamilton had nothing to lose as to his reputation for
chastity. The world had fixed a previous opinion of that."
James Callendar

Actually Callendar had some basis for doubting that Hamilton
would pay any hush money, but for another reason. Contrary to
charges by his political opponents that Hamilton was getting rich by
embezzling public funds-- they accused him of pocketing 100,000
pounds from one deal-- his bank accounts certainly didn't bear out
any such prosperity. In fact, after his death, his assets were so
downright pitiful that friends passed the hat to raise a little money
to help his widow and children.

For Jefferson; Against Burr
Hamilton could be a hard man to get along with. He was often
impatient with others, strong in his views, sensitive to criticism and
quick to lash back.

He made bitter enemies of powerful people. Thomas Jefferson
and the growing Republican party strongly disliked Hamilton's
Federalist ideas. Their constant attacks finally drove Secretary
Hamilton to resign from his Cabinet post. Within his own party, the
Whigs, John Adams was continually at odds with Alexander.
Adams never forgave him for pulling support away from him in his
run for the presidency.

Neither did Aaron Burr like it when Hamilton threw his political
weight against him in favor of old adversary Tom Jefferson in the
presidential election of 1801.

Burr Almost Became President
Burr almost became the third president of the United States. He
missed by just one vote!

In the presidential election, Burr and Thomas Jefferson ended up
with a tie vote in the Electoral College. To break this impass, the
outcome then had to be decided in the house of Representatives.
There the deadlock persisted for 36 roll-calls. Finally, Alexander
Hamilton persuaded the representatives to give the victory to
Jefferson by a single vote.

Q: How did Burr become vice-president?
A: According to the rules at that time, the candidate with the most votes became president, and whoever was in second place became vice president. So Burr, much to his disgust, ended up with the nothing-to-do vice-presidential job

Burr burned even more a few years later when Alexander made public statements that questioned his integrity. Those remarks squelched Burr's hopes of getting the Republican nomination for the important governorship of New York State, a post he coveted.

"Aaron Burr is a man of irregular and insatiable ambition who ought not to be trusted with the reins of government."
Alexander Hamilton

Burr was so furious over Hamilton's remarks that he claimed personal insult, and challenged his political adversary to a duel. Hamilton was strongly opposed to the practice of dueling; his son had been killed in a duel just three years previously. Yet he felt that as a public figure he couldn't refuse Burr's challenge. Reluctantly he agreed to face Burr with pistols.

He shouldn't have. On the dueling field, Hamilton did not take aim, but merely fired a shot in the air. Burr was out for blood, and he got it. His shot hit his opponent, and Hamilton died the next day.

Q: Was Hamilton's pistol bad luck?
A: Definitely! His 54-caliber weapon was the same one his 19-year-old son, Philip, had used in a duel that cost him his life. Oddly, Alexander's brother-in-law had also borrowed this pistol for a duel he fought with Aaron Burr.
Fortunately in that fracas, as often happened, neither contestant was injured.

Alexander Hamilton was only 49 years old when his brilliant career ended. His widow, who lived to be 94, survived him for another 50 years.

Strangely, Burr and Hamilton had been friends at one time. They'd known each other both as officers in the Continental Army and later as lawyers in New York who sometimes worked on cases together.

At the time that he killed Alexander Hamilton, Aaron Burr was vice president of the United States!

6
Aaron Burr Wanted to be
an Emperor

Shooting and killing Alexander Hamilton was only one of Aaron Burr's indiscretions. He became involved in a variety of scandals. For one of them, an attempt to set up his own empire, he was arrested at the special request of President Jefferson, and tried for treason against his country.

At the beginning, Aaron had it all. He was rich, talented and charming, That was an ideal combination for a young man with unlimited political ambition.

He came from a distinguished family. His father, the Reverend Aaron Burr, had been co-founder and the second president of the College of New Jersey, later to become Princeton. Both of his parents died when he was three, and he went to live with an uncle, the Reverend Timothy Edwards.

A precocious boy who throughout his life was a rebel, Aaron escaped from Uncle Timothy's strict discipline by enrolling at the College of New Jersey at the age of 13. He graduated with honors at 16. Brought up by churchmen, it's understandable that he started out studying to be a minister himself, but he changed that for the law. However, before Aaron could begin his career as a lawyer, the War for Independence intervened.

From War to Marriage and Politics
Burr had a relatively short military career, but met several interesting people in the army. He served on Benedict Arnold's staff and also briefly with Washington. Rising to Lieutenant Colonel, he commanded a regiment at the Battle of Monmouth.

In ill health (records of his illness are not clear, but our ancestors suffered from endless ailments) Aaron resigned from the army. It took him three years to recover his health, resume his law studies and gain admittance to the bar in New York.

Shortly thereafter, he married a widow, Theodosia Prevost, who was ten years his senior. Theodosia already had five children, so the young attorney, who was only 26 at the time, took over as big-daddy to a sizeable bunch of kids.

Theodosia bore him a daughter, named after her, whom Aaron doted on. He also seemed devoted to his wife until her death after a dozen years of marriage.

Aaron's law practice flourished. He became one of the two most successful lawyers in New York City. The other leading barrister was Alexander Hamilton. Both of them were up to their ears in political activities.

Headed for Political Success
Within a few years after setting up his law practice, Burr was appointed Attorney General of New York by Governor Clinton. Two years later, he was elected to the U.S. Senate. The man he defeated for that post was Hamilton's father-in-law, Philip Schuyler.

Q: What political machine boosted Burr's career?
A: In the same year Burr entered politics, the Tammany Society was founded. Aaron molded it from a social club into a potent political machine which supported him and eventually gained notoriety as Tammany Hall, the long-time powerhouse of New York politics.

As you learned in a previous chapter, Burr suffered two major political set-backs. First, he missed becoming the president of the United States, tying with Thomas Jefferson in electoral votes, and then losing the tie-breaker in the House of Representatives. Next, while the vice president, he tried to change that job for one considered more important; he wanted to be elected governor of the great state of New York.

His political enemy, Alexander Hamilton helped to frustrate his ambitions both times, and the animosity between the two led to the famous duel in which he killed Hamilton.

The duel, since Hamilton fired his shot into the air, was regarded by most people as murder. Public disapproval of the killing of the Secretary of the Treasury by the Vice-President pretty much finished Aaron Burr's political career in Washington or his home state. However, never one to give up easily, Burr turned his eyes toward more distant fields.

Just Like Napoleon

His aim was to regain popularity and power in a major way. As were many of his countrymen, Burr was also hungry for land, and he envisioned a way to become the powerful monarch of tremendous expanses of land. He looked toward a career like that of Napoleon Bonaparte, who had recently been crowned an emperor.

Burr's plan was to conquer and seize Spanish-controlled territory in the West and in Mexico. *For himself.*

America had just purchased the huge Louisiana Territory from the French. However, Spain still held vast areas in the Southwest, and was attempting to grab more in the lower Mississippi Valley, a situation that was bringing the U.S. and Spain to the brink of war.

Ex-Colonel and almost-President Burr thought he spotted a rare opportunity to beat the two feuding countries to the draw. While they were arguing about borders and territories, he'd raise his own army and grab off enough Southwestern and Mexican land so he could set up his own fiefdom.

His plan was to set himself up as the Napoleon of a vast new Empire of the West.

Thinking like an Emperor

Not one to dream little dreams, the out-of-work politician (having been dumped by Jefferson and his party) approached Britain to go into partnership with him. He knew that the Brits hated France and Spain, and certainly weren't fond of the new government in

America either. So Burr figured they'd be likely to help him if he proposed a scheme that would enable them to damage all three of their enemies. With British aid, he thought he could bite off a big chunk of the western United States and some of Mexico too.

The Brits said *"No thanks,"* to the out-of-favor American politician with the wild ideas. But Burr pushed ahead anyway. He decided he could enlist support from other influential people.

Triple-Agent Wilkinson

Ex-Colonel Burr contacted General James Wilkinson, a cagy old friend who was not averse to working a double deal. Not only was General Wilkinson on the U.S. Army payroll, but he was also secretly collecting from the Spanish in New Orleans, who wanted to gain control of the lower Mississippi Valley. Since he was already playing two sides, Wilkinson was easily persuaded that he could also profit from helping a third player, Burr.

Heading for New Orleans, Burr purchased a riverboat on which he cruised down the Ohio and Mississippi Rivers. Along the way, he recruited a small fighting force of adventurous frontiersmen and out-of-work soldiers like himself, looking to make a buck any way they could. The scheme in which he enlisted them was a wild one, but the fact that it was headed by the former Vice-President of the United States gave it some credence.

To pick up much needed funds, debt-laden Burr paused along his journey down the Ohio to stay for a few months with a wealthy Irish emigrant, Harman Blennerhassett. Harmon agreed to help with finances for the new risky venture. He did, and with additional funds from Burr's son-in-law, Aaron was able to buy more than a *million* acres of land in the Louisiana territory. That provided a start for his scheme of empire.

Q: What additional success did Burr have in Ohio?
A: Evidently not only Harman but also his pretty young wife, Margaret, was fascinated by charming Aaron. The baby she bore the following year was reputed to have been fathered by Aaron during his visit.

Tried as a Traitor
As Burr solicited many prominent people to finance his growing private army, his scheme became widely known. He was taken to local courts a few times, but always acquitted. That was until Burr's talkativeness got triple-dealing General Wilkinson into trouble.

Afraid he'd soon be court-martialed and nailed for treason, the General reported all the details of the plot to President Jefferson. Of course, he laid all the blame on Aaron Burr. President Jefferson promptly ordered the arrest of Burr. Aaron jumped bail and made a bee-line for the border, but he was apprehended near Natchez, Mississippi, just before he could slip across to the safety of the Spanish territory.

The man who would be Emperor was tried by the Chief Justice of the United States, the famous John Marshall. In some ways, it seemed like an open-and-shut case. There was little doubt that Burr had schemed to seize territory to which his country was laying claim. His conviction on a charge of treason seemed like a simple and quick matter.

Politics Enters the Picture
Political considerations changed the odds, in Burr's favor. Chief Justice Marshall, in charge of the trial, was not about to help the President who had requested it.

Justice Marshall was a Federalist who favored a strong central government. Jefferson was the leader of the Democrat-Republicans, fighting for states' rights and against the ideas of Marshall, Hamilton, etc. That made them political foes. Therefore, Marshall was not inclined to make it easy for Jefferson to gain public plaudits with a speedy successful trial of a noted traitor.

Marshall had the ability to screw up the trial, and he did. On behalf of the plaintiff, he decreed that President Jefferson must appear in his court to substantiate the claims against Burr.

There was no way Jefferson was going to subject himself to public questioning by his enemy, Marshall. *He refused the court summons*, a precedent followed today by his successors in such affairs as the Iran-Contra trials.

It would seem that Jefferson's personal testimony wasn't crucial; after all, he only knew what General Wilkinson had told him. That's what many American thought. However, it was ruled that though Burr might have made plans, he'd actually committed no act of treason.

Burr went free. It was a political fluke that freed him. Many of his countrymen recognized that and still considered him a traitor to his country.

One Last Try

Burr was not a man to give up easily. His credibilty gone in America and harrassed by creditors, Burr headed for Europe, where he tried again to enlist support for a scheme to capture a chunk of Mexico. He had no success there.

After six years, he returned to the U.S. under the assumed name of *Adolphus Arnot*. His new moniker didn't fool anyone. Recognizing that his masquerade didn't work, he soon returned to his true name. He also returned to practicing law in New York City where, in spite of his bad record, he managed to achieve a moderate degree of success.

He even married again. At the age of 77, Burr married a wealthy widow, Eliza Jumel. This late marraige may have boosted Burr's anemic fortunes, but evidently it was no great romantic success. Three years after the wedding, Eliza sued for divorce. She needn't have bothered. *On the day the final decree was granted, Burr died.*

The brilliant man who could be so charming, who almost became President, and who desired to be a Napoleon, never quite succeeded in his grand plans. The lasting legacy he left in history was as a treasonous smooth-talking rogue.

One distinction he has always retained. Aaron Burr was *the biggest stinker* of all the Vice-Presidents of the United States.

7
Lust for Land

It's impossible to understand the American people of 1776 without considering their absolute fascination for owning land.

Wherever you went in the Colonies, land and how to get more of it was a constant subject of conversation. It was an obsession which affected the lives of many famous people you'll read about here, as well as those of countless nameless families who braved incredible dangers to push westward into the wilderness so they could lay claim to a few acres of their own.

The big wheelers and dealers we have in real estate today were pikers compared with those in colonial America.

The size of some of the land holdings in our Colonies boggles the mind. However, until after the Revolution, it wasn't the colonists living in America who owned the really huge chunks of land. It was *absentee* land barons who stayed in England or Europe who controlled the really large holdings.

Carving Up the New Continent
The system for carving up the land started with the kings and queens you'll be reading about. Ask the King of England (or of France, Spain or Holland) who owned a certain area of America, and they'd all say "ME"!

That was a logical conclusion. After all, the first European ships' captains to land here always jumped ashore, planted a flag and proclaimed, "I claim these lands in the name of my king" That was the precedent-- all the territory belonged to one of the major kings to have and to hold (if he could) and to do with it whatever he damned well pleased.

What the Kings Wanted

What pleased each of the four major kings was to populate as big an area as possible. Just as quickly as possible. With enough loyal soldiers and settlers to keep it out of the hands of his enemy kings.

All of the monarchs figured the huge wilderness across the ocean (nobody knew exactly how huge) might come in handy some day. At some distant time, it might even prove as valuable as the tiny "Sugar Islands" of the West Indies, such as Barbados, whose rich tropical fields supplied the cane and molasses which were the backbone of the lucrative rum trade.

Of course, the monarchs themselves were too busy with their local wars to pay much attention to the distant American lands. So they made it worthwhile for their relatives and friends to do the colonizing job for them. Very worthwhile.

Wealth Beyond Imagining

The size of the land grants that British and Dutch monarchs handed out to favored friends is difficult for us to imagine. As a matter of fact, they themselves often didn't comprehend the magnitude of their gifts, for they might describe a land grant as *"extending to the Mississippi river, or to the mountains"*, and no one had an accurate idea of how far away that might be.

In some instances, the vast parcels of land they generously gave away to their freinds were as large or larger than entire countries in the Old World!

Q: How did American land areas compare with British?
A: Just the area which the Duke of York changed in name from Niew Amsterdam to New York is larger than all of England and Wales combined, or about twice the size of Scotland. New Jersey, which he gave to his friends, was a smaller piece of land, but still considerably larger than Northern Ireland. William Penn did okay too. He got more than five times the area of New Jersey.

For example, Charles II of England hated the Dutch and decided to take away from them the land they were settling in America. To try to accomplish this, he gave his brother, the Duke of York, all of what is now New York State... plus a few million acres south of it. The Duke of York, in turn, handed an ownership charter for all of New Jersey to his pals, Lord John Berkley and George Carteret

Let's Buy Albany

Before the Duke of York and his friends drove them out of Niew Amsterdam, the Dutch didn't do too badly in the land-grab business. The patroons the Dutch King set up in the New World lived like kings. Killian Van Renssalaer stayed in Holland, but he had his agents buy a few lots for his son who needed a place to get started in life. He purchased 700,000 acres, which we now know as Albany and its environs. Another lucky patroon owned a nice stretch of riverfront property--- 15 miles of shoreline along the Hudson.

> **Three-fourths of all the land in New York State was owned by about 30 people.**

Many of the rich patroons who bought vast estates from the Dutch East India Company were able to hold onto them when the British took over. Devoted business men, they didn't let any foolish patriotic notions interfere with whatever they had to do to keep their holdings under the new regime. As a matter of fact, they quickly fitted in with the rich gentry arriving from London.

They consorted with the royal governors and became loyal supporters of the British regime. So much so that when the Revolution broke out, the wealthy Dutchmen became the most rabid Tories in New York, and strongly opposed the rebellion.

Nobility, Old and New

Not only in New York, but in the southern colonies as well, the nobles of England became the landlords of America. Lord Fairfax, young George Washington's benefactor, was an absentee landlord on a grand scale.

From his mother, Lord Fairfax inherited *six million acres* of choice land between the Potomac and Rappahannock rivers. That enormous area, near present-day Fairfax, Virginia, was only a part of his holdings. In addition to that, he also owned almost the entire Shenandoah Valley.

Despite owning all of this valuable real estate, Lord Fairfax paid little attention to it. Except for a couple of visits to these shores, he stayed in England and left the operation of his American interests in the hands of his younger brother. In that respect, he was much like other British noblemen who enjoyed their life in England too much to venture overseas to check on their colonial holdings.

A New Nobility

In South Carolina, ownership of land became the means for some commoners to acquire titles of nobility. A peculiar system of peerage was set up in that state to encourage people with some money to settle there.

By buying land, you could buy a title. Naturally, the prestige of the title depended on the amount of land you purchased.

The strange new titles created for this incentive program were as follows. To become a *Landgrave*, the top title, a man had to own 48,000 acres. A *Cacique* had to buy 24,000. A *Baron* needed 12,000 acres. That might sound like a lot, but land near Charleston could originally be bought for as little as a penny an acre, so even people of moderate means could aspire to a title of nobility if they became landowners.

Way down below the lords of the manor were the *Freeholders*. They won the right to vote if they purchased merely a piddling 50 acres. Compared to their former status, that was a move up. For just half a dollar, they became *somebody*-- a recognized land-owning member of society with a vote in affairs of the community. Better than being a peasant in the Old Country!

The Irresistible Magnet

It wasn't just the very wealthy who wanted land in America, and got it. The big rich might hold title to vast areas of wilderness, but they had to populate it in order to hold it against the claims of enemies from other countries.

That meant they had to inveigle poorer people to sail to our shores to develop and defend the land, often a requirement their king insisted on when he made a grant. Or they had to sell parcels of their holdings to settlers already here. In either case, there were plenty of people who'd do almost anything to realize their dream of owning land, the precious commodity available in abundance only in the New World.

Ask most people why the early settlers came to America, and they're likely to answer, "to find religious freedom." That's a fine-sounding motive, which applies to some of our ancestors. *But it's not true for most!*

Even the *Mayflower* carried not only religious escapees, but also immigrants who came aboard for strictly economic reasons. By far the majority of those who followed had no special problems with the churches of their native lands... or cared little about religion.

By 1776, most Americans didn't even attend any church regularly. It was lust for land that brought them here. And a lust for ever more of it constantly drove them westward.

Raping the Land
Our pioneer heritage of destroying the environment grew out of the seemingly limitless acreage available to the west. Little thought was given to preserving the rich virgin soil as long as it was easy to get more.

Early settlers adopted the labor-saving primitive farming methods of the Indians. Often they didn't bother to clear their farms completely of trees, a difficult task. Instead, like the Indians, they'd cut down only the brush and small trees: merely kill the bigger ones by slicing away a ring of bark and hacking or burning the roots. The big dead trees would soon lose their branches and fall. With a semi-clearing created, the farmers would plant their crops in the loose ground between tree stumps.

They didn't bother with manuring their fields either. When nutrients in the rich soil were used up, they turned those butchered areas into pasture. Like the transient Indian tribes, they moved on to a new clearing. Early on, when white settlers were few, that wasn't too difficult. The space to the west was virgin forest where titles to land, if any, were hard to enforce.

The only obstacles the settlers faced in grabbing off new lands were the Indians. They posed no great problems. The settlers possessed the fire arms with which they could simply drive the natives off their land, or kill them if that proved to be necessary.

Push to the West

Gradually, as settlements expanded and courts of law were established, it became harder and harder simply to reach out for some adjoining free land. This was especially true in the Southern colonies where large-scale farming developed and planters needed to add many hundreds of acres for their crops. Any sizable expansion wouldn't go unnoticed. People like Lord Fairfax held legal title to the land, and he prosecuted squatters.

Still, planters in the South continued to ruin their fields with repeated crops of tobacco. A few scientific planters like George Washington adopted crop rotation. Eventually Washington turned entirely away from tobacco, and planted only grains and other crops that were easier on the soil.

Wasteful farming methods that destroyed the fertility of fields near the coast created more and more pressure for exploration into the wilderness toward the Mississippi. There was money to be made by those who could lay claim to fresh lands in the West. As you'd expect, that drew a host of entrepreneurs eager to make a buck (or a few gold sovereigns).

Rise of the Speculators

To make money on these virgin lands, you didn't have to go out there yourself. You could join with others in *financing* the surveying expeditions that plotted and laid claim to the new acreage.

Land speculation became the favorite way to gamble. In those days, if you had some extra dollars to risk, you couldn't wager them on a stock market. But you could hope to get rich by buying shares in a land company. Some whopping big ventures were launched. A prime example is the Ohio Company. This Virginia-based group of big-time speculators laid claim to *a million and a half acres* in the Ohio Valley.

As in playing the stock market today, you could make a bundle. Or lose it all on such ventures! They were totally unregulated. You placed your bets and took your chances.

Q: Who participated in the big land speculations?
A: Just about every wealthy person of that era. George
   Washington, Thomas Jefferson, Aaron Burr, Robert
   Morris and many others of our founding fathers were
   all up to their eyebrows in land speculation.

Most speculators didn't do very well at the land game. That's putting it mildly. Their headlong pursuit of land literally made paupers of some of the richest of them.

A Lesson in How to Go Broke

Robert Morris was called the *Financier of the Revolution*. He was called an economic genius, and he truly was one. But land speculation did him in.

At the beginning of the War, Morris was a very wealthy Philadelphia merchant and an important congressman. When our fledgling Continental Army ran into financial difficulties (which happened almost instantly) General Washington turned to Morris. He needed Morris' help in coaxing money and supplies for his army from the individual Colonies.

When the money pinch became most precarious, rich Robert Morris even obtained personal bank loans to carry the cost of the War. It's generally agreed that without his financial help, the Continental Army would have been forced out of existence.

Despite this, Morris was criticized because his firm received several profitable contracts for supplies while he was involved as a congressman in military procurement. Despite the fact that he was perhaps the only man with enough financial clout to get any supplies, he was accused of profiteering. Eventually though, he was vindicated by Congress.

At the war's end, President Washington offered Morris the chance to become the first Secretary of the Treasury of the United States. Morris decided he'd had enough of straightening out the country's financial affairs. He turned down the President's offer, and became a senator instead.

The Downfall of Robert Morris

Late in life, financial genius Robert Morris made some of the same mistakes that had ruined other men. He speculated dangerously in lands in the west and around the new city of Washington, D.C.

In doing so, he overextended his credit, considerable though it was. Then his investments soured, and he couldn't meet his loans. Things got so bad that the famous financier even tried to hide from his creditors. But they tracked him down, and *had him thrown into debtors' prison in Philadelphia* where he languished for three years.

Q: Who visited Morris in prison?

A: His old friend George Washington, by that time the ex-President, had dinner with Morris in his jail cell. Morris might have stayed in prison for many years if Congress hadn't passed a new Federal bankruptcy law that put an end to the old English system which kept debtors in jail indefinitely.

By the time Morris got out of prison, his fortune was gone. So was the magnificent Chestnut Street mansion he was building, which came to be known as *Morris' Folly*.

The man who saved America financially ended his days living in a small house in Philadelphia, skimping along on an annuity obtained for his wife by sympathetic friends.

Lust for land was an obsession with many of our ancestors. It led to bloody battles with the Indians and arguments with the British who tired of sending troops to protect their Colonists from Indian raids. It was also the driving force in the relentless push westward.

That driving force, called *the westering,* was what eventually created a vast nation of 48 contiguous united states.

8
A Tough Sailor Named Jones

Captain John Paul Jones, America's greatest naval hero, enshrined in a special grave at the U.S. Naval Academy, exemplifies the international makeup of the Colonial armed forces. During his varied careers on the high seas, he commanded ships for three widely-scattered countries-- England, America and Russia.

In all his commands, he was one rough tough guy. What else? No other sort would have the guts to take a little ship and harass the mighty navy of Britain. Our Patriot ancestors loved him and his daring escapades that took him inside English waters. And so did other enemies of King George, those European rulers you'll read about in a later chapter.

Jones was also a man of mystery-- one of the strangest officers ever to sail under an American flag. *To start with, his name wasn't Jones.* Born in Scotland as the son of a gardener, the lad was christened John *Paul.*

Off to Sea at 13
When the boy was only 13, he left home to become part of Britain's maritime service. He signed on as an apprentice seaman, *bound over to serve a ship owner for seven years at miniscule pay,* for the privilege of learning to become a mariner.

Learn he did, moving along steadily in his profession. Serving aboard a brig hauling sugar, rum, tobacco, pig iron, timber and other commodities back and forth from the West Indies and America's southern colonies to England, he learned the basics of navigation and trade. Young John Paul also read extensively and taught himself to write well.

. During his trips to the southern colonies, he often visited his brother who was a tailor in Fredericksburg, Virginia. Introduced to some of his brother's wealthy customers, young John Paul learned to dress well, and tried to observe how gentlemen talked and acted. He quickly learned to love Virginia, and vowed that he too would live in America some day.

A Move Up-- in Slave Ships

About halfway through his apprenticeship, John Paul got a break. His merchant master went bankrupt and freed the young seaman from the remaining years of his contract.

So, at 17, the mature teen-ager was free to seek out some way to better himself; he wanted to become a ship's officer rather than just a seaman. Opportunities were limited, so he took what he could get. He signed on as third mate aboard a slave ship, a tiny 50-footer that packed 77 negroes below decks.

That was a hard life, but young John Paul survived, though he hated the stench and inhumanity of the "abominable trade". After a couple of years aboard two slave ships, he quit. Stranded in the Indies, he met a fellow Scot who owned and commanded a brig, on which young John Paul was allowed to hitch a free ride back home. Coincidentally, the brig on which John Paul got his free return trip was named the *John*.

Master of a Ship at 21

Again John Paul had a stroke of good fortune, because of his new friend's bad luck. Fever broke out aboard ship and killed both the owner-captain and the mate. That left no one who knew how to navigate, except passenger John who took the helm

When he sailed safely into port in Scotland, the owners were so pleased to get their ship back intact that they offered its substitute navigator a permanent job as her skipper. John Paul became captain of a merchant vessel at the very early age of 21.

He must have looked more like a boy than the master of a ship. Though strong and tough, he was short and boyish in build. His face was boyish, still with a few freckles, though the sandy hair of his childhood had changed to reddish brown. He had prominent cheekbones, a rather sharp nose and a cleft chin. Always neatly dressed, he wore a sword (rare for a merchant captain) perhaps to achieve a military look or maybe so he could present a more mature air of command.

The heroic Captain may have inspired similar tender thoughts in the Parisian women ladies whom he met later during his long stay in their country. But what he might have lacked in bulk, Captain Jones more than made up for in spunk. No man or any ship was too big for him to tackle .

No Nonsense Aboard John Paul's Ships

The young captain earned a reputation for running a tight ship. Remembering his disgust at horrible conditions on slavers, he insisted that everything be clean and neat aboard his vessels. He took good care of his crews, but they encountered an explosive temper when he spotted slovenly work.

That temper opened Captain Paul to his first difficulties with the law. When one of his crew continually shirked his duties, Paul had him flogged with a cat-o'-nine tails. After arrival in port, the crewman protested to the vice-admiralty court about the severity of his punishment. After Captain Paul explained that his crewman was both lazy and disobedient, the court agreed the man got what was coming to him.

That should have been the end of the matter. However, while sailing back to England on another ship, the man contracted a fever and died at sea. When his body arrived in London, his father concluded his death was the aftermath of the flogging. Again Captain Paul was hauled into court; again he was cleared. However, he'd been charged with murder, and the story that John had flogged a sailor to death continued to surface at inopportune times throughout his life.

Big-Time Trouble

Captain Paul's reputation for violence was enhanced by a second incident. He was charged with a second killing. Even in a day when a ship's commander could do almost anything to discipline his crew, that raised eyebrows and got him into deep trouble.

He'd progressed to command of a larger ship by that time, which he owned with a partner. At just 25 years of age, he'd become a ship owner, but that's what led to the problem. Laying over in Tobago to take on cargo, he needed all his cash to pay for the merchandise. So he refused to give his crew an advance on wages they wanted for a spree on shore before departure: he said he'd pay at the end of the voyage.

His crew, many of them natives of Tobago, were determined to go ashore with money in their pockets to entertain their friends. Defying their Captain, they attempted to launch a boat. John claimed their ringleader attacked him with a cudgel. Whatever happened, it's certain that Jones drew a sword and spitted the rebel leader with the weapon, killing him on the spot.

Again John would have to face a murder charge, only this time there was an added hazard. The trial was scheduled to take place in a civilian court in Tobago where the dead man had friends and relatives. Rather than face a trial with hostile local witnesses and a jury who might hang him, John Paul figured it would be smarter to hide out someplace. Taking only 50 pounds with him, he left his ship and possessions and disappeared.

A Fugitive on the Lam

He fled to the American Colonies where nobody was likely to recognize him, especially if he changed his name. So John Paul decided it would be wise to switch things around.

He dropped the John, and kept Paul as his first name. Then he picked the very common English surname of Jones for the end. Do you follow that? *John Paul*, fugitive from justice, disappeared, and in his place emerged the new *Paul Jones*.

Under that pseudonym, he became a criminal on the lam!

Whether his past impetuous escapdes were recognized or not, who'd care in his new surroundings? There should be a need for a skilled ship's captain in the New World, but for nearly two years the newly-named Jones found no takers. Not until nearly the end of 1775, as America moved toward open rebellion and established a tiny naval force, did he get his commission. He signed on, as John Paul Jones, Esq., as a first lieutentant in the Continental Navy.

Offered command of a small ship, Jones promptly sailed it across the ocean to the British Isles to the ports he knew so well, and began raising havoc there. To the delight of his new Colonial friends, who badly needed a few victories to lift their spirits.

Sailing Right Into English Harbors

Daredevil Jones' strategy was to shock the English by striking at their small vessels right in their own waters... then disappearing before any big warships could catch him.

With his first tiny ship, *The Providence*, Jones attacked English fishing boats and scuttled 16 of them. That wasn't any great tonnage of shipping, but Jones audacious acts thumbed the nose at mighty Britain. The American press had a field day in reporting his exploits.

A pleased Continental Congress gave the bold captain a larger vessel, the Ranger. It was provided by our friends, the French, who allowed Jones to operate from French ports. With his more powerful ship, flamboyant Jones sailed right into English and Scottish harbors and attacked anything anchored there. He even captured a British naval sloop. Both Congress and the British-hating French loved the cocky captain's audacious style..

Q: How big was John Paul Jones?

A: Though mighty in deeds, he was was only five feet, five inches tall and slight in build, though wiry, according to biographer Admiral Samuel E. Morrision. John Hancock referred to him as "Little Jones", and Abigail Adams described her surprise at his small stature when she first met him. " I expected to see a rough, stout, warlike Roman. Instead of that, I should sooner think of wrapping him in cotton wool and putting him in my pocket than sending him to contend with cannon balls. "

Our French allies were so pleased with the troubles Jones was causing their old enemy Britain that they gave us several vessels. Jones was put in command of this small fleet.

It included a large but decrepit merchantman that had been fitted for battle. The old hulk was patched up and equipped with 42 guns.

It was renamed the *Bonhomme Richard*, after *Poor Richard's Almanac*, the famous publication of Ben Franklin, who was then the very popular Ambassador to France.

Winner of a Hopeless Battle

With his new flagship and other smaller craft, Jones took 17 more British ships before the powerful enemy warship, the Serapis, finally caught up with him. The contest was hopelessly unequal. Jones was outgunned, and his Bonhomme Richard was soon about to sink.

John Paul Jones leading his men in a hand-to-hand
charge as they board the British ship, the Serapis.

Jones refused to quit. He slammed his shattered ship against the Serapis, and lashed the two vessels together.

In the midst of the bloody tumult, with the Serapis' guns still pounding the Bonhomme Richard to pieces, one of Jones officers screamed wildly to the British to stop and accept the Americans' surrender. Jones hit the man in the head with his pistol to shut him up. Supposedly he then shouted his famous defiance.

"I have not yet begun to fight!"

Scrappy Captain Jones drove his men to continue the battle hand-to-hand aboard the Serapis, which they'd climbed onto as the Richard sank lower and lower in the water. With muskets and swords, the desperate American crew finally overpowered the British sailors and took control of the Serapis.

Switching ships from a sinking one to a conquered one was an unprecedented feat. Jones had accomplished the impossible.

When he sailed the captured Serapis to a harbor in France, Captain Jones and his men received a tumultuous welcome. In fact, King Louis XVI himself presented the popular scourge of the British navy with a gold-hilted sword bearing the inscription: *Vindicati maris Ludovicus XVI remunerator strenuo vindici"* ("Louis XVI recognizes the services of the brave maintainer of the rights of the sea"). Enjoying his hero's status and great popularity with the French ladies, Jones stayed in France for three years before finally returning to America.

Advice From Franklin and Jefferson

The lionized Captain presented both opportunities and problems for America's ambassadors to the court of France. His great popularity was a public-relations plus for the new country. But he was a difficult personality to control, a loose cannon.

Unhappy with the percentage of prize money from his raids that was allotted to him and his crew, he badgered both French and American politicians to change the arrangements. He was probably justified, but made a nusiance of himself.

Unhappy with the lack of impetus back home to expand America's pitifully small navy, he bombarded congressmen to speed things up. When that didn't work, he tackled French officials, urging them to get involved in joint ventures. He may have been right in his advice, but irritating.

When he first arrived in Paris, he knew scarcely a word of French. Ambassador Franklin, always a practical man, gave him some advice on the best way to learn a new langauge, presumably based on experience. Here's what he indicated:

"The best way to learn a new language is to share a bed with a pretty teacher. The best way to get things done in France is with the connivance of the ladies."
Benjamin Franklin

Ben may have regretted his advice because Jones proved to be a remarkably fast and far-ranging learner. In fact, when Ben left France and turned his duties over to new ambassador Jefferson, it's said that he told Thomas one of his prime duties would be to keep an eye on Jones and his current mistress, whoever she might be, to make sure they were discreet.

In later years, when he became a celebrity, John Paul Jones wore a fancy wig that had curls at the sides, and a ponytail.

Ambassador Jefferson's problems with Jones included helping him elude persistent Madame T_____ who probably bore the captain a son, and thought he should marry her after her husband died. Jones paid her a little money when she needed it, but then left Paris. When he returned, he hid out in an inconspicuous hotel until his friend Thomas Jefferson could advise him the coast was clear of the ardent want-to-get-married widow.

Q: How many known French mistresses did Jones have?

A: The first was probably Madame de Chaumont, pleasant for a time but an embarrassing friend after he had to engage in business deals with her husband. Then La Comtesse de Nicholson who in torrid letters said she'd live in a cabin with him or hock her diamonds if he needed the money. Also the pretty 17-year old wife of ugly sextenarian Jim Moylan. Certainly a Madame T____, later identified in Jefferson's papers as Madam Townsend.

A Russian Admiral

Adventurer Jones saw no further American service on the high seas, except for commanding a vessel during his trip home. He was awarded a gold medal for his exploits, and given the job of supervising construction of a new warship. But it was never finished, and Congress never found another appointment for him.

He never became an American admiral, although he's regarded as the founder of the United States Navy, and in it his fame is higher than that of any flag officer we've ever had.

Searching for employment after the War, Jones was hired by Russian Empress Catherine the Great. She wanted to build a navy to make the Baltic a Russian sea. So Jones finally made it to Admiral's rank... but in the Russian navy.

He became Kontradmiral Pavel Ivanovich Jones, but he was an unhappy man. He was angered by the sniping of other admirals who were jealous of him. And he was frustrated by Catherine's lover and powerful chief aide, Grigori Potemkin, who never liked Jones.

False Charges of Rape

His service to the Russian Empress ended after a few years, in a strange manner. He was accused of raping a young girl-- a most improbable charge which was thoroughly discounted-- but it hit the papers not only in Russia but throughout Europe.

In all likelihood, the whole affair was orchestrated by someone who wanted to see Jones ousted from his job and from Russia. The girl's mother admitted under questioning that she set up the scam, possibly hoping to blackmail the Admiral. She further disclosed that she'd been encouraged in her plot by an unidentified important gentleman who had paid her money to get the scheme started. After the accusations, no one in the legal system seemed the least bit interested in finding out who that might be, or in letting the Admiral have his day in court to clear his name.

Despite the lack of evidence, everyone in St. Peterburg turned their backs on Jones. *That included the Empress.* Although she herself had a reputation as a libertine, she expected the hired help to be circumspect at all times.

A Sad End in France

In ill health, Jones moved to France, where he was still a celebrity. He died there in 1787, away from his native England and far from his adopted country of America.

His last years were pitiful. The gay days in Paris were long gone, ended when the French Revolution decimated his titled friends. Most of his funds were gone too. In its attempts to pay off the war debt, the leaders he still knew in America were pinching the budget and had closed down the Navy, so there was no chance there for employment, even for a great hero.

Jone's funeral was pitiful too. The American minister to France, Governeur Morris, did come to see Jones briefly when informed the old sailor was on his deathbed. But after death occured that same evening, on July 18, 1792, Morris ordered that Jones be buried as cheaply as possible. He also decreed that most of Jones' valuable items be auctioned off to pay bills he owed.

Indigant that America would toss one of its most illustrious citizens into a pauper's grave, the commissaire of the town district where Jones lived dipped into his own pocket to pay for the funeral.

102

Still, it was good there was no viewing. To preserve Jone's personal effects for his heirs-- though, of course, the bachelor Captain had no identifiable children-- he was clad in neither his fancy uniforms nor with his many decorations. His body was simply wrapped in a linen winding sheet.

Belated Remembrance By His Countrymen

Not until more than a century of oblivion did any American make any effort to honor John Paul Jones. The American Ambassador, General Horace Porter, began trying to find his grave in the long-abandoned cemetery where he'd been interred. Simonneau, the French official who'd paid for the funeral was finally proved right; the Americans would sooner or later attempt to remedy their neglect of the famous hero.

Amazingly, when they located and dug up one of several likely coffins, doctors from the Ecole de Medicine were able to identify Jones. Simonneau had the foresight to seal the body in a lead coffin filled with alcohol. Thanks to the preservative action of the alcohol, Jones' face remained fairly intact.

President Theodore Roosevelt became interested in the resurrection. He dispatched four cruisers across the ocean to bring the body to the Naval Academy at Annapolis where elaborate ceremonies were held on April 24, 1906, almost 114 years after his death. It took another six and a half years before an impressive tomb was built in the chapel at Annapolis to house a marble sarcophogus. As midshipmen march near this hallowed spot, they sing an irreverant song to their hero.

> "Everybody works but John Paul Jones
>   He lies around all day,
> Body pickled in alcohol
>   On a permanent jag, they say.
> Middies stand around him
>   Doing honor to his bones--
> Everybody works in 'Crabtown'
>   Except John Paul Jones. "

As the young warriors-in-training at Annapolis parade past the grave of America's greatest naval hero, they fantasize that someday they may perhaps be as valiant as he. They dream of becoming another John Paul Jones, who was one of our most wierd and wonderful ancestors. A legend without equal.

9
God Bless the Women

Most histories of the American Revolution deal almost exclusively with the exploits of males-- the speeches men made, the battles they fought and hardships they endured. Give them their due, the heroic men of the 1700s deserve all the praise of the history books. But without their women folk, they'd have gone nowhere!

From the earliest days in the Colonies, those women who accompanied their families to the New World faced the same hazards and struggled just as hard as their husbands. Laboring alongside their men, plus handling the problems of child-bearing and child-raising, they had an even tougher time

As the land became more settled, things didn't get much easier for most American women. A very few were rich, with servants to do the heavy work. However, about 90 percent were poor farmers' wives, and most of the others were married to craftsmen and small shopkeepers of modest means. Surrounded by our modern labor-saving devices, it's hard to comprehend how difficult life could be for a home maker at the time of the Revolution.

Work from Dawn to Exhaustion

In Colonial America, a housewife's duties were endless. They ran from dawn to exhaustion.

Besides working inside the house, it fell upon her (and her children) to feed the chickens, milk the cow, tend the vegetable garden, fetch water from the well. She and the older kids might also chop wood for the fireplace, if hubby was too busy with farming and hunting, or was away soldiering.

Store-bought clothes were a rarity, especially for poorer families. In those pre-shopping-mall days, mother and her daughters carded wool, spun yarn, wove and knitted fabric, tailored new garments and repaired old ones. They also made soap and boiled laundry. Made candles too. And cooked, canned, swept, scrubbed, etc... without a single electrical appliance to make things easier.

Even wealthy families such as those who lived on large plantations in the South had to supply many of their own wants. There was no handy store to which they could run for household or personal supplies.

Q: Where did rich Martha Washington buy clothes?
A: Occasionally from London. But even though she was a multi-millionaire by today's standards, Martha knitted George's stockings, and in the early days at Mount Vernon she operated what amounted to a clothing factory for the whole plantation. During one year, she and her spinning and weaving crew turned out 815 yards of linen, 365 yards of woolen, 144 yards of linsey and 40 of cotton. Besides keeping everyone clothed, it was the duty of good housewife Martha to see that the dairy supplied enough milk and the smokehouse enough hams... while Master George kept an eye on the crops and workshops.

Living Alone Was Scandalous
There was only one acceptable life style for men and women in early-day America. That was to marry young, stay married no matter what, and produce numerous offspring.

Living alone was considered scandalous in the 1700s. Bachelors were frowned upon, because hot-blooded young men on the loose represented potential trouble. Maryland levied a heavy tax on bachelors over 25. Other parts of the country didn't use economic pressure, but they considered evasion of matrimony as flouting the sacred command to multiply the human race.

Young women usually married earlier than they do today. In some backwoods areas, brides were very young. There were no laws setting any minimum age requirements to protect child brides. Age disparities were common.

Sometimes, however, the difference in ages was not between an old man and a maiden, but between an impecunious young man and an older rich widow who seemd a likely meal ticket.

**"Yesterday was married, in Henrico, Mr.William Carter,
third son of John Carter, to Mrs. Sarah Ellyson, aged 85,
a spritely Old Tit with three Thousand Pounds Fortune."**
The Virginia Gazette, May 15, 1775

More often it was a young woman who became the second, third or fourth wife of a middle-aged widower, especially one whose previous spouse had just died from childbirth fever or other complications.

Varied Courtships

Courtship practices varied widely in different regions and different strata of society. At the lowest levels, that of slaves and other bound servants, there was no courtship of women. Sex, yes.

Illegal but unstoppable affairs between partners in servitude existed, as did illegal but winked-at sex at the whim of a man who owned a desirable woman. She might be either a black slave girl or a pretty white maidservant bound for a number of years, as you'll read later.

A step up from that bottom rung, was the *bought bride* who had no choice in the husband she was joined to. A poor immigrant who couldn't pay her way to the New World, her courtship (?) lasted but a few minutes while a ship's captain haggled with prospective suitors over her passage price.

Where freer choice existed, the curious habit of *bundling* was one practical method of courtship widely practised in early days. It's discussed in a later chapter.

Among the gentry, of course, courtship was an altogether different story. Where large landholdings or prosperous businesses provided money and leisure time for high society to develop, the girls and young gentlemen partied and danced and indulged in elaborate pre-mating maneuvers. They had fancy weddings too.

Marry for Money, Not Love

In old-country tradition, marriages were arranged for young members of substantial families. If parents disapproved, it's rare that young lovers dared to defy them.

One reason for this was that newly-married couples generally were financially dependent on their parents. The groom almost invariably worked for his father, and anticipated inheriting the family business or farm. Usually the young couple went to live at the home of one set of parents until they could manage a house of their own, probably financed at least partially by Dad.

"How big is your bankroll?" was the first question asked of a prospective groom. "How large is your dowry?" of prospective brides. This emphasis on money versus love was especially hard on the second and later sons of wealthy families, whose inheritances were negligible.

Q: What wedding custom predicted the next marriage?

A: It was similar to the present-day practice of tossing the bridal bouquet and the bride's garter, only with a reverse twist. The bridesmaids did the tossing. They turned their backs to the bride and tried to hit her with a rolled-up stocking. The first to do so would be the next to marry. A similar routine then took place between the groom and his attendants, but that occured upstairs in the bridal bedroom at nightfall. The newlyweds were left there, but the party resumed with feasting, tippling and dancing until the next morning when bride and groom were brought glasses of liquor to revive their strength.

Smock Weddings

Along with the traditions of arranged marriages and dowries, there was another old English wedding custom related to money. It was the *smock wedding.*

There was precedent in English tradition (not in the law) that a husband wasn't obligated to pay off his bride's debts if she came to the wedding wearing only a smock, the type of under-garment we'd call a slip or chemise. This symbolized that she came to their union with nothing. Therefore, the groom would be unaware that such a poor person could have financial dealings, and he'd be free of any entanglements if they existed.

Evidently this old English custom, assuring that a bride's creditors couldn't hang her bills on the new groom, was accepted in some American colonies. Smock weddings were performed in parts of New York, Pennsylvania and throughout much of New England up until the time of the Revolution.

Forget the Smock

Some smock weddings attracted more attention and comment than others. To establish that everyone knew that debt obligations were going to be denied, some couples felt it necessary to hold the ceremony in broad view of a large audience. The wedding might take place out in the yard or on the highway. In a time when ladies underclothes were not discussed, the sight of a young woman clad only in her chemise must have caused some gossip.

Other debt-laden brides went even further. They wanted to express in unmistakable fashion that they had brought *absolutely nothing*-- not even a chemise or smock-- to their union. So they stripped completely before the ceremony.

Their nakedness was not clearly displayed to everyone, however. It was only vouched for by female witnesses who accompanied a bride while she hid in a closet or behind a screen. To the rest of the wedding guests, the bride revealed only her naked hand which she held out to receive her wedding ring.

A Dozen Kids, or More

Childbearing, unlimited and uncontrollable, was the lot of married women in early-day America. Often it was the death of them.

Scant statistics available indicate the average family had seven or eight children. But that may have meant only the *living* offspring-- frequently fewer than half of those conceived. A birth every year or two soon added up to double-digits, but attrition cut that total down from huge numbers to merely sizable ones.

Peter Kalm, a Swede who visited the Colonies and kept a diary of his "Travels in North America", was surprised at the number of very large families he met.

> **"It is not difficult to find the reasons why people multiply faster here than in Europe. As soon as a person is old enough, he may marry without any fear of poverty. There is such a good tract of ground yet uncultivated that a new-married man can, without difficulty, get a spot of ground where he may sufficiently subsist with his wife and children."**

An example of this is the childbearing history of Eleanor Laurens, wife of Henry, who was president of the Continental Congress in 1777. Eleanor bore 12 children before she died at the age of 39, but only five of the dozen lived. This occurred in a well-to-do family receiving the best available medical care.

Broods of far more than a dozen were common. Patrick Henry of oratory fame was one of 19 children. John Marshall, who was to become Chief Justice of the United States, was the eldest of 15. Benjamin Franklin's father was one of 18.

A girl who married at 15 or 16 could easily become a great-grandmother in her forties. If she lived that long.

Q: What was considered a really big family?
A: One New England woman (who lived to be 100) boasted of 500 births in her family. Of course, that half-a-thousand infants didn't all survive the hazards of colonial life. By the time of the old lady's death, only 250 of her children, grandchildren, great-grandchildren and great-great-grandchildren were still alive. Another matriarch boasted that her modest brood of only seven living children (from the 16 she'd borne) had produced 127 descendants.

Quick Remarriages

There were many second and third marriages in the 18th Century. Not because of divorce, which was practically unknown. Untimely death was the cause.

Diseases such as smallpox, diphtheria, typhus and tuberculosis were constant threats and very often fatal. Hazardous occupations killed many husbands. The most hazardous occupation of all, motherhood, finished many women in their twenties and thirties.

Whether it was a widow or widower who survived, there was nearly always a large brood of children in the household. They needed a replacement parent, *quickly*. The idea was to get the funeral over with, line up a new mate without delay, and arrange for a not-too-distant wedding date.

Story of the Thrifty Widow
One story from Revolutionary days recounts the exceptional speed and exemplary frugality of one thrifty widow. She must have set a record for speedy remarriage.

It seems that this woman had considerable food left over from her husband's funeral party. Loth to allow expensive groceries to spoil, she figured the economical thing to do was arrange an *immediate* remarriage so the victuals left over from the funeral could be put on the wedding buffet. She found a widower as anxious as she to tie the knot without delay. So it was off with the widow's and widower's black attire, and on with a new wedding ring. No waste of time, no waste of food.

Q: What profession helped with child rearing?
A: Wet nursing was an occupation much in demand in 1776. Before the days of infant formula and bottles to dispense it, newspapers were full of ads by amply-bosomed women who, for a fee, offered to provide a "good breast of milk" for infants whose worn-out mothers lacked a sufficient supply.

Because of the extreme hazards of childbirth, there were more widowers than widows. Many a man had a succession of wives, often two or three or more. An older wife would be replaced by a younger one, and the cycle of frequent pregnancies, illness and early death proceeded.

Considering the risks and the hard labor involved, it seems incredible that there was a steady supply of applicants for such a job. A typical woman of 1770s who married in her late teens spent half of her childbearing years either pregnant or nursing an infant..

Populating the New Country

Contraception was not unknown. Products for it were available in Europe, which exported all sorts of other goods to America. Yet in Colonial annals, birth control is an unmentionable. It was a subject not discussed, not used. This created a population explosion which became a major factor in moves toward independence.

As the Colonies grew in size and prosperity, with their cities beginning to get bigger than most in England, the Colonists no longer felt like little outposts that had to be silently subservient to Parliament and King. They grew impatient with restrictions imposed on them.

So it was the quiet child-bearers of America who stimulated much of the loud revolutionary rhetoric of their husbands. Our prolific women also made it inevitable that, sooner or later, America would be a sovereign nation.

> **"In the campaign where the British eventually took Bunker Hill, they killed 150 Yankees. During that same time, our women gave birth to 60,000 little Americans"** Benjamin Franklin

During the War, the women of America contributed greatly to the cause of the Revolution. *Thousands* of them actually followed their husbands into army camps, a fact rarely acknowledged. They provided many of the housekeeping services, such as cooking and laundering clothes, which our modern armies delegate to support squadrons. You'll read more about that in a later chapter.

The Civilizing Influence

However rough their backgrounds may have been, the women landed on our wild shores did their best to improve the habits of their even rougher menfolk. Those who prospered, as many did, strove to instill a few social graces in their children.

Their dream was not so much that of their husbands-- acquiring more and more land-- but of establishing a decent, civilized family. After the first generation of immigrants managed to hack a farm out of the wilderness by sheer perseverance, life generally became a bit easier for their children.

Compared to the worn-out acres of Britain and Europe, the new land was rich and bountiful. And there was so much of it that the second and third generations often began to enjoy a standard of living they could never have dreamed of attaining when they were back in the Old Country.

They got what their folks had come to America for-- a chance to move up in the world.

Q: What protection did wives have against beatings?
A: Although wife-beating was accepted as the logical way to emphasize who was in command in early American homes, the law restrained the husband from inflicting undue damage with too large a stick. He was not supposed to supplement his fists with a rod thicker than a finger.

The fortunate ones were able to buy fancy clothes and to enlarge their homes. They equipped their homes with good furniture, porcelain plates and glassware or pewter cups to replace wooden ones. Particularly among the prosperous merchants of the North and the plantation owners of the South, a new High Society arose which supported a much higher standard of living..

The Revolution Helps Women
To a few merchants, the war meant primarily gaining freedom from certain import taxes-- a limited goal that's often blown up as the main reason for the Revolutionary War. It's true that those very influential merchants, along with wealthy plantation owners, took the major role in getting the rebellion started. But they weren't the only players in the revolt.

To most ordinary folks, who'd never even seen one of the King's customs collectors at the harbors, the motive in fighting was more a desire to be rid of any governance from overseas. After the war, the *men* of America (the only *voting* citizens) won their freedom from interference from distant officials and regulations.

But women wanted some new freedoms too! In a world where both laws and customs decreed that the man of the house was to be undisputed boss, women suffered many indignities.

As happened when American women took on new roles during World War II, the women of the Colonies felt more independent at the end of the Revolutionary War. While their husbands were away, they'd handled all the responsibilities of family life, and had done it well. As a consequence, they questioned old restrictions.

Abigail Adams, who was perhaps the first prominent American proponent of women's rights, expressed this attitude forcefully to her husband, John Adams, when he and other powerful men in Congress prepared to draft laws for the emerging nation.

> **"In the new code of laws which I suppose it will be necessary for you to make, I desire you would remember the ladies and be more generous and faithful to them than your ancestors. Do not put such unlimited power into the hands of husbands. Remember, all men would be tyrants if they could. If particular care and attention is not paid to the ladies, we are determined to foment a rebellion, and will not hold ourselves bound by any laws in which we have no voice or representation."** Abigail Adams

Abigail didn't foment the open rebellion she threatened. But she and her sisters did move a few steps closer to the freedoms they desired. More and more states began to recognize that daughters as well as sons were entitled to receive inheritances. Wives, who had previously been viewed more like children than responsible adults, began to gain freedom to sign deeds, contracts and other legal papers without authorization from their husbands.

Abigail's determination to have a true voice in formulating the laws had to wait quite a while though. It took more than a century before one state, Colorado, granted women the right to vote. No woman was elected to Congress until 1916 when Montana sent Jeanette Rankin to Washington D.C. And not until 1920 did the 19th amendment to the Constitution guarantee American women the right to vote.

10
Dangerous Doctors and Terrifying Dentists

A major reason why you can be thankful you didn't live at the time of the Revolution is the dangerously low quality of medical care then. One did not go to a doctor in those days except as a last resort. And it could prove to be the last thing you ever did.

The lack of good medical care was a major factor in the lives of all the people described here. It also played a big role in the conduct of the Revolutionary War. Disease killed more soldiers than bullets did. No wound was a minor one, because chances were high that it would become gangrenous and probably fatal.

Q: What were the odds of death in the Revolutionary War?
A: It's estimated that a soldier had a 98 percent chance of coming through combat alive (because of the high turnover, most were in the army for only a brief time). However, any soldier unlucky enough to land in a sickbed, for whatever reason, stood only a 75 percent chance of leaving while he was still breathing.

Physicians in the army, exposed constantly to severe diseases amidst poor ventilation and awful sanitation in crowded hospitals, suffered a much higher mortality rate than did officers of the line.

Unlucky George Washington
The medical vicissitudes of our first president illustrate how poorly even those in the highest strata of society fared. Washington was

lucky so far as the dreaded smallpox was concerned. He contracted the dread disease in his youth, but escaped alive and with only a few pox marks on his face. This early attack gave him immunity for the rest of his life, so he escaped the epidemics that killed so many of his colleagues, especially in army camps.

On a wet snowy December day in 1797, when he was 67 years old, Washington went for his usual morning horseback ride. When he came inside, his neck appeared wet and snow was hanging from his hair. He admitted his throat felt raw, but never imagined this would be the beginning of the end for him. Here's what he said to Tobias Lear, his secretary, who urged him to take some medicine for his sore throat. It was a macho mistake.

> **"You know I never take anything for a cold.**
> **Let it go as it came."** George Washington

That night, between two and three in the morning, he was shivering, could scarcely speak and breathed with difficulty. He awoke Martha, but wouldn't let her get out of bed to call a servant for fear she might catch cold.

Early the next morning, Washington summoned his overseer to bleed him. A full pint, he insisted. Then his friend and family physician, Dr. Craik, was sent for. Craik bled him twice more before sending for backup-- two additional doctors. So our First President received care from three highly-regarded physicians, but their cures were fatal.

They diagnosed his illness as quinsy, an extreme form of tonsillitis. They purged him and bled him, several times more. They had him gargle with hot sage tea and vinegar. They blistered his legs and feet with poultices of hot wheat bran. His inflamation was cauterized with Spanish Fly, to raise a blister that would bleed inside his throat.

Bleed Him Again!

One of the three doctors argued against further blood-letting, because it was weakening Washington. His two colleagues overruled the more cautious Dr. Craik, and the lancet was used again and again. Washington himself realized it was a losing battle.

116

George Washington on his deathbed, was attended by three
doctors who could do little but bleed him, again and again.

On the third day after contracting his cold and sore throat,
Washington died in the night. He had been drained of more than
four pints of blood-- *more than half of his body's supply*-- in a very
brief time. He simply didn't have enough energy left to fight his
severe infection and the strain of his labored breathing.

With his usual stoicism, Washington's last words to his doctors
were calm and uncomplaining. On his deathbed, he even took time
to thank his physicians politely for their efforts, ineffectual as they
were.

> **"I die hard, but I am not afraid to go... Thank you for
> your attention. Let me die off quietly, I cannot last long."**

If you think the number-one personage in the United States was
short-changed in his medical treatment, consider what ordinary
people must have endured.

> *Q: How healthy was George earlier in life?*
> *A: Not very. Like many of his compatriots, he suffered*
>   *constant illnesses. When he courted Martha, he was home*
>   *from the French and Indian War briefly to recover from*
>   *dysentery. During his first presidency, he almost died*
>   *twice-- from an infected carbuncle on his thigh, in 1789,*
>   *and the following year from pneumonia.*

Anyone Could Be a Doctor

There were no legal restrictions on the practice of medicine. Anyone who wished to do so could peddle homemade pills or drugs, diagnose illnesses, or even wield a surgical knife.

Most of the people who provided what we'd consider basic medical services didn't even call themselves physicians. They might be barbers, experts in the highly-regarded practice of blood-letting. Or they might be ministers. As the best-educated people around, clergymen were the ones to whom people went for drugs and medical advice about as frequently as they did for spiritual guidance.

One of the most common sources of medical help was the neighborhood "healer". Generally she was an old woman familiar with English folk remedies and Indian medicines. She was often the first source tried if salves, cathartics and potions from the family medicine cabinet failed to produce results.

Painful Operations

In the days before anesthesia, you can imagine that any surgical procedure was a horror. Often the patient couldn't survive the trauma..

Doctors carried opium or laudanum to counteract pain. A bottle of whiskey, gulped down rapidly, might also be used to knock out the patient before an operation. Since even these depressants failed to deaden all sensation, two or three strong heavy men would hold the patient down while the surgeon sawed off a festered limb or sliced off a tumored breast. Then, to stop the bleeding, the wound would be *cauterized with a red-hot iron.*

Doctors of the 1700s, properly attired in wigs and long coats, prepare to amputate (without the benefit of anaesthetics) a man's arm, neatly held above a catch basin.

Internal operations were practically unknown. No use in attempting to remove anything such as "gout of the stomach". Opening of the abdomen would have been as fatal as the disease. Pain killing drugs or alcohol were the only recourse.

Getting Rid of Morbific Matter

No matter what your illness, it was assumed to be caused by something bad inside you. That was "morbific matter", material which caused disease. There was plenty of it around.

Colonists suffered severely from Ague, the Gripes, Distemper, the Bloody Flux and Putrid Quinsy, along with a host of other illnesses. Those included such strange-sounding maladies as the King's Evil, the Running Evil, Bilious Colic. Jail Fever was another dreaded ailment, said to be spread from the foul convict ships that landed in American ports loaded with sick and dying passengers.

To cure any of these ailments, all the bad morbific matter had to be gotten out! First on the list was bad blood. Maybe you went to the barber to be bled. (His red and white striped pole advertised his expertise in cutting and bandaging.) Or a doctor would oblige. Or you might get out your own basin and knife and slit a vein. If the first bleeding didn't seem to help, you repeated the process the next day. And the next. For pleurisy, you were "bled by the quart."

Vomits and cathartics, such as castor oil, were also standard treatment for everything. Amply imbided, they got rid of a lot of morbific matter. When anyone was ill, the privy became a busy place.

Wierd Medicines

Laudanum and opium were the staples in the doctor's satchel. That made sense. If you couldn't cure an illness, as was often the case, you could at least alleviate the pain with strong sedatives.

Blisters and clysters were popular remedies too. Blisters were poultices that burned the skin, presumably causing enough irritation on the outside so you forgot about the pain inside. Clysters were enemas. Good for anything that ailed you..

Foul-smelling concoctions were highly regarded. It was generally agreed that the stronger the potion, the better. So curatives with really stinking odors were preferred.

One concoction, made from burnt leather and asefetida, smelled so bad it was called Devil's Dung. A small bag of Devil's Dung hung around your neck was reputed to clear the illness from your head. It also kept everyone a distance from you.

Q: What were Martha Jefferson's favorite remedies?
A: To restore hair, she recommended that a bald man wash his head nightly with a solution of rosemary; then bind it up in flannel. For anyone bitten by a mad dog, she advised that the animal be plunged into icy water for 20 days. (What that accomplished after the dog completed his attack isn't known.) The bite was to be smeared with a mixture of wood ashes and hog's lard. Mrs. Jefferson claimed this remedy saved a boy who'd been bitten on the nose.

Some pharmaceutical geniuses reasoned that if artificial dung worked good, then *the real thing* should be even better. A poultice of cow dung was preferred to heat the pain and swelling out of a bruise. Either chicken dung or goose dung could be dissolved in wine and *swallowed* as a draught. This particular potion was considered to be especially effective for clearing up infections and weaknesses.

New Medicines of the New World

In addition to the medicines they brought from the old country, settlers in America naturally tried others made from herbs and animals endemic to the new world.

Indian remedies were popular. Many of these utilized parts of forest animals. Turkey buzzard eggs. Earth worms dissolved in wine. A necklace of wolf fangs to keep children from being frightened. Broth made from rattlesnake meat. Turnip broth for coughs. A mash of rotten apples applied to the eye for a sty.

Snake oil was recommend for the gout. Eating snakes was regarded as a way to increase sexual potency.

Plants such as senna, rhubarb, onions and garlic were raised in colonial gardens for their medicinal values. They were used for brewing elixirs and teas. For strains and muscle aches, every household kept a supply of plasters and poultices. These might contain deer fat, goose grease or honey.

What might be considered the ultimate remedy, however, was a sure cure for fevers. It required the patient to swallow a spider-- *a live spider*-- encased in a spoonful of syrup for easy swallowing. It's not known whether the cure was supposed to result from the venom of the spider or from its final perambulations inside the stomach.

Modesty Versus Medicine

The idea that any male, physician or not, would be allowed to examine a woman's vaginal area was unthinkable. As a consequence, assisting at childbirth or treating female infections or illnesses was taboo to doctors in colonial times.

For assistance at childbirth, women went to a midwife. They also confided in her if they had any "female problems", which they couldn't possibly discuss with a male doctor. The midwife would provide whatever salves or medicines she might think useful.

Midwives were pretty good at normal births. However, if any unusual difficulties showed up, that was just too bad for the child. Oftentimes for the mother as well.

High Early Mortality

Midwives certainly got enough practice in delivering babies in pre-contraception days, but infant mortality was scandalously high. With no concept of cleanliness, childbirth fever was rampant.

Burial plots were filled with tiny headstones with such inscriptions as "Baby Jones". With no first name listed, these headstones indicated the infant died either at birth or perhaps just a few days thereafter, before the parents had time to Christen their newborn child.

Don't Look

It was not until just before the Revolution that obstetrics appeared on the curriculum at a couple of the more advanced medical schools. This led a few venturesome pregnant women to visit a male doctor. Usually they did this only after a midwife had foreseen some special difficulty with childbirth.

That was a drastic step because obstetricians were known to use not just their hands at delivery, as midwives did, but instruments as well. Women remembered that forceps had always been the brutal tools for dismembering a child to save a mother's life.

A physician assisting at childbirth while handicapped by a "blanket of modesty".

It's a wonder the early male obstetricians could accomplish anything at all. They were *not supposed to look* while they examined a woman or assisted at the birth. One widely-used medical textbook stated that the ideal obstetrician would be blind, and therefore not subject to peeking where he shouldn't.

Difficult as it must have been, a proper woman about to give birth would be attended in a darkened room with a sheet covering her lower torso and limbs. The proper physician then did his best by feel alone. It was obstetrics by Braille.

Germs? What Germs?
In all medical treatment, lack of cleanliness probably killed more patients than did the crude procedures and potent potions they endured. Surgeons were not particular about washing their hands between patients. Or about sterilizing instruments.

On the battlefields in the War for Independence and around the camps, chances for any type of sanitation were slimmest of all. A vistor to one of the Kentucky forts in 1779 wrote that the place was filthy. Putrified dead dogs were left in the street. There was an abundance of excrement from horses, cows and hogs near the water supply. Privies could be located anywhere, and many soldiers didn't even bother to walk to one.

Disaster at Valley Forge
The camp at Valley Forge was among the worst. When General Anthony Wayne arrived there to aid Washington, he said he'd rather go into battle than make an inspection tour of the huts, because the stench was so bad. Half the men were so sick with dysentery that they stayed in their beds all day, with no one to clean or care for them.

The surgeon general of the army, General Benjamin Rush, attempted to improve sanitary conditions in the camps. He advised officers to get their men out of their tents or crowded blockhouses as much as possible. He observed that there was less sickness on marches, when soldiers were out in the fresh air, than when they huddled inside between actions.

One of Dr. Rush's suggestions for warding off disease: wearing a flannel shirt next to the skin fends off fevers.

Hard Work, Low Pay

Despite the criticism we might have of the scandalously low quality of early medicine, the doctors did their best with what they had. They tried to discover more about the human body, and gradually did. They adopted new ideas, such as vaccines for smallpox. They studied, dissected, tried new medicines and methods.

No one envied the physicians who ventured into houses filled with pestilence to care for the sick and dying. They risked their own lives often, and their death rate was high. Their income was not. Physicians did not get rich in early-day America.

Receipt books of Colonial doctors show that most of their patients were either unable or reluctant to pay them generously for service rendered. At least, not in money. The doctor got what the patient could spare. Since more than 90 percent of Americans were farmers until the time of the Revolution, the doctor received the produce of the fields. It might be vegetables, eggs, chickens, a pig. Maybe even a cow for major surgery.

You could call it a living, though often a meager one. Few doctors drove around in fancy expensive carriages with a lot of horsepower, but at least they ate regularly.

Barber's Knife and Pliers

Getting a haircut or shave was not the only reason you went to a barbershop in the 1700s. Along with his scissors, your barber was also handy with a knife and pliers. If you suffered any sort of sickness, those were the tools he used to remedy your problem.

It was much easier to find a barber to treat your illness than to locate a physician. And the treatment would probably be the same.

Bleeding was the universal first step taken for any illness, and barbers were adept at that. In fact, the symbol used to advertise their shops, centuries ago and even today, was the red-and-white striped barber pole that symbolized blood and bandages.

Not-So-Painless Dentistry

Barber shops of 1776 often sported signs that claimed "Painless Tooth Pulling". That was false advertising. The only pain-killer was a slug of rum or whiskey, possibly laced with an opiate. And the

124

operation was not likely to be very quick or neat, since a big pliers was the only tool used to yank your molar.

Q: *How troublesome were George Washington's teeth?*
A: Pain from his teeth and gums plagued him constantly. It was so severe that he kept having teeth extracted in futile efforts to relieve the discomfort. By the time of his death, Washington had only one tooth left in his mouth-- an inadequate anchor for the clumsy artificial plates that flopped about and caused him to keep his lips clamped shut most of the time. He was a man of few words partly because it was awkward for him to talk a lot.

The almost complete absence of personal dental hygeine, and poor diets, meant that there was a lot of tooth decay to be dealt with. After most of your teeth were removed, you'd be restricted largely to soft "spoon foods" such as soups, stews or mush, which formed a major part of the Colonial diet. Or, if you were rich, you could try to supplement your sparse natural teeth with artificial ones. False teeth might not be much better than no teeth at all. Even a rich man such as George Washington had to suffer terribly with his artificial molars.

With no plastics that could be molded to fit your mouth snugly, springs were the only means of keeping hand-carved dentures (made of bone or ivory) from falling out. But can you imagine what they must have felt like in your mouth? No wonder poor George Washington had such a lumpy-looking mouth, and in his later years feasted mostly on bread and milk for his supper. Washington was by no means the only prominent American who suffered from bad, or non-existent, teeth. His successor as President was equally plagued with a bad mouth.

By the time John Adams became president, he'd lost almost all his teeth to Pyorrhea. Stubborn John tried dentures but hated the ill-fitting contraptions so much that he refused to wear them. As a result, our second president, appearing practically toothless, spoke with a lisp! His smile must have been a killer too.

Q: Were Washington's false teeth made of wood?

A: Definitely not! Being a wealthy man, he had several sets of artificial molars made as he kept losing more and more of his teeth. Dentists often used elephant ivory or cows teeth in their creations. They also salvaged human teeth, if they pulled ones in reasonably good condition. The myth about Washington's wooden teeth may have started because dentists somtimes used little wooden pegs to wedge a false tooth tighter onto its supporting plate.

11
The Multiple Lives of Benjamin Franklin

When the Patriots gathered at the Second Continental Congress on the tenth of May in 1775, the patriarch of the gathering was a venerable 69-year-old diplomat and man of many talents.

Just five days earlier, the esteemed Dr. Franklin had returned to Philadelphia from England. He received a tumultuous welcome from his fellow townsmen, complete with fireworks and a parade. But he almost didn't make it home.

Only eight days after his ship docked, an order for his arrest was posted in London. If the English authorities had moved more quickly, they'd have caught him before he sailed. In that case, Ben Franklin would have gone to the gallows or spent the war in prison. Instead of causing no end of problems for the British... and no end of help for us.

A Reluctant Rebel

The irony of England's displeasure with Ben Franklin is that he tried loyally for years to patch things up between the Mother Country and her obstreperous offspring in the New World. In fact, some volatile rebels accused Ben of unpatriotic tendencies.

That too was ironic, for Franklin had spent 11 years as a very successful representative for Pennsylvania and other colonies at the English court. He did his best to stave off repressive laws and taxes. But after violence erupted at the Boston Massacre and the Boston Tea Party, Parliament was in an angry mood with Ben and all other Americans.

Reluctantly, he had to accept the fact that there was no longer any road open except the one to rebellion.

Engraving of Benjamin Franklin from a painting by
Duplesis made while the diplomat lived in France.

The Incredible Dr. Franklin

If some modern-day author were to write a novel about a character
like Franklin, it would be ridiculed. We'd find it hard to believe that
any one person could lead so many different lives. Or could in one
lifetime accomplish such astounding things in not just one but
several different fields of endeavor.

It's no wonder that Ben was one of the most talked-about people of his time. Not just in America, but throughout the world. And not just because of his great accomplishments.

Ben was also a constant subject for juicy gossip. Earthy and ribald, he gave the tongue-waggers of his day plenty to speculate about. As he skipped amazingly from one prodigious task to another in his 84 years, Ben never changed his fondness for three things: mellow Madiera wine, ribald songs and stories, pretty women.

From Zero to First Successes

The man often called "the smartest American who ever lived" didn't enjoy a very auspicious start.

Benjamin was the youngest son of 17 children sired by a poor Boston candlemaker who placed little value on education. The lad's maternal ancestors were better educated. His maternal grandfather, Peter Folger, was a schoolteacher and later the town clerk at Nantucket.

Q: How much did Franklin's grandmother cost?

A: She was purchased for 20 pounds sterling when Benjamin's grandfather, Peter Folger, bought himself a serving maid. Eventually Peter married his maid servant. Similar instances occured in other families whose progeny rose to prominence. For example, the Sullivan family, begun by both a mother and father who'd been indentured, produced two sons who became state governors and a grandson who was a congressman.

Young Benjamin was allowed just two years in school, where he excelled, before his father decided that was enough. Daddy put the lad to work pouring wax and trimming candle wicks in his shop-- a dull job that little Ben hated.

Benjamin was only 10 years old when he began laboring in the candle shop. But in a couple of years, he had an opportunity to move to a much more stimulating career that was destined to change his life. At the age of 12, he was apprenticed to his brother, James, a young man of 21 who'd just returned from England where he'd learned the printer's trade.

His brother and the print shop opened up two fascinating new vistas to the eager apprentice. One was the trade of printing and publishing, in which he quickly became expert. The other was the world of books which became the key to a whole new life.

Ben Franklin read voraciously all his life, and in doing so he educated himself on every subject he possibly could. That included just about everything you could imagine.

Successful Grade-school Drop-out
Eventually the dropout with two years of formal education came to be regarded as the most learned man in America. He taught himself to read Latin, French, Spanish, Italian and German. He also became a renowned scientist, philosopher and statesman, showered with honorary degrees from prestigious universities around the world.

By the time he was 27, Ben had published a newspaper, founded the first subscription library, been appointed public printer for the state of Pennsylvania, written and published his *Poor Richard's Almanac* which became the most popular book in the Colonies for the next quarter of a century.

That would have been a fabulous lifetime career for most people, but it was only a starter for incredible Ben Franklin.

Sexual and Marital Entanglements
Although he achieved early success and prosperity as a publisher and author, Franklin was not so lucky in love. In fact, for all of his 84 years, Ben's love life was a titillating source of speculation and gossip widely enjoyed by his countrymen. Franklin himself acknowledged a strong sexual appetite.

> "That hard-to-be-governed Passion of Youth hurried me
> frequently into Intrigues with Low Women that fell in
> my way, which were attended with some Expence and
> great Inconvenience, besides a continual Risque to my
> Health by a Distemper which of all Things I dreaded,
> tho' by great good Luck I escaped it." Benjamin Franklin

Considering the generous amount of venereal "distemper" that abounded in London when young Ben spent a year and a half there, sowing his wild oats, he was indeed lucky to escape a dose of it.

Excitement in London

At 18, Franklin sailed to Britain on a false hope that contacts there would help him get financing for a printing operation. Before the voyage, Ben had been talking marriage with his landlady's daughter, Deborah Reed, but his going away for an undetermined length of time ended any wedding plans. Deborah was not to see him again for nearly two years.

Although his hopes for financing fizzled, young Ben discovered life in London too exciting to leave. He found work as a printer, and forgot his fiance. The friend he traveled with, James Ralph, was also forgetful. James forgot all about the wife and child that he'd left behind in Philadelphia.

Both Ben and James enjoyed a randy time sampling London's pleasures. After about a year, James married a wife in England who never found out about the old one he still had in America.

London was a wide-open city. So many prostitutes peddled their wares there that a booklet, *The Covent Garden Ladies*, was published yearly to advertise their appearances, dimensions and special abilities. As you might guess, it was a bestseller.

One verse that appeared in Poor Richard's Almanac ten years later must have been based on memories of Ben's adventures in London Town.

> **Some of our Sparks to London town would go**
> **Fashions to see, and learn the World to know;**
> **Who at Return have naught but these to show,**
> **New Wig above, and a new Disease below.**

Before Franklin finally returned to Philadelphia, after 18 months in London, his sort-of-fiance Deborah had written him off and married a potter. Unfortunately, Deborah's husband earned very little and soon squandered her dowry.

Worse than that, she learned that he was, like Benjamin's friend, an across-the-ocean bigamist. It turned out that the potter had a wife and family in England.

Deborah left her no-good husband, but that left her in a nebulous situation. She never obtained a divorce. So, although the returned Franklin showed signs of remorse about leaving her, and an inclination to take up where they'd left off, that wasn't possible. Since she was a still-married woman, any new marriage would be bigamous, and Ben and Deborah would be liable to prosecution.

Like a Soap Opera

That's not the end of the soap-opera saga of bigamies and escapades. While he waited and pondered the situation that existed between himself and Deborah, Ben evidently made other friends.

He fathered a bastard son named William. No one knows for sure who the mother was. Later in a political campaign, an election pamphlet claimed that a prostitute named Barbara was William's mother, and that she was kept as a servant in the Franklin family. A close friend of William's disputed that, and wrote that his mother was a woman "not in good circumstances" but that some small provision is made by him (William) for her. In his Autobiography, Ben Franklin never said a word about William's birth.

To compound the mystery, Ben took Deborah as his wife. And it was Deborah who raised Ben's illegitimate child. That strange situation raised quite a few eyebrows.

Gossip About Ben's Wife and Son

Ben and Deborah's marriage was not announced nor recorded in any church. They simply entered into a common-law agreement and lived together. Thereafter, Deborah always called herself Mrs. Franklin. Fortunately, her earlier, legal husband never showed up again.

When Franklin became famous and a controversial political figure, gossip was renewed about his loose marriage arrangement and the strange situation of a wife raising another woman's child. It has also led to speculation that William might really have been Deborah's baby, conceived while she still lived with her potter husband, but not acknowledged publicly to avoid embarrassment.

William's birth was not the only instance of bastardy in the Franklin clan. William followed in Ben's footsteps by also fathering a son out of wedlock. That didn't go unnoticed either. Since William became an important political figure, the Royal Governor of New Jersey, his continuing the family penchant for anonymous sex partners provided more fodder for the scandal mill.

The Smartest American
After his first career as a printer, publisher and writer, Franklin branched out into many other directions. He maintained his print shop and never stopped writing. That's an understatement; Yale University's collection of *The Papers of Benjamin Franklin* fills 20 volumes.

Franklin constantly developed new interests. In everything! Any one of his new careers would have been lifetime occupation for an ordinary mortal. It's no wonder he's been called "the smartest American who ever lived."

He was America's outstanding scientist of the time, actually acknowledged to be one of the major scientists of the world. His experiments with electricity, of which the famous flying-a-kite episode is only one, enabled him to change the basic concepts of electricity which scientists had believed for centuries.

He studied the common cold, wrote scientific papers on sunspots, ocean currents, tides in rivers, earthquakes, geology, population trends, insects, astronomy.

Franklin was constantly inventing things. Among his best-known inventions are bifocal glasses, the lighting rod and the Franklin stove.

Q: How much did Franklin earn from his inventions?
A: Nothing! He didn't collect a cent in royalties. Franklin
never attempted to patent any of his many inventions. He
believed his ideas should be free to anyone who wished to
use them.

Another of Franklin's inventions was a musical instrument named the Armonica. It consisted of rotating glass globes the player rubbed with fingers to produce melodious tones.

This became a very popular instrument. Both Mozart and Bethoven wrote compositions for it; Marie Antoinette was fond of its soft warbling tones, which Franklin himself described as "incomparably sweet beyond those of any other". However, rubbing constantly against the vibrating globes caused a tingling in the musician's fingers. Some found this soothing, but it bothered other players who started a rumor that the vibrations could cause insanity. Gradually the Armonica fell out of favor.

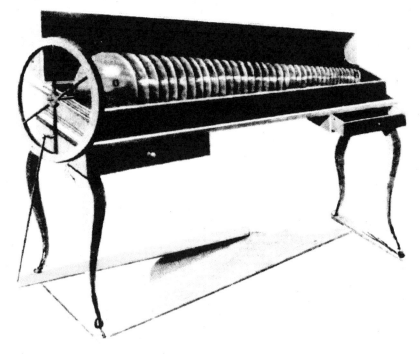

The Armonica was a musical instrument invented by Benjamin Franklin, which enjoyed wide popularity for a number of years. To produce its soft warbling tones, musicians rubbed their fingers at varying pressures against rotating glass globes.

50 Years of Public Service

Ben Franklin's second "life", a life of public service, began when he was 30 and lasted for 50 years. At various times, he was clerk of the Pennsylvania General Assembly, Postmaster of the United States and the President of Pennsylvania's Commonwealth. He was also an ambassador extraordinary.

Franklin was also a great founder of new institutions: He started the first hospital in Philadelphia. Franklin founded the first public library in America and its first fire insurance company. He launched the American Philosphical Society. He founded a school which became the University of Pennsylvania.

As if this wasn't enough, Franklin is credited by many historians as doing more to help win the Revolutionary war than any other American. Without his diplomatic success in wheedling money, guns, soldiers and ships from the French, who hated the English, our thin tired troops could never have won the crowning victory at Yorktown that led to the end of the War..

This recounting of Franklin's accomplishments is far from complete. There's not room here even to list them all. This makes one wonder, how could he live so many lives-- become an outstanding printer, publisher, author, scientist, inventor, philosopher, postmaster, politician, diplomat-- and still find time for a family life?

The truth is that while genius Ben Franklin was busy solving the problems of the world, he short-changed his family.

Did Benjamin Love Deborah?

When they began living together, both young people were poor and had little education. As he moved along in life, brilliant Benjamin eventually travelled with the famous and grew to be an intellectual giant, while Deborah stayed home and kept house.

Today such a union probably wouldn't have lasted. However, Ben didn't abandon the woman he never took with him in his social travels. Deborah meekly accepted her role as the loyal helpmeet, thankful for the man who gave her a home when she had none.

Did Ben love Deborah? That question has often been asked,but it's difficult to determine. Its answer depends on how you define love. Despite his voluminous writings on most every subject in the world, Ben never said much about his private affairs. His autobiography is almost void of family references. In it, Benjamin mentions his wife Deborah only once.

A letter to her that survives indicates that Ben appreciated the pleasing plumpness of his wife. He sent the letter from London along with an amply proportioned blue and white beer jug. Not exactly a love note, since most women wouldn't like to be compared with a beer jug, but Ben evidently intended this as a compliment.

> **"I fell in love with it at first sight, for I thought it looked like a fat, jolly Dame, clean and tidy, with a neat blue and white Calico Gown on, good natured and lovely, and just put me in mind of -- somebody."**
> Benjamin Franklin, February 19, 1758

Nowadays, if a man far away on a lengthy business trip sent his wife such a note-- comparing her to a beer mug and calling her a "fat jolly dame"-- he'd be inviting not just a divorce but a homicide. Deborah, however, was truly good-natured.

If not passionate in their relationship, Benjamin and Deborah seemed to be genuinely fond of each other. During their multi-year separations, they corresponded constantly, frequently calling each other "my dear child."

Perhaps that term gives us a clue as to their true feelings toward each other. Benjamin was protective of the gentle child-like woman he'd far outgrown. She wanted still to mother the man who'd left the nest to go wandering far away overseas.

No Time for Family

Those who criticized Franklin-- and great men, especially those in politics, always have detractors-- pointed their fingers at the scandalous way he ignored Deborah. For a total of *more than 15 years,* he was absent from her while he was overseas on various assignments.

The first separation, spent in England as agent for Pennsylvania and other colonies, lasted more than five years. Ben returned to America for about a year, but spent much of that time away from home to inspect and regulate postoffices throughout the colonies. Then he took off again for another diplomatic stint of a little more than ten years that required him to live in London, Paris and other European courts.

Deborah wrote her busy diplomat husband pitiful letters, never complaining, but asking when he'd come home. They had no effect. She wrote this when he'd been absent for six years.

> "I am very sorry to think that I should not have it in my power
> to attend on you. When will it be in your power to come home?
> I long to see you but I would not say a word that will give you
> a moment's trouble. If you are having the gout... I wish I was
> near enough to rub it with a light hand."
> Your A Feck Shonet Wife, August 16, 1770

During the last four years of this long separation, Deborah was seriously ill. Even after he received word that she'd suffered a stroke, he still stayed away for a while. *Benjamin finally returned four months after Deborah died, a situation which caused some tongue-wagging.*

Her adopted son William buried her. William, who was never close to his father, wrote to him after the funeral. That occured just before Christmas in 1775. It took two months for William's letter to arrive in England, and then another month before Ben even got on the boat to head for Philadelphia. Here's an excerpt from that letter.

> "Her Death was no more than might reasonably be expected
> after the paralytic Stroke she received some Time ago, which
> greatly affected her Memory and Understanding. She told me
> that she never expected to see you unless you returned this
> Winter, for that she was sure she should not live till next
> Summer. I heartily wish you had happened to come over in
> the Fall, as I think her Disappointment in that respect preyed
> a good deal on her Spirits."
> William Franklin, December 24, 1773

The learned man's relationship with the woman he lived with for 44 years (minus 15 overseas) was a strange one.

The Darling of Other Ladies
One of his characteristics that the made Old Ben one of the most-talked-about men of his day was his reputation for romantic escapades. These may have been more imagined than real, but Ben

didn't spend much effort in trying to refute his fame as a lady's man. Undoubtedly it helped his diplomatic efforts in the sophisticated courts of Paris and London, which you'll read about in a later chapter.

If Ben engaged in any serious liason in his years far from home, as was often assumed, it was with his London landlady. Gossips on both sides of the ocean speculated as to whether anything more than a warm friendship existed between the famous American diplomat and Margaret Stephenson. Obvious he liked being around her and her daughter, who seemed closer to him than his own.

For sure, Franklin spent much more time with Mrs. Stephenson during his later years than he did with Mrs. Franklin. He roomed with the English widow for five years, then later for ten more.

Whether founded or not, rumors reached Deborah. However, with her usual smiling calm manner, she ignored the gossip. In fact, she sent a succession of jolly notes to her husband's possible paramour, along with gifts of jams and other colonial goodies. Mrs. Stephenson reciprocated by shipping Deborah many presents of ribbons and fashionable fabrics from the London metropolis.

The Distant Father
Franklin's relationships with his children were unfortunate. He had a small family, although he approved of large ones. In his best-selling Almanac, he has his alter-ego, Poor Richard, state this attitude.

**"A Ship under Sail and a big-bellied Woman are
the handsomest things that can be seen common."**

Ben Franklin's brood, compared with the 17 his father sired or the ten Deborah's mother bore, was tiny. Ben and Deborah had a son, Francis Folger Franklin, two years after their union. They doted on him, but the boy died of smallpox at the age of four.

Another seven years passed before they had a daughter, Sarah, usually called Sally. From the time she was a teenager until she was in her 40s, Father Franklin saw little of Sally. His admonitions to her came mostly by overseas letters.

These missives were not generally welcomed, because Benjamin and daughter Sally had different ideas as to whom she should marry. Ben and his best friend, William Strahan, who owned England's premier publishing house, envisioned a marriage of their children.

Neither the young girl nor the young boy, who'd never met, were consulted. When Sally was 16, the two fathers wanted her to come and meet her intended, but neither Deborah nor her daughter would board a ship for the long voyage to England.

Sally fell in love with a young American, Richard Bache. Ben tried to squelch this marriage to a man with little fortune, and in Ben's opinion, little future. Sally married Richard anyway. Daddy Ben was miffed at this show of independence; it was a year before he wrote to his son in law to welcome him into the family.

Embarrassed by a Loyalist Son

William, Franklin's illegitimate son, seemed closer to the woman who adopted him than to his father. Of course, he saw more of her than he did of Ben.

William and Ben never seemed to get along very well. This was despite the fact that the two of them worked together at times. Perhaps it was because the critical father took his son's efforts for granted and rarely handed out any praise.

Son William was an active partner with his father in the famous electrical experiments. While Ben travelled as Postmaster, it was William who charged foil-lined jars with electricity gathered during thunderstorms. Contrary to some pictures you see, it was not Ben but William who flew the famous kite, taking his chances of being fried by lightning, while Daddy Franklin stayed safe and dry in a nearby shed.

Ben was not unmindful of his fatherly obligations however. He used his considerable influence to give William a good start on his way in government service.

When Ben was elected to the Pennsylvania Assembly, under the customs of his times, he was able to turn his old job of Assembly Clerk over to his son. A few years later, when William was only 23, Ben was able to appoint him to another job. William Franklin became the Postmaster of Philadelphia and also the Comptroller of the entire postal system of the Colonies. Those were important and lucrative positions for a lad so young.

Q: How fast and sure was the postal service?
A: Not very. Before Franklin was appointed Postmaster General in 1773, it took two weeks to get a letter from Philadelphia to New York. Efficient Ben cut that to three days. There were no stamps. You paid the local postmaster in cash, an arrangement which sometimes resulted in embezzlement. A single sheet of paper, folded and sealed, could go from London to America for a shilling. Delivery of the letter took two months or longer.

Like many fathers, Benjamin tried to give his son a hand up in life. Yet a coolness developed between father and son, and intensified as the war with England grew near. Ben, cautious at first about rebellion, became a leading advocate for freedom from the mother country. William remained a staunch Loyalist. In fact, William became successful in politics and was appointed to the high post of Royal Governor of New Jersey

This greatly embarrassed the elder Franklin. His son's Tory associations opened the way for unpleasant aspersions from those rabid revolutionaries who'd always questioned Ben's early reluctance to support a plunge into Revolution. They pointed to Royalist William as proof that the Franklins were all supporters of the King.

Ben tried to persuade William to come to the Patriot's side, but his son refused. To cap it off, William warned the British that his father was going to Canada to enlist support for the American cause, which could have resulted in Ben's capture by the British.

Removed from his governorship by the Patriots, he was branded a traitor to America, and placed under house arrest. Influential Benjamin probably could have helped him, but he would not intercede in any way to aid his son.

Franklin's bitterness toward son William lasted right up until Benjamin's death. When Franklin died, he disinherited his heir. He left *nothing* in his will to son William.

> **"The part he (William) acted against me in the late war,**
> **which is of public notoriety, will account for my leaving**
> **him no more of an estate he endeavored to deprive me of."**
> from Benjamin Franklin's will

A Doting Grandpa

The elder Franklin's only really close relationship to his descendants was with his grandson, William Temple Franklin. Temple was the illegitimate son of William.

Although William always supported the boy, he never publicly acknowledged him. Perhaps that wouldn't have been wise for a rising politician. To get his grandson out of the public eye, Temple was shipped off to England to be raised by Ben Franklin's good friend, William Strahan.

Eventually Ben acknowledged Temple as his grandson. As you'll read in a later chapter, the boy then came to live with his grandfather and aided him in his diplomatic work. The two became great friends. It seemed almost as if Old Ben, who'd distanced himself from his son, now discovered the fatherly role he needed in this companionship with William's child.

Two Or Three Bottles At Dinner

Heavy drinking was no big deal in colonial America. But even at a time when everyone shunned water, Ben Franklin was noted for his capacity to enjoy the fermented fruit of the vine.

Today the same amount of imbibing by a famous public figure would generate scandalous cluckings from columnists and other media types. In 1776, however, the fact that the good doctor was accustomed to polishing off a couple of bottles of Madiera wine each night with his dinner raised few eyebrows.

At the taverns, his verses about the joys of drinking were much appreciated. So were some of the remarks of Poor Richard in Franklin's Almanac. One favorite: *"There's more old Drunkards than old Doctors."*

Alcoholic consumption didn't seem to bother Doctor Franklin. Certainly it didn't hamper his mental acuity. However, the large quantities of wine and rich foods he put away no doubt contributed to the attacks of gout he suffered.

In his youth Franklin had been a powerful man. He was noted for being an especially strong swimmer. In fact, during his first trip to England, his skill in the water attracted considerable attention. So impressed were some of his friends that they encouraged him to start a school to teach swimming. But Ben didn't have time for that.

Even as he grew old, although his love of good food and wine added to his waistline, Franklin remained a rugged man. That was a characterisitic which must have helped him greatly when he had to stand up under the stress of long journeys and frustrating diplomatic negotiations. But like so many of his peers, he suffered from illnesses that came from imbibing and eating too well.

Q: What was Ben's physical fitness regimen?

A: In Philadelphia, he'd started each day with a swim in the Delaware. Following that came a workout with dumbbells and an "air bath" in the nude-- a prescription he favored even in his old age. As a youth he was also a vegetarian, mostly for economic reasons, though he later abandoned that habit when he could afford a rich diet.

One of a Kind

In every way, Benjamin Franklin was a unique character. His personal life was certainly unconventional. His intellectual accomplishments were incredible-- doubly so considering that he had virtually no formal education. His scientific discoveries and many inventions have rarely been matched. His successes in both business and government are remarkable.

He was unique too in his energy and devotion to a multitude of projects for the betterment of his fellow citizens. No one served longer or better as a leader in government.

Justifiably, many historians are firmly convinced that Benjamin Franklin's contributions to our nation's success make him one of the greatest of all Americans. Certainly the good doctor was undeniably one of our most wonderful ancestors, though also a bit wierd at times.,

142

12
Samuel Adams
The Number - One Rebel

More than anyone else, it was Samuel Adams of Massachusetts who lit the fuse that set off the rebellion. He's often rightly called the "Father of the American Revolution." Therefore, you might picture this giant of American history as resembling an impressive hero, such as George Washington, in physique or personality. Not so. At least in outward appearances, Samuel was exactly the opposite.

If you could have walked past Sam Adams on the streets of Boston, you'd see little to impress you. He was a man of stocky build and medium height, with a prominent nose and hair already turning gray by 1776. He suffered from a peculiar tremor, most apparent in a quivering of his hands and head. His clothes were so old and unkempt that you'd never imagine this shabby-looking character would ever play an important role at anything.

From most perspectives, Sam Adams seems the unlikeliest person to succeed in fomenting a revolution, or anything else. He certainly didn't look like a leader. Nor did his early record indicate any great talents. Until middle age, Samuel failed at everything he'd tried. And he'd tried a variety of careers.

Heading in All Directions
Samuel Adams, the cousin of President-to-be John Adams, came from a well-known Boston family. His father, also named Samuel as his grandfather had been, was a prosperous merchant who operated a malt house. He supplied essential ingredients-- barley or other grain steeped in water until it germinated-- to the scores of

breweries that constituted one of the busiest industries in Massachusetts.

When his son was 14, Samuel Sr. sent him to Harvard to prepare for the ministry. Records show that Daddy paid Junior's college tuition with flour and molasses, not exactly what Harvard registrars prefer to receive today.

Q: How much was college tuition?
A: It cost $12 per year to go to Harvard in 1770. That was for
tuition only. A year's board, lodging and laundry added
about $50 extra. Students were required to attend both
morning and evening prayers every day, and to doff
their hats to instructors. They were not to use profane
language or leave the area without permission. Until about
this time, seating was still by social rank; students from the
best families sat in front, poorer ones in back. At
graduation, listings were according to family prominence,
not by scholastic rank.

Adams career goal in the theological field didn't last very long. After graduating with an MA degree, the young scholar lost his early enthusiasm for a ministerial life and decided to study law.

His switch in career goals from church to legal work represented quite a drastic change. While ministers were highly regarded (though miserably paid) in colonial days, lawyers were held in low esteem. In fact, an early statute in Connecticut listed lawyers along with drunkards and brothel keepers as undesirable citizens to be watched carefully. Even Samuel's cousin, John Adams, who was to become one of the most esteemed Americans, ran into this prejudice as a young lawyer. When he wanted to marry, his future father-in-law was reluctant to have his daughter wed a lawyer.

But Samuel didn't pursue his studies of the law for very long. He figured that a commercial enterprise was the most promising field for a young man in bustling Boston, so "successful business man" became his third goal in life. That career choice didn't work out well for young Adams either.

No Head for Business

Samuel Sr. helped 21-year-old Sam get his first job, in the counting house (business office) of a prominent Boston trader named Thomas Cushing. It lasted only a few months. Cushing soon concluded that his new employee spent more time thinking about politics than about business matters, so he fired him.

Maybe his son would do better working for himself, thought Samuel Senior, so he gave Junior the significant sum of 1,000 pounds to set up a business of his own. Instead, soft-touch Samuel loaned half of his grub-stake to a needy friend. Unfortunately his friend never repaid the loan. That was a substantial financial loss, and it ruined any plans for starting a new business. For the next three years, Sam worked for Daddy at the malt house.

From Riches to Rags

Samuel came into money when he was 26. His father died, leaving him the malt company and a substantial home on Purchase Street overlooking Boston Harbor.

Samuel didn't take good care of either the malt company or the house. The business dwindled away, not because Bostonians didn't guzzle enough beer, but because Samuel continued to devote most of his energies to political activities. And he had neither time nor money to keep the family home in good repair.

Q: How bad did Sam Adams' finances get?

A: Sometimes gifts of food and clothing from solicitous neighbors helped to keep the Adams family afloat. Taxes on their house slipped far in arrears. In fact, the sheriff put the house up for sale four times, though each time Samuel managed to stall the foreclosure.

He did marry, twice. First to the daughter of the minister of Boston's New South Church. His wife, Elizabeth Checkley Adams, died after six years, leaving him a son and a daughter. The fact that she'd had five pregnancies in those half-dozen years may have contributed to her demise.

The second Mrs. Adams was another Elizabeth, from the Wells family. Fortunately for Samuel, who had run through nearly all of Father's money by this time, Elizabeth the Second was a thrifty woman. She proved able to stretch a very few dollars to keep their household going, most of the time.

Samuel Adams, who originally studied for the ministry, changed careers to became a lawyer, a failed business man, a politician and America's fiery preacher of rebellion.

In spite of his financial problems, Samuel was well-liked. This probably was due to the fact that he was often more concerned with the welfare of his community than of his own family. At one time, friends built him a barn. Consistently, his fellow citizens selected him for municipal offices. They were very minor ones.

Small-Time Politician

Samuel Adams' first public job was to oversee the sanitation of the town, making sure that streets and commons were kept clean. He also served on two town committees. One dealt with fire hazards from faulty chimneys, and the other with small-pox inoculations.

Surprisingly, the failed business man and future fighter against taxes was also elected repeatedly as a *tax collector*. That was a job that provided some badly-needed family income, but it seems a strange vocation for a man who's noted for his battles against taxes.

Perhaps his fellow townsmen liked the fact that sympathetic Samuel neglected to press them for tax payments when times got tough. However, the authorities didn't approve of the slipshod way he kept his ledgers. There was even some talk of prosecuting Adams over a shortage of funds. However, that never came to pass, probably because any unaccounted-for money obviously never found its way into Sam's pockets.

Although Samuel would have made no ripples whatever in the stream of American history if he'd died at 40, he was destined soon thereafter to stir up a great turbulence.

Passionate Preacher of Rebellion

It was not until Adams was 42 years old that he found his true calling in life. The British Parliament passed the Sugar Act, the first of several arbitrary laws and taxes destined to irritate many Colonists and infuriate volatile Samuel.

Maybe Adams, the former divinity student, was never suited to be a minister. But in his middle age, he became a *preacher of rebellion*, calling down hell-fire and damnation on the British with all the passion of a Puritan pulpit pounder. He was one of many who began to question the new taxes. Samuel's loud dissension soon reached the ears even of the Governor of Massachusetts, who was not amused by it. That didn't bother Samuel. He despised the Royal appointee. And the feeling was mutual.

> **"He (Samuel Adams) is a dangerous incendiary."**
> Governor Thomas Hutchinson
> **"He (Governor Hutchinson) is an enemy of freedom."**
> Samuel Adams

Samuel had always been an avid member of the discussion and debating clubs at which civic-minded men spent much of their time in those days before TV sportscasts. A thinker and idealist, Adams expressed himself well in those discussion groups, and also in neighborhood taverns where it is said he drank little but talked much.

He was a diffident man, which made his arguments palatable, even though they tended to be on the extreme side. Unlike other civic leaders who flaunted prestige and wealth, unprepossessing Samuel could win the confidence of laborers, craftsmen, farmers, dock workers and other ordinary people who were to become major factors in the defiance of London. Though he was a highly educated man, Samuel Adams never talked down to the unschooled majority, so they listened to his ideas.

A Prolific Writer

In addition to being a charismatic speaker, Samuel Adams was also a prolific writer. He expressed his criticisms of the British government in more than 40 articles in Boston newspapers.

He also churned out numerous leaflets railing against the Sugar Act, the Stamp Act, the series of Townshend Acts and the arrogant attitude of Parliament. These were widely read, and influenced the thinking of prominent people in the Colonies.

Q: Who first said, "No taxation without representation?"
A: That famous rallying cry was coined by James Otis. A prolific writer and fiery speaker, he became an inspiration to his friend, Sam Adams. Although a prime force behind the revolt, Otis faded away while others moved on to fame and high office. Otis attended the Stamp Act Congress, but later became mentally deranged. His rhetoric escalated into wild ravings during which he fired pistols and terrorized his neighbors. Eventually his family committed him to an insane asylum.

However, Samuel wanted not just new thoughts, but *action!* And he knew that the place to get actual acts of violence against the Crown was not from the educated upper classes. It had to come from rougher folks such as carpenters, coopers, cobblers and other craftsmen (known as "mechanics") plus the roustabouts around the harbor and the unhappy unemployed.

He used his persuasive verbal skills to enlist those malleable men into groups he called *"The Sons of Liberty."*

"My Mob, the Sons of Liberty"

If a Tory official or a Loyalist merchant needed scaring, the fellows Sam often referred to as "his mob" were always ready and delighted to take on the job.

Their approach was direct. They'd threaten the British sympathizer, and if that didn't work, they'd beat him and break up his house. They might even tar-and-feather him.

An unlucky Loyalist gets tarred and feathered. The rod held by one of his tormenters indicates he might be beaten too. The noose at rear symbolizes the possibility of an even worse fate.

So feared did the *Sons* become that often a Loyalist sympathiser could be silenced, or a merchant selling British goods could be made to clear them off his shelves, merely by sending him a *feather*. That symbol of tar-and-feathering served as a chilling hint of what could happen if he didn't change his ways.

Samuel was the brain in the drive to suppress any opposition to rebellion. The *Sons* were the muscle.

A Genius at Organization

Samuel didn't stop at organizing his trained mobs in Boston, which became the pattern for similar Sons of Liberty groups in other colonies. He looked beyond his local area for support in distant places. He created a *network of committees* of prominent citizens throughout America.

These committees started late in 1772, just before the Tea Tax was passed. At a Boston town meeting, Samuel presented the motion to initiate a *Committee of Correspondence*. It's purpose was to draw up a statement of the rights of Americans, and to broadcast this manifesto as widely as possible.

The idea caught on. Similar committees were set up not just in other Massachusetts towns, but throughout the Colonies. They began to communicate with each other and share ideas for opposing British restrictions.This sparked the beginning of cooperation between different areas of the country. The Committees played an important role in the drawing together of 13 distinctly separate Colonies, and uniting them in a common cause.

Onward and Upward to Philadelphia

The Committees of Correspondence that Sam Adam started led to an actual gathering together of delegates from various Colonies. That gathering occurred at the First Continental Congress. Convened on September 5, 1774 this historic meeting was attended by 12 of the 13 colonies. Only the Royal Colony of Georgia decided not to participate.

Samuel was one of five delegates chosen to represent his state at the Congress in Philadelphia. Then 52, he possessed ample brains, spirit and eloquence for his new assignmnt, but was sadly lacking in appearance for such an important event.

His friends came to the rescue. They persuaded Sam to discard his disreputable old clothes-- he was always seen in the same ratty red suit and an equally shabby red cloak. They outfitted their delegate in a new suit, shoes and silk stockings.

Garbed in suitable splendor, Sam set out for his very first trip far from Boston. He was to travel far along the road to sedition. Along with his Boston friend John Hancock and General George Washington, he became one of the three Americans most "wanted" by His Majesty's executioners.

Fortunately none of the these three most notorious rebels were ever caught by British authorities. The penalty administered to traitors to the Crown was not just an ordinary death. That was too easy; instead they faced *drawing and quartering.*

That was a very unpleasant procedure in which the victim was disemboweled and literally cut up into quarters. Usually the quarter of him containing the head would be hanged, though doesn't that seem to be a bit redundant?

Almost a President

Samuel Adams, debater extraordinary and firebrand of the Revolution, went on to an illustrous career. With friend John Hancock, he was appointed a distinguished delegate to the Second Continental Congress.

Enroute to Philadelphia that second time, the two Bostonians were nearly nabbed by the Redcoats. They outdistanced the soldiers, thanks to advance warning by a horseman named Paul Revere. You'll read more about him later.

After the war, the formerly shabby bankrupt brewer became a state senator. He was elected Lieutenant Governor of Massachusetts, and succeeded to the Governorship when John Hancock died in that office. Governor Adams was subsequently elected for three more terms, so his performance must have pleased the electorate.

At the end of his career, esteemed Samuel Adams came close to holding the highest office in the United States. While serving his last term as Massachusetts' Governor, he was nominated for the office of President of the United States. Fellow Democrat Thomas Jefferson was his chief competitor for the office. As you know, Jefferson won.

When Jefferson assumed office for his first term in 1801, he invited the old rebel to become one of his cabinet members. But Samuel, who was 74, decided it was time to retire from public life. The President expressed his regrets.

> **"How much I lament that time has deprived me of your aid...**
> **But give us your counsel, my friend, and give us your blessing,**
> **and be assured there exists not in the heart of man a more**
> **faithful esteem than mine to you, and that I shall ever bear**
> **you the most affectionate veneration and respect."**
>
> President Thomas Jefferson

In his last years, even the Federalists, the party opposing Democrat Samuel Adams, expressed their regard for the aged revolutionary and statesman. When he died, at 81, the military drums beat a dirge at Faneuil Hall for the "Father of the American Revolution" as his funeral cortege rolled by.

Appropriately, Samuel Adams lies at rest in the heart of his beloved Boston, in the old Granary Burying Ground near the graves of the five victims of the Boston Massacre.

13

Strange Manners and Customs

Whether it be pigs roaming the streets, a lack of forks and separate bowls at the table, or bugs in the bedding, you'd have been jolted by some eye-opening surprises in even the finest communities of America in 1776.

To be sure, the "better sort" were aspiring to higher standards of dress, dining and deportment than early settlers had enjoyed, but they still had a long way to go by present-day yardsticks.

For example, society's standards were at their apex among the prosperous plantation owners and their wives in Virginia. Yet primitive customs prevailed even there, as indicated by a set of rules copied down by one of our most distinguished ancestors.

Rules of Civility

George Washington is often lauded for a list of 110 maxims on polite conduct which he presumably wrote during his brief teen-age schooling. It's doubtful they were original, since they closely resemble an old Jesuit Latin text and also a popular set of rules by an Englishman named Hawkins.

However, George's youthful observances illustrate actions that had to be warned against even among the upper classes of Virginia. Here are just a few of these 110 Rules Of Conduct young gentlemen ought to observe:

> "When in Company, put not your Hands to any Part of the Body not usually discovered.

> "Spit not in the Fire, nor Stoop low before it neither Set not your Feet upon the Fire especially if there be Meat before it.

153

> **"Bedew no mans face with your Spittle by approaching to near to him when you Speak.**
>
> **"Kill no Vermin as Fleas ticks lice &c in the Sight of others.**
>
> **"If you Cough, Sneeze, Sigh or yawn, do it not Loud but Privately, and Speak not in your Yawning, but put Your handkerchief or Hand before your face and turn aside."**

Young Master Washington also included several rules for proper decorum while dining. Here are some of the table manners that young George recommended:

> **"Cleanse not your teeth with the Table Cloth Napkin Fork or Knife but if others do it let it be done with a Pick Tooth.**
>
> **"If you soak bread in the Sauce let it be no more than what you put in your Mouth at a time and blow not your broth at Table but stay till it Cools of it Self.**
>
> **"Put not your meat to your Mouth with your Knife in your hand neither Spit forth the Stones of any fruit Pye upon a dish nor cast anything under the table."**

As you may have noted in the above list of maxims, our first president's two or three years of formal schooling left him poor at spelling. However, he was always noted for his neat appearance and gentlemanly manners.

Strange Dining Habits

In a day when forks were a rarity, even in the finest homes, you'd have noticed that fingers often came into play at the dining table. They had to be used to chase down an elusive piece of meat before it could be speared with a knife-end and lifted to the mouth. Almost anything could be classified as a "finger food".

Most foods the "middle folk" and the "lower classes" subsisted on, however, were not roasts but stews, soups and other spoon food. Most folk didn't eat sumptuous meals. Their daily diets tended to be both simple and monotonous.

Meat, if available, was likely to be cut up into small pieces and cooked with vegetables to make a stew. That made it easier to eat.

Corn bread or corn meal mush was also a staple in many households, eaten not only for breakfast, but also as a main meal. Even rich George Washington very often had only a bowl of bread and milk for his late supper.

Q: What did you share with a trencher mate?

A: In Colonial days, when few families could afford pewter or stoneware dishes, most ate from a trencher. That was a block of wood ten or twelve inches square, gouged out in the center to form a shallow bowl. But you seldom got a trencher all to yourself. In a typical large household, there wasn't enough room for that at the dining board-- literally two or three boards fastened together and perched atop a couple of trestles. To save space, only one trencher was placed between each two diners. So you and your trencher mate scooped a quantity of stew into your common bowl, and vied with each other as you attacked the food with spoons and knives.

Don't Drink the Water

Among our distinguished forefathers, there were no Alcoholics Anonymous. Just alcoholics.

Even little children drank hard cider. Both milk and water were regarded as unsafe, with justification. So the little ones, as well as adults, needed to drink liquids that had been purified. The answer, of course, was to drink only those containing alcohol. Watered wine, beer and cider all fit that category.

Not even infants were excluded from alcoholic drinks. It was a common practise to give babies a few sips of hard cider at bedtime to insure a sound sleep.

Cider was so cheap that it was given as freely as water to any thirsty traveler who stopped at a farmhouse along the road. A whole barrel of it could be purchased for a few shillings. Hard cider was considered a mild drink. Even the rare man who advocated temperance, such as John Adams, believed that a drink of hard cider was needed to start the day.

**"John Adams took only one large tankard of hard cider
when he first arose, but nothing more the rest of the day."**

Other "small drink" favored by moderate imbibers was beer, wine or mead. The latter, a drink rarely heard of today but common in 1776, was made from either fermented honey or from the bean of the honey-locust plant. Beer was so popular that there were more than 60 breweries in Massachusetts alone at the time of the Revolution.

For Heavy Topers

A quart of beer or hard cider or a light wine might be all right to wash down a meal, but for serious drinking our forefathers preferred a more potent brew.

Rum was the main drink of the colonists. Appropriately, it was commonly called *Kill Devil*. Another term for cheap rum was *Bumbo*. Rum was either slugged down straight, or combined with other liquids to form a wide variety of drinks.

Bartenders back in early times had to know how to mix many kinds of beverages. *Stone Wall* was a simple but potent concoction. It consisted of half rum and half hard cider. *Toddy, Sling* and *Grog* were all rum-based drinks.

Flip was a popular drink. It was made of a pitcher of strong beer, sweetened and fortified with molasses or sugar or sometimes dried pumpkin. It was then given some bite by adding a gill (a small glass-full) of rum. The flip was finished by dipping into it a red-hot poker, which gave the mixture a scorched, bitter taste that was much admired by some topers.

Punch was another favorite. It had many variations. All contained rum, sugar and "sourings", which could be any type of citrus juice. Brandy or Madeira wine were often added. So were spices, especially nutmeg. Punch was usually mixed in a large bowl. At a party of mixed company, punch cups were used. But in keeping with colonial ideas of friendliness and sanitation, all-male groups usually skipped the use of dainty cups. It was their habit to quaff in turn from the lip of a communal punchbowl.

Bars at taverns offered many strange drinks. They had strange names, such as *Calibogus, Ebulum, Metheglin, Mumbo, Rumbullion* and *Switchel.*

Spirits for Every Occasion

The serving of alcoholic refreshment was expected at every social occasion, whether it be a wedding, funeral, political election or the ordination of a preacher.

George Washington was reminded of this to his sorrow. In his first attempt to be elected to Virginia's House of Burgesses, thrifty George tried to skimp on campaign expenditures by not offering drinks to his supporters. He was defeated at the polls.

Next time around, in 1758, candidate Washington loosened his pursestrings and bought a round for everyone-- a quart and a half of whiskey for each supporter. This added up to 160 gallons of whiskey, but it got him 391 votes. Of course, he won.

Other famous government figures also believed in treating the voters at election time. Thomas Jefferson, James Madison and John Marshall were known to offer cheap but potent Bumbo to all comers on election days. After all, they didn't want to be known as cheapskates and get defeated at the polls.

One of the few politicians who spoke out against this practice of soliciting votes with hard drink was abstemious (hard cider only) John Adams. He even railed against that sacred bulwark of Colonial society, the tavern.

> "These taverns are become the nurseries of our legislators. An artful man may by gaining a little sway with the rabble of a town, multiply taverns and dram shops and thereby secure the votes of taverner and retailer. Here diseases, vicious habits, bastards and legislators are frequently begotten."
>
> John Adams' diary

Whether Adams liked them or not, taverns abounded in the towns of 1776. They were the social centers of the community... *where the action was!*

Besides being a combination of restaurant bar and hotel, the taverns also served as neighborhood clubs. For example, they provided a place to gamble at cards, dice or billiards.

Taverns also served as the centers where important news was posted. And of course, they were the gathering spots for festive occasions. Even the places where chilled church-goers stopped to warm up with a potent hot toddy before and after a long Sunday sermon they'd sat through in an unheated church.

Even for the Church

When a young minister was ordained, it was customary to throw a party for the occasion. Usually it was held in a tavern conveniently located near the church. With drinks, of course.

In fact, there was a special brew called "ordination beer", which presumably was a milder watered-down beverage. However, the regular type of alcoholic beverage--- flip, punch or wine-- was served at many ordination parties.

One account of such a party, held near Boston for a freshly-appointed minister, reveals that those attending did not hold back in attacking the bar. They consumed 30 bowls of punch and ten bottles of wine during the preliminaries, 44 bowls of punch and eight bowls of brandy while at dinner. Six spoil-sports drank tea.

Benjamin Franklin, who was an enthusiastic toper as well as a prolific author, expressed the prevailing sentiment about liquor in a short song he wrote that became a favorite in the taverns.

> 'Twas honest old Noah first planted the Vine,
>   And mended his morals by drinking the Wine.
> And justly the drinking of water decry'd,
>   For he knew that all Mankind by drinking it dy'd.
> From this piece of History plainly we see
>   That Water's good neither for Body nor Mind;
> That Virtue & Safety in Wine-bibbing's found
>   While all that drink Water deserve to be drown'd."

Part of the Employment Contract

Along with their pay, which might be meager, workers of all types expected to be supplied with stimulating refreshment on the job.

Soldiers refused to go into battle, especially on a hot day, without the stimulus of a tot of grog beforehand. This was not considered mutinous behavior. Just what anyone should expect.

George Washington, not one to pamper his employees, jotted in his journals that when he hired Philip Bader as his gardener at Mount Vernon, the employment contract included terms for drinking on the job. Bader agreed "to partake of no more than one dram of grog in the morning and another at noon." Except on holidays. A dram is 6.25 ounces, so those morning and noon pick-me-ups were each equivalent to *six shot glasses* of potent rum.

Washington's journal details further that as a Christmas bonus, his gardener was to receive a special allowance of four dollars. That would be *"enough to enable him to keep drunk for four days and nights."* He'd also get two dollars at Easter and Whitsuntide for the same relaxing purpose.

Pigs and Cows in the Streets

Visitors from England and Europe, where sanitation was far from good, were horrified to find an almost complete lack of it in scruffy American cities. Cows and pigs meandered on Boston Common, and wherever else they pleased, since it was unlawful to erect fences that herds couldn't pass around.

Presumably the animals were kept somewhat under control. A cowherd was hired by the town to watch the bovine herds. A hog-reeve performed a similar function for the pork crop. Besides growing up to be pork chops and bacon, pigs served another useful function. They'd eat almost anything. That helped with the garbage problem. There was plenty of refuse around. Even in a cosmopolitan center like New York, people just tossed their slop and refuse into the streets.

Despite the best efforts of the porkers, the garbage got deep at times and combined with mud and manure to make an awful mess that was difficult to wade through. Add horses and chickens to the mix of animals on the unpaved streets of a typical American town, and you faced a stinking mess. Needless to point out, that was not a very sanitary situation either.

Little Wigs and Big Wigs

An abundance of hair, natural or artificial, had been regarded as a mark of wealth and prestige for gentlemen in England and Europe. As a consequence, those in America who followed the fashions of the mother countries wanted to show off with abundant coiffures too, and they did with elaborate wigs.

Staid elders in New England ranted against the vanity of "long-haired" youth (just like the 1960s). They likened the affectation of wigs to the perfumed ringlets of English lords and dandies, or to the barbarous customs of feather-topped Indians. These admonitions had no effect.

The European trend of men wearing wigs spread in New England, as elsewhere, as a prosperous citified class grew in America. Every colonist with any pretensions at all to fashionable dress, wore a wig. Even some slaves who were personal servants in rich families were fitted out in wigs.

A Multitude of Styles

As in the mother countries, the bigger the wig, the bigger the gentleman. You might see a small neat wig on a man of modest pretensions. On the other hand, you'd expect a big high-piled mass of hair, or a curly billow down the shoulders, on an important magistrate or rich merchant.

At least that was the case when wigs first became popular in the colonies. Later, the practical Americans wanted something smaller and neater than the long, loose curly types. There were a multitude of styles available.

Gentlemen in the 1700s all wore wigs, which were often expensive.. They could take their pick from a large variety of styles, ranging from the "bag wig" shown at left, to the long full "barrister" style pictured at the right..

Some gentlemen adopted knotted wigs that didn't have loose hair to flop around so much, or bag wigs in which the long end of the hair was gathered up into cloth or netting. Some simply tied the ends of their hair neatly with a ribbon. Not everyone liked the new hair styles.

> **"Imagine me wearing a little bag wig showing my naked ears."**
> Benjamin Franklin

Costly and Stealable

Everyone had to have a wig. Obviously, though, everyone couldn't afford one. The finest cost as much as $200. As a result, wig stealing became a common problem. The newspapers contained notices offering rewards for the return of a costly prized wig that had been lifted, presumably not while on the owner's head.

Intricate headpieces were made from either human or horse hair. They might be natural in color, but mostly they were powdered white. Powdered by those who could afford it. Wigs were often whitened with *flour* by those who had to skimp on cost. Powder or flour was often applied also to natural hair, perhaps along with Pomatum, a thick perfumed grease.

The wearer of a wig shaved his head to accommodate it. (Perhaps that was also intended to help solve the prevalent problem of lice?) Then he applied a lacquer which was supposed to keep the wig from slipping on his bald dome.

Can't Outdo the Ladies

Though the men might want to show off as "Big Wigs", colonial dames knew how to put them in their places! At parties, they affected wigs that enabled them literally to tower over their husbands. Appropriately, these super-tall hairdos were called *Towers*. Some were two or three feet high.

It was reported that certain ladies of fashion had such enormous hairdos that they couldn't fit under the roofs of their carriages. They'd have to stick their heads out of the window (not safe on a breezy day) or kneel on the carriage floor.

THE PREPOSTEROUS HEAD DRESS, or the *FEATHERD LADY*.

An extreme example of the towering wigs worn by ladies of fashion.

The ladies also went their menfolk one better by adding decorations to the mass of hair they wore. Their coiffures were topped with plumes and feathers, especially peacock feathers. Stuffed birds and sculptured objects, such as cupids, might be added. The vanity of colonial dames, but not the men, was bound to reap the scorn of church fathers.

> **"Will not the haughty daughters of Zion refrain their pride?**
> **Will they lay out their hair and wear their false locks,**
> **their borders and towers like comets about their heads?"**
>
> Rev. Cotton Mather

Fragile Towers

The extreme height and complex structure of the most fashionable ladies' wigs posed problems. A strong wind, or an accidental bumping, could mess up a costly masterpiece of entwined hair, fluff and fancy decorations. Something was needed to bind the ladies' towering wigs securely together no matter what the weather.

Lard was the answer. Not nearly as neat (or non-smelly or non-sticky) as our present-day hair sprays, but the fat of the pig was readily available. And it glued things together.

Of course, the lard created problems of its own. No mention in literature of that time talks about the smell it must have created, especially after ripening for a few days or weeks. However, there is mention of a rodent problem. It seems that rats and mice were attracted to the well-larded towers the ladies stored in their closets between dress-up parties. This must have been a common problem, because wire "rat screens" were sold. Placed over the wigs, these screens were intended to keep the larded wigs from being gnawed to pieces.

Q: What was the "Hairdress a la Independence?"

A: Introduced in 1776 by politically hip hairdressers, this popular coiffure featured 13 curls at the lady's neck, symbolizing the 13 colonies.

Patches of Beauty

Another fashion Colonial dames adopted from European noblewomen was the use of beauty patches. These were little bits of silk, often in the shape of stars, that the lady would stick onto her face.

They were considered to be decorations. You've probably seen pictures of famous women of the French Court, such as Marie Antoinette, adorned with such beauty patches.

Besides their decorative aspect, these little bits of silk had a practical purpose. They were handy cover-ups for pimples or especially bad scars from smallpox which disfigured many people in the 1700s.

Soaps and Smells

There was not much of the former, an overabundance of the latter. When the British blockaded the rebellious American Colonies, they cut off the main source of hard soap for personal bathing. (As opposed to soft home-made lye soap used for washing clothes.) Not that a great deal of bathing soap had been used before. No one, of course, believed in daily baths or showers. Even if facilities had been available, such over-scrubbing of the skin would have been considered unhealthy.

Not much soap was wasted on clothing either. The usual schedule for washing underclothes was *once a month.*

The infrequency of washing was covered over by perfume. Although the British blockade also reduced supplies of imported perfumes, the colonists could resort to a variety of local products.

Rose petals were used abundantly. So were bunches of fragrant herbs and blossoms, called "simples" which were hung from rafters as well as placed around a room. The colorful simples were decorative as well as fragrant. Aromatic gums and oils were burned to freshen the air in early mansions.

From every aspect, the standards of personal cleanliness in 1776 were scandalously low.

14
The "S" Word - Sex

Sex was not talked about in "mixt gatherings" of polite society in the 1770s. But in the rougher milieu of the frontier, or if you were at the local tavern enjoying the alcoholic male comraderie there, would you hear about it? You bet!

The population of our country didn't multiply more than a hundred-fold, from only about 2.5 million in 1776 to more than 250 million today, via sexual abstinence. What our ancestors called by such strange names as "sexual congress, venery or wenching" was as popular a form of sport in their day as it is now.

Two centuries ago, there were many activities between American men and women that we'd consider very strange. Others we might call up-to-date!

Multiple Husbands
The scarcest and most sought-after commodity in the Colonies was women. In the very early days this sometimes led to a scandalous custom never mentioned in your schoolbooks. *Polygamy.*

You may think of "Groupies" and communal living as outgrowths of the promiscuous 1960s, but some of our ancestors were way ahead of Hait Asbury. The fact that polygamy was against the law, then as now, did not stop the practice in the lower strata of society in some colonies.

Several potent factors were involved. First, the young women who came here alone from the Mother Country, were almost invariably poor. As you read earlier, they might even be paupers, petty thieves or prostitutes cleaned out from English jails. And they

165

owed the ship's captain for their passage money, so they were available for purchase when they stepped off the gangplank.

An eager crowd of men would gather to greet any vessel landing with a fresh cargo of women. Most of those poor fellows meeting the boat were likely to be riff-raff too. Not picky about the beauty or backgrounds of the ladies for purchase, and lacking enough coin to pay the going marriage price.

Solution: two or three ardent males would pool their resources to buy a wench to become their communal wife.

A lonesome man could buy himself a wife, or split the cost with a friend.

If she were willing, this could provide a happy answer to the financial difficulties of both the male and female participants. There's no indication that the authorities tried to stop such arrangements. Or that the ladies found them other than pleasant.

Red "A" for Adultery

In contrast to the rather loose views on polygamy in the early days of some Southern Colonies, New Englanders were *death* on adultery. Sometimes literally.

The early Puritan laws in Massachusetts decreed that females who committed adultery were to be lashed by whips. In public, to discourage others from similar peccadilloes. Afterward, they were made to wear a red "A" for all to know their shame. They might even be branded on the cheek with the letter.

Q: Were there any sex manuals in 1776?
A: Of course! One, supposedly written by that smart Greek, Aristotle, enjoyed wide readership. It contained many cautions against too frequent enjoyment of "sexual congress" which could cause blindness and brain damage. Those who might be tempted to indulge too often were warned that copious copulation would shorten their lives. Perhaps there's some truth in that? Our forefathers and foremothers certainly must have gotten together frequently to produce so many children, and its' true their average lifespan tended to be brief.

Lest you think that Puritan laws punished only women, consider the penalty for men. In old New England, an overly ardent male faced *death* if caught between the sheets with a married woman. The possibility of hanging from a gibbet was designed to cool the ardor of a fellow who might covet his neighbor's wife. Cool other things as well.

Note, however, that this penalty applied only if a married woman was involved. It was up to an unmarried woman to put her foot down, and keep her skirts down. Otherwise the man was absolved. Not what we'd consider a fair ruling.

Adultery was by no means the only activity forbidden in old New England. Any public affection, even between spouses, was verboten. In one instance, a lonesome seaman coming home from a long voyage made the mistake of ardently hugging and kissing his wife when she greeted him at the door. Unfortunately a nosy nieghbor spied this unseemly show of ardor. The ardent husband was reported to the church elders. He was called before them and sentenced to spend a period of repentance in the stocks until he cooled off..

Any pleasurable activity that took place on Sunday was especially frowned upon by the church elders. For example, children were not allowed to run and play on that day. And above all, of course, sex was strictly forbidden on the Sabbath.

Q: How did the Puritans know if you had sex on Sunday?
A: It was common knowledge in the 18th Century that a child
was always born on the same day of the week on which it
had been conceived. Ergo, if a Sunday birth occurred,
everyone knew you'd been doing what you weren't
supposed to on the Sabbath. In old Boston Town, you'd be
in deep trouble.

No Shortage of Bastards

Despite the severity of laws against adultery, it obviously flourished. Life was rough for many of the offspring. Since they were an embarrassment, bastard children often were shunted off to an orphanage. As soon as they reached working age-- maybe five or six-- they were likely to be "bound out" to some family that was looking for cheap labor.

Until able to live on their own, they received room, board, discipline and spiritual instruction. While they labored in the fields, the kitchen or as an apprentice to a craftsman.

Public views about illegitimate births varied widely in different areas of colonial America. They were far more liberal in rural areas of Pennsylvania, for example, than in Puritan New England. In the western stretches of Penn's Commonwealth, practical German farmers wanted to be certain that a prospective daughter-in-law was capable of bearing strong children to share in the workload.

To make sure that marriage would result in a large family, parents encouraged a courting couple to produce a pregnancy, and possibly even a birth, before the wedding banns were posted. If a prospective bride couldn't deliver such proof of fertility, with one swain or another, she'd be apt to end up as an old-maid.

Beware of Hookers
The Revolutionary War created an unwelcome by-product. That was the considerable increase in Syphilis and Gonorrhea that appeared where troops were concentrated, and spread from there.

Prostitutes, though by no means unknown before the war, faced restrictions then. In the small towns and rural areas which made up most of America in 1776, everyone knew what everyone else was doing. There might be hanky-panky between friends, and frequently was, but any professional provider of sex who showed up was likely to taste the whip and be driven out of town. Therefore the populace was shielded from the likeliest purveyors of venereal disease.

Since townspeople and farmers seldom traveled far, they had little opportunity to visit the raunchy taverns and brothels of seaports where the "unfriendly diseases", as they were called, were imported. The war changed all that.

Some medics maintained that Hessian mercenaries, a loutish unpopular lot, brought venereal diseases with them. Undoubtedly they and their British comrades contributed their share, for tea wasn't the only thing that came from across the ocean. But wherever the problem came from, it was the professional ladies following the troops who spread it around.

When lads left the farm to experience life in the army, they had ample oportunity to pick up new friends and other things. If there was any shortage of prostitutes or other willing women in camp, they could always be located nearby.

They were a rough crowd. Annals of army life in the brief New York campaign show that colonial soldiers quickly located a red-light area known as Holy Ground. At that popular gathering spot, prostitutes murdered two soldiers, probably to rob them. As if that wasn't bad enough, they *castrated* one unlucky lad. He must have really made them angry.

A Colonial Cross-Dresser
One of the most-publicized scandals of Colonial America was the fondness of an early Governor-General of New York for wearing women's clothes.

Edward Hyde, the Viscount of Cornbury, was Queen Anne's cousin. At the beginning of the Eighteenth Century, she sent Lord Cornbury to Manhattan where he governed for six years. The fact that Cornbury proved to be a grafter and a drunk was not regarded as unusual for a high official of the Crown. However, when he presided at the New York Assembly *dressed in drag*, that was regarded as a bit strange.

For this important occasion, the Royal Governor wore a beautiful satin gown with a hoopskirt, and also sported a fancy tall hairdo with a jeweled bauble atop it. In his graceful hand with very long fingernails, he waved a lady's fan. He tottered about on high heels.

Even the Governor himself recognized that his feminine costume at the Assembly might set tongues to wagging. He attempted to explain why his attire was appropriate. Since he represented Queen Anne, he maintained it was proper to dress like her. The New Yorkers he governed did not like this illogical claim. However, people in the other colonies did. They thought it was hilarious.

Many Complaints, But a Lucky Ending

Lord Cornbury's appearances in fancy women's attire were not limited to a few government or society affairs. He was also spotted numerous times late at night in the raunchy dock areas of New York City, decked out like a hooker. Eventually, the State Assembly complained so loudly about Cornbury's peccadilloes that it persuaded the Royal Privy Council to replace him as Governor.

It was not only his peculiar dress they objected to. He spent far more money than his income allowed, made up the difference by embezzling state funds, granted large tracts of land to his friends, and otherwise infuriated the people of New York. It looked as if the weird governor had come to the end of the road. He was even thrown into debtor's prison for a while, but then his luck turned.

His father died, making him a rich heir and the Earl of Clarendon. That stroke of luck changed everything for Cornbury. When he returned to England, his cousin Queen Anne appointed the new Earl to her Privy Council, the powerful body that had supposedly punished him by ordering him back to England. You figure it out!

Other Transvestites

Lord Cornbury was not the only transvestite who occasioned speculation. During the Revolutionary war, one of the interesting characters involved in our getting munitions and money from France was the Chevalier d' Eon. No one knew for certain what D'Eon's sexual orientation really was. It seemed to change from time to time.

He'd been a diplomatic agent, a job limited to men in those days. D'Eon was also a champion fencer. Moreover, he was a captain in a regiment of French dragoons, an extremely masculine occupation. Right? However, when the dashing chevalier entered fencing tourneys, he registered in the *female* category. That confused people a bit.

Chevalier D'Eon's split personality is featured in this old magazine illustration which pictures him as half woman and half man.

Evidently some of his close friends were confused also. He was reputed to have a love affair with a prominent (male) playwright. What's more, one of his fellow captains in the Grenadiers fell madly in love with D'Eon and wanted to marry him.

Want to guess as to which sex the female fencer and masculine warrior really was? At his death an autopsy was performed, to satisfy public curiosity which had even escalated into big-time betting. The autopsy revealed that D'Eon was undeniably equipped with male plumbing.

Scandalous Bundling

An odd practice of the eighteenth century which evokes a chuckle and a snicker nowadays is the custom of *bundling* a young courting couple together in a cozy bed. Of course, with appropriate restrictions placed between them.

Bundling was controversial in colonial days, and not practised by "people of quality". But it was a sensible courtship custom among the common folk who lived in crowded, poorly-heated homes. In summer months, lovers could stroll in the woods for their sparking. But in rain or cold, they could get together only in a house that might have just one or two downstairs rooms, jammed with several younger children plus the parents. That offered no privacy at all.

With a large brood in a small house, parents might be anxious to marry off an excess daughter of nubile age. Therefore, if a respectable suitor came calling, Momma and Poppa wanted to encourage him.

Sensible Solution

The hospitable thing to do was to invite the young man to stay the night in the only available warm place, daughter's bed. That had several advantages. After all, it wasn't safe for a young man to travel back to his home after dark. Either a highwayman or the local watchmen might shoot him, eliminating a good future son-in-law. Also, things got quieter and more conducive to romance after the family went to bed. And after the fire smoldered down, a bed was a warm safe haven. Or was it?

Of course, one potential problem presented itself. Could a curious young woman and her warm-natured young man be trusted alone together when they shared a bed, while weary parents fell into a deep sleep? This worry didn't necessarily upset the parents too much. After all, they did want to promote a marriage. And a quiet midnight scamper by an approved suitor would be regarded as no great catastrophe, so long as any unplanned increase in daughter's waistline led to matrimony.

Jokes were plentiful about the tendency of brides to deliver their first children prematurely, but little stigma was attached to the their offspring. They were jokingly called *"seven-month babies."*

After all, our religious ancestors pointed out that the biblical precept was *increase and multiply.* Based on this Bible verse, *Increase* was one of the most popular names bestowed upon female babies in the 1700s, a strong hint as to what was expected.

The Bonds of Non-Matrimony
The famous bundling board was supposed to be the major safeguard. Extending down the middle of the bed, this heavy plank was fastened into place so neither occupant could crawl under or over it. Reaching over was okay, but no snuggling together.

Stricter colonial mothers figured out various additional ingenious safeguards to assure that adventurous questings in the night wouldn't go too far. Or so they hoped.

The young couple might be put to bed fully clothed as an obstacle to romance. Extra cautious mothers sometimes took the additional precaution of knotting the bottoms of their daughters' petticoats. Although such an impediment to roaming hands could be undone, untying was difficult unless both paries cooperated.

Publications of the time frequently published little poems that questioned if such restraints really worked.

> You don't undress like man and wife,
> That is your plea, I'll freely own,
> But who's your bondsman when alone,
> That further rules you will not break,
> And marriage liberties partake?
> You will say that I'm unfair,
> That some who bundle take more care,
> But bundler's clothes are no defense,
> When unruly horses push the fence.

Despite such speculations, bundling remained a popular custom. Safely tucked away under a warm quilt, a young courting couple could lie cozily together in a chilly house and get to know each other better, though presumably *not too well.*

Ben Franklin Helped to End Bundling
Of all people, it was free-thinker and scandalously romantic Benjamin Franklin who was more responsible than anyone else for the demise of bundling. His Franklin stove made homes easier to heat and safer at night, without the hazard of wood burning in an open fireplace. This meant that young lovers no longer had to climb under the covers to keep from freezing. They could sit on the sofa and carry on their romancing.

Did this greatly raise the standard of morals? Evidently not. With no bundling to rail against, strict moralists switched their suspicions to the new-fangled upholstered sofas that had became popular.

Our ancestors determined that since they could no longer blame sexual transgressions on the old bundling boards, it must be the snuggling on the new upholstery that was creating an atmosphere conducive to temptation.

15
The Loyalists

Victory was sweet for the Patriots who fought for separation from Britain. But it was a catastrophy for those numerous Americans who called themselves Loyalists or Tories.

They were a large segment of society in 1776, those conservative ancestors of ours. As big a segment as the Loyalists. In fact, Patriot heroes whose exploits we know so well were *outnumbered* in many localities by the thousands of citizens who remained loyal to our Mother Country, Britain.

Q: How many Loyalists actually fought for the King?
A: At times there were more Americans bearing arms for King George than General George had in active service. At least 30,000 Loyalists served with British troops at some time. They formed the basis for more than 50 companies named for localities throughout America-- the Maryland Loyalists, Carolina King's Rangers, Loyal New Englanders, Buck's County Light Dragoons, the Queen's Loyal Virginians, etc.

There were more Loyalists than Patriots in the Southern Colonies of Georgia and South Carolina. The Loyalists were also strong in the Middle Colonies of New York, New Jersey and Pennsylvania. They came from all areas of the country and all walks of life, those citizens who refused to change their loyalties when the War for Independence erupted.

175

War Against Their Own Relatives and Country
Remember, this was a not a fight against a foreign land. What the citizens were planning was a *revolution* against their own country, England, of which they'd always been proud to be a part. Most of them had either been born in England, or their parents had come from there. They had relatives in the Mother Country. George III was not a foreign monarch; he was *their* king, and they'd been taught since infancy that he ruled by divine right.

They had no great quarrel with the existing government, and certainly no desire to join a group of hot-heads intent on picking a fight with King George's mighty army.

Prominent Loyal Citizens
Those at the highest levels of government in the Colonies tended to be Loyalists. After all, the governors of the various colonies were appointed by the King. They and their helpers were all employees of the existing government-- not keen on losing their jobs. Not only were a wide range of political jobs controlled by the Crown, but religious positions were also.

Anglican ministers, appointed as part of the official state Church of England, were naturally British sympathizers. Almost unanimously, they preached a conservative gospel that labeled as blasphemous any rebellion against the existing government.

When the War really got underway, against their warnings, many a preacher paid dearly for his support of the Crown.

> **"I have been obliged to shut up my churches to avoid the fury of the populace. Every clergyman of the Church of England, who dared to act upon proper principles was marked out for infamy and insult... Some have been dragged from their horses, assaulted with stones and dirt, ducked in water, obliged to flee for their lives, driven from their habitations and families, laid under arrest and imprisoned."** Rev. Thomas Barton of Lancaster, Pa.

Divided Families
As in the Civil War several generations later, the Revolution resulted in bitterness and even bloodshed within families.

You've already read about two prominent examples of this. One was Mary Washington, George's cantankerous Tory mother, who believed that her son would and should be beaten by the King's forces. Another was William Franklin who became the King's Royal Governor of New Jersey while his father, Benjamin, labored valiantly to win French support for the Patriot side.

Countless other families were divided by their views of the War. For instance, when Lucy Flucker, daughter of a Tory known as the most hated man in Boston, fell in love with patriot Henry Knox, trouble was inevitable. She had to marry in secret and run away with her sweetheart. Henry became a Brigadier General and Washington's Chief of Artillery.

Lucy never saw her family again. She became one of the many casualties of America's first bitter civil war.

A Time to Choose

The Fourth of July in 1776 was a time of catastrophy for the Loyalists. Until that date when all 13 colonies agreed to a formal Declaration of Independence, it was permissable to argue about the pros and cons of rebellion. Even some famous signers of the Declaration initially voiced great doubts about fighting against England.

A few members of the Second Continental Congress refused to go along with the Declaration, and resigned when it was adopted. One of those congressmen who protested the signing was John Alsop from New York.

> "As long as a door was left open for a reconciliation with Great Britian, on just and honorable terms, I was willing to render to my country all the service in my power. But as you have closed the door, I must beg leave to resign."
> John Alsop

Even as late as the winter of 1775, after some fighting had started, Washington's officers in the new Continental Army continued the custom of raising a toast to King George at their mess. Till the last, many hoped that the bitter arguments and battles over taxes could somehow be settled. They hoped the Crown would soften its stance and allow some sort of reconciliation. That hope went down the drain once the Declaration of Independence was signed. After that, it became treasonous to side in any way with the British.

Those who professed continued loyalty to the Crown were *traitors* who faced four tough choices:

(1) They could sign an Oath of Allegiance, agreeing to support the Revolution and fight in it if required. Many signed this oath only out of fear, but kept their mouths shut thereafter and stayed out of trouble.
(2) They could leave the country. Tens of thousands did.
(3) They could join the enemy army. Tens of thousands more followed that course.
(4) They could refuse to sign the oath, but stay home, perhaps giving clandestine support to the enemy when they could. This group took a chance on being harshly abused by their neighbors, jailed or maybe even hanged.

Goodbye to Home and Friends
A sad by-product of our first American civil war that's usually mentioned briefly, if at all, in schoolbooks, is the fact that it ruined many American families. Their exodus from the land they loved was a rough ordeal.

> **"Tories with their brats and wives
> should fly to save their wretched lives."**
> Popular ditty of 1776

Their lives were wretched indeed, because they lost everything they'd worked for. Somewhere between 80,000 and 100,000 colonists who remained loyal to the King packed up and left the country. About half of these emigres fled to Canada, where they received some assistance toward a new start in that English colony. Others went to the British West Indies, Bermuda or the Bahamas. Some returned to England.

At war's end, the British insisted in the peace treaty that Loyalists returning to America should get their possessions back. Few of them ever received much of a settlement.

Sentiment against Tories still remained high, and their confiscated land and goods had been sold while they were gone.. In New York, for example, the state raised $3.6 million from the sale of Loyalist/Tory property-- a vast sum in those days. By War's end, the money had disappeared. It had been used to buy badly-needed supplies for the Continental army.

Any valuable possessions left in the Loyalists' homes when they fled would be long gone-- stolen by the mobs that drove suspected Tories out of town.

Committees of Safety

With about a third of their neighbors favoring victory by the British, it's easy to imagine how concerned the Patriot third was about "fifth columns" in their midst. To guard against saboteurs, communities throughout the colonies formed Committees of Safety patterned after those Samuel Adams started in Boston.

These Committees didn't worry much about justice or civil and human rights. Those accused by anyone of loyalty to the Crown could be summoned before the local Committee to explain their offenses. These offenses could be so slight as drinking tea (imported from Britain) or charging high prices, or being overheard saying something critical of the war.

The Committee of Safety served as both accuser, judge and jury. Punishments meted out depended on the whims of Committee members. The mildest punishment meted out for any reported lack of enthusiasm for the war was public humiliation. The accused would be forced to recant his actions, apologize and sign an oath of loyalty. He might also be beaten or whipped by ardent rebels after his "trial". Maybe even *before* it!

Newspaper accounts indicate that attacks on Tories often showed no respect for circumstances or persons. At Roxbury, Massachusetts, a Mrs. Brimley, lying in for the birth of a baby, was upbraided by a band of drunken rebels who stripped her and her children of their clothes. An Anglican minister in Hartford, Dr. Joseph Clark was jounced around town on a rail -- seated astraddle a sharp board. When finally dumped off, after fainting several times from the pain, he was described as "injured in a Manner unfit for Description in a Newspaper."

Confiscation of property was provided by law in almost every state. In some, a blacklist of Loyalists was posted publicly. Those named were given a few hours to pack up and leave their country. They were threatened with death if they returned.

Q: What prominent Patriot defended Tories in court?
A: Young lawyer Alexander Hamilton agreed with many Americans that not all Tories should be punished for continuing to feel loyalty to the King. He maintained, personally and also in court, that Loyalists who refrained from active opposition to the Revolution deserved the protections guaranteed other citizens. Of course, defending such people was good for business. New York, where he practised law, was loaded with Tories. As Hamilton once stated, the beatings and other attacks on British sympathizers "brought a plentiful harvest to us lawyers."

Prisoners at Symsbury Mines
Prisons during the Revolution were dreadful places. The worst of them were reserved for convicted Loyalists who escaped the death penalty. Worst of all was the prison at the abandoned copper mines at Symsbury, Connecticut.

The unlucky Loyalists dumped there likened them to living tombs. Prisoners at Symsbury were lowered by a windlass down into cold, wet cells, more than 100 feet below the surface, that had been gouged out of the earth by the copper miners.

The prisoners saw daylight only when brought up to the surface to work, chained and fettered by the leg or neck. Their food-- chunks of bread and meat-- was thrown down to them. As you'd expect, the survival rate was poor at Symsbury. Most prisoners died after a few months there.

Cruel as this imprisonment was, it was condoned because it served its purpose. Washington endorsed the Symsbury Mines Prison when he requested the Connecticut Committee of Safety to "confine some atrocious villains sentenced to court martial to the mines, so that they cannot possibly make their escape."

Soldiers of the King

The most fortunate of the Loyalists may have been those men who were able to join the British army. They were able to blend in with their comrades, and so attracted no special retribution if captured.

When we think of non-English soldiers that the Royal Army recruited, the Hessians generally come to mind. In reality, the ranks of the British army contained many more Americans who were loyalists than it did German mercenaries.

This big influx of American turncoats was especially apparent in Southern campaigns late in the War. For example, in the Battle of King's Mountain, *all the soldiers on both sides were Americans!* Only one man, the commanding officer of the British forces, was a royal regular. That battle was truly one that arrayed Americans versus Americans.

A Resource Wasted

Despite a few instances such as the use of many Tory soldiers in the Southern campaign, the British mostly ignored the vast potential offered them by the thousands of American Loyalists.

From the beginning, they'd *said* that Colonists loyal to the Crown would rise up against their trouble-making Patriot brethren and put an end to the rebellion. But the English didn't really *do* much to use the Loyalists fully. That was a big mistake.

Q: How were Loyalist women protected in New York?

A: The stationing of large numbers of British soldiers in New York created a considerable increase in rapes. This was especially undesirable in a Loyalist stronghold. The British counted on the New York Tories to help them; they didn't want to lose that support by having unruly soldiers violate Tory wives and daughters. Solution: the British War Office sent 3,500 prostitutes (20 shiploads) to Manhattan to act as the "intimate property" of the army there. This served a dual purpose, for this exodus somewhat thinned out the over-abundance of hookers who innundated England's cities at that time.

It's true that some Loyalists were enlisted to serve as spies. And tens of thousands actually bore arms in Redcoat units at one time or another. But the professional British officers tended to look down on such recruits as amateurs not to be trusted on their own. They set up few all-American units.

Had the British forces armed and really encouraged separate Loyalist units, it's speculated that King George's predictions of an early end to the War might have come true. Remember, there were *several hundred thousand Loyalists*-- perhaps as many as there were Patriots. Right at hand in America, they were potential combatants who didn't have to be transported 3,000 miles from England, a tremendous problem with regular British troops.

Hatred that Never Faded

Hatred of Loyalists who fought for the British was bitter and unforgiving. Instead of being taken prisoners when Continental soldiers triumphed in battle, they were likely to be butchered. The Patriots hated them more than they did even the detested Hessians.

> **"No quarter for Tories!"**
> A common battlecry

If they were captured and later identified as American turncoats, their treatment was so bad that several American regiments formed in Canada were dissolved. The soldiers in them became anonymous members of regular British units, a safer situation. They couldn't risk being taken prisoners because it was almost certain they wouldn't live long once they fell into Patriot hands.

Many captured English soldiers and many Hessians chose to remain in America after the war, and were accepted with little fuss by their neighbors. On the other hand, American traitors who served with the British were not welcome to return home. The war that pitted neighbor against neighbor and brother against brother inflicted deep scars that lasted for many decades.

16
Life at the Bottom

To understand our ancestors of 1776, we need to look at *all* of early America's melting pot. Not only the few famous people at the top, plus the substantial merchants and land-owning farmers just below them, but those at the very bottom of the pot as well.

There was a multitude of them. Not only black slaves (discussed in the next chapter) but thousands of whites in bondage too. Lower than the underclass of today, they performed America's hard dirty tasks. They had no vote and no voice in the building of a nation or in arguments about a revolution. But their sweat became a key ingredient in the building of America, the supplying of its army, the battle to establish a new nation.

Semi-Slaves Called Indentured Servants

Everyone knows about the disgraceful practice of buying Africans from the slavers to obtain a cheap supply of laborers in America. It's a scandal we can never forget.

What few people realize is that a form of *white slavery* also existed. It was a big part of America! *At least half, and maybe as many as two thirds, of all the white immigrants to the colonies came here as indentured servants.*

The agents who transported them to America sold these indentured servants to the highest bidder, usually for a price between 15 and 20 pounds. The word "sell" was avoided in regard to white laborers, as opposed to black slaves. The euphenism used to cloud the transaction was that white servants were "set over"-- not sold. But however the deal was described, like the Africans *they were property.*

They had to serve their masters without pay and with no personal freedom, typically for four or five years. Like a horse or a piece of real estate, they could be resold ("set over") to someone else if their masters wished to do so.

Their lot was not as horrible as that of the Africans. For one thing, white servitude lasted for a specified number of years, not for life. Also, the white Europeans generally were not treated so inhumanely as the Africans. However, in many other respects, there was not a great deal of difference.

Yet many of those indentured servants came voluntarily to these shores, in order to escape conditions which were even worse across the sea. Others had no choice. But all arrived here to solve the biggest problem in the early Colonies.

A Shortage of Muscle
America offered an abundance of land-- undeveloped areas many times greater than all of England or the European countries from which the settlers came. But always there was a shortage of labor.

Unlike the crowded homelands, America had no surplus of unemployed people that landowners could hire to clear and work their fields. A few free laborers, mostly craftsmen, came to these shores to earn double the wages they'd made on the other side of the Atlantic. But most of those with money for ship's passage didn't want to work for someone else, especially not as field hands in the hot sun of the Southern plantations.

They came here to get their own plot of land, often appropriating an open forest patch without bothering about titles. These newly-arrived small farmers also needed strong hands to help them with their crops.

With an endless demand and no adequate supply of free workers, the solution became obvious. One way or another, they had to get people who could be *forced* to work the fields of America.

Four Possibilities
The first source of forced labor tapped by the colonists was the native Indians. The earliest white invaders, including the pious Puritans, attempted to force captured Indians to work for them-- to

make them slaves. But the stupid savages were too smart to learn the back-breaking techniques of farming; at the first opportunity, they'd sneak back into the forest. If kept locked up in the white people's houses, they also had a proclivity to catch the white's diseases which caused them to die off quickly.

A second source of forced labor-- one we all know about-- came from Africa. However, the African slave trade didn't get underway in big volume until well into the eighteenth century.

Until the 1700s, the number of African slaves in the colonies was just about equaled by laborers obtained from two other sources. These two added sources of muscle were easy to obtain. They were provided with the enthusiastic assistance of the English authorities.

To the Gallows... or America
One commodity England had in over-abundance was criminals. As a consequence, we American share some of the same sort of heritage given to Australia a century later.

Many of our ancestors were thieves, whores, debtors, vagrants and other riff-raff. Whatever the English authorities wanted to clean out of their goals.

During the wars with the French, English criminals were routinely shipped into the army for a stint of soldiering. With a smaller peace-time force, this outlet dried up. In 1713, Parliament thought of a new way to dispose of felons. They might receive Royal clemency, but only if transported to the colonies for a specified term of forced labor.

The convicts were sold at the dock in America. to anyone willing to pay the passage money, plus a profit to the ship owner, for a worker of dubious quality. The average price for a convict laborer was equivalent to about 15 dollars.

His Majesty's Seven Year Passengers
The usual term of indenture for criminals was seven years of hard labor. For this reason, those shipped to American shores were often referred to a *His Majesty's Seven-Year Passengers*. However, any criminals under death sentences, which were meted out for dozens of offenses in England, had to serve twice as long. They received indentures of 14 years.

Those hard characters usually ended up in labor gangs in the fields of Virginia, Maryland and the Carolinas. About 50,000 of them arrived in America by 1776. Working in the hot southern sun, many didn't survive long enough to serve their full terms. If they did make it through their indentures, they could become free laborers or farmers, with the gift of a few dollars and a few acres mandated as their take for a new life. They were a prolific group, and their children multiplied rapidly, along with those of the more prosperous immigrants.

The 50,000 convicts, shipped to America like cattle, often in chains, included only those who arrived *alive* after a rugged sea voyage.

> **"Planters fortunes here consist in the number of their servants, who are purchased at high rates, much as the estates of an English farmer do in the multitude of their cattle."**
> The Governor of Maryland, 1759

A Growing Big Business

Even the considerable supply of white felons who could be forced to come to the new land couldn't satisfy all of the the needs for labor before the African trade developed. Colonists had to seek another source of workers.

Volunteers, or semi-volunteers. were needed to increase the number of indentured servants.

To meet the demand for laborers, recruiting agents teamed with ships captains and merchants to get thousands of poor people to come to the New World. No passage money was needed, but the immigrants, like the criminals before them, would have to pay for the trip by the sweat of their brows. Whoever bought them on the western shore would get their services for a specified period. The typical term was five years, although it might vary from four to as much as six or seven, for the indenture was a business contract with flexible terms..

The booming industry in importing indentured servants began in England, and then it spread to Ireland, Germany, the Netherlands and Switzerland.

Q: How profitable was the trade in indentured servants?
A: Very! It cost a merchant only six to ten pounds to ship
someone to America. There an indentured man or woman
who survived the voyage could be sold for as much as 20
pounds. Maybe more at harvest time or when shortages of
labor existed. Profit was good for the purchaser too. Since
he paid no wages and provided only minimal subsistence,
he could make as much as 50 pounds per year on his small
investment, for perhaps as long as five years.

No Need for Volunteers

Some of the most aggressive recruiters, called Spirits or Crimps, did not depend much on volunteering. They scoured the taverns for gin-sodden wretches they could spirit aboard a ship before they sobered up.

Sometimes the Spirits literally kidnapped their cargo. Children on the loose-- and there were many of them wandering in impoverished areas of Britain and Europe--were especially easy prey. They might be lured to a gathering depot or ship with candy. For that matter, the government might lend a hand to get rid of orphans, who were a nuisance and an expense to the state.

> "The authorities of London packed off more than 100 orphans,
> in one roundup alone, to the docks to be shipped to the colonies
> and there bound out as servants."

Recruiters posted advertisements and otherwise dazzled potential emigrants with stories of fabulous opportunities in America, contrasted with their present wretched lot.

All they had pay for their transportation to paradise was several years of their lives. Once they signed the Certificate of Indenture, which few of them could read, they became the property of their new master to be worked as he desired and sold to someone else if he wished to do so.

A Family Deal

Indentured servants of a special type were enlisted from a level of society that was slightly more prosperous. They were called *Redemptioners.*

One step up the social ladder, the Redemptioners were individuals or families who could pay some but not all of their passage money. As partially-paid-up passengers, they agreed to settle up and *redeem* their debt shortly after arriving in America.

Sometimes they had relatives or friends in the new world-- people they counted on to loan them money to pay the shipping merchant what he was owed. If not, he could sell them to the highest bidder to get his money back, plus a hefty profit.

The whole family was then obligated to serve their new master for a term that depended on the amount to be redeemed. Their servitude might be for as little as two years, but four was typical.

First Hurdle-- the Sea

White Indentured Servants and Redemptioners headed for our shores were not chained as later African cargoes would be. Ships captains didn't fear they'd mutiny or jump overboard, as captured Negroes might do. Of course, some white passengers posed a hazard. Like the captured Africans, convicts were shackled at the neck and chained in place to make sure they caused no trouble.

The captain's only concern for any type of forced laborers in which he had an investment was that too many of them shouldn't die enroute. He didn't get paid until his wretched cargo, white or black, hit the wharf. Hopefully still in salable condition.

It's estimated that at least one sixth of the convicts shipped to America died enroute and were tossed overboard. Sometimes the death rate reached one third or more. The African death rate was worse.

Short Rations

The first shock that faced the Indentured Servants and the Redemptioners who thought they were headed for a good deal was the rations they were fed aboard ship. Skippers in the flesh trade didn't want their passengers to starve to death... not quite. But wormy meat, moldy bread and scummy water were par for the course. If storms slowed a voyage beyond the estimated 15 weeks or so, even those supplies ran out.

**"We ate the mice, we ate the rats,
And through the hold we ran like cats."**
Sailor's song

During one voyage from Rotterdam to Philadelphia of a scow with the delightful name of *Love and Unity*, it's recorded that rats, mice and water were sold to the starving passengers. The ship's crew broke open and plundered the trunks of the dead or dying.

On another vessel, *the Sea Flower* sailing from Ireland, storms kept the ship at sea for 24 weeks. By that time, 46 of 106 passengers starved to death. Presumably the death toll might have been higher, except that some of the survivors cannibalized six of the corpses.

Pest Houses
After months of suffering under such conditions, it was inevitable that passengers arrived at port with every sort of disease imaginable.

To protect their citizens, officials at port cities tried to separate the sick arrivals and quarantine them. Boston kept a pest house on an island in the harbor, and fined skippers of human-cargo ships who failed to stop there for inspection. Philadelphia also set up an island pest house.

The states of Virginia and Maryland, where most convict ships landed, tried to quarantine all such ships, keeping everyone on board as long as deemed necessary. However, the English parliament didn't like this impediment to their jail-emptying program. They overruled such quarantine regulations.

The Soul Drivers
Once they made it to port, the immigrants faced further shocks. They were cleaned up a bit and auctioned off to buyers who came on board.

That was always a hectic scene. In the confusion of being dragged off by their new masters for debarking, the new servants often lost baggage that contained treasured possessions, or their articles of indenture. Sometimes families were split up between more than one master.

Probably the unluckiest immigrants were bought up by the Soul Drivers. Those tough characters were aptly named. Acting as retail merchants in the big business of forced labor, they bought up packs of immigrants and drove the poor souls out into the countryside for sale to outlying farmers.

After they were puchased, or "bound over", the new farm hands generally faced rough working conditions. The sort of treatment they received depended almost entirely on who bought their contracts. Their new masters decided on the kind of work to be done, on the hours to be worked, and on their food and lodging.

Better Not Run Away
If he didn't like his working or living conditions, an indentured servant better not run away. When caught, the law permitted his master to lash him with a whip. In addition to that painful punishment, his length of servitude would also be extended, in such a way as to give his master a generous bonus of extra labor.

Servants who skipped out repeatedly for short periods of absence greatly multiplied their length of servitude. In some cases, penalties added up to several extra years.

Q: What penalty did a runaway servant pay?
A: In some states, the extra time a runaway had to serve was twice the time he'd been away. That was the easiest penalty. Pennsylvana added a five-time penalty. Maryland extended the term of indenture by ten times the length of absence.

Chances for a servant getting away for good were very slim. You might imagine that a white person on the loose could easily blend into the landscape. That wasn't true. Identity cards were required for travelers in early America. Shades of the totalitarian state!

Whenever the local sheriff spotted a stranger in town, he was likely to demand to see an identity card. Maybe he'd collect a reward for apprehending a runaway servant.

As with negro runaways, rewards were often posted for the return of runaway indentured servants who "took off" from their unpleasant unpaid jobs. For example, in the Virginia Gazette in April of 1775, George Washington advertised a reward for return of two Scotsmen who'd run from Mount Vernon before their indentures were up.

A Long Day's Work
There were no 40-hour weeks and no coffee breaks in 1776. The length of the work day was governed largely by the rising and setting of the sun. In fact, during harvest season, the laborers would be out in the fields even *before* sun-up.

Fifteen hours was a typical work day at peak periods, both on the farm where most people worked and in a Colonial shop. It could be longer if circumstances required.

Just before the Revolution, a few Colonies attempted to place some limits on the work day. South Carolina showed the most concern. Its legislature decreed that 15 hours was enough during planting, cultivating and harvest seasons, with 14 the maximum in late fall and winter. Georgia decided that 16 hours per day were needed for the laborers on its plantations.

However, there was no enforcement mechanism of any sort, anywhere. This meant that if the boss wanted a longer work day, he got it. One famous plantation owner's opinions on a worker's obligations have been recorded.

> "To request that my people may be at work as soon as it is light, work till it is dark, and be diligent while they are at it, can hardly be necessary... the presumption is that every laborer does as much in twenty-four hours as his strength, without endangering his health, will allow."
> Planter George Washington

Problems of Sex
As usual in centuries past, women got the worst deal. Although maidservants (far fewer in number than men) were highly prized,

they faced special hazards. They might escape the heaviest types of work, but were always vulnerable to sexual abuse.

Many a master bid highly at the auction for a pretty young maid. She might become his mistress, or in time, even his wife. Often, however, a comely maidservant remained just a captive diversion.

A maidservant made pregnant by her master could go to court and accuse him. If her story was believed (by a court composed of men who all owned indentured servants) her master would be punished for adultery. Even then, she was likely to regret her action, for she'd be removed by the court and resold. Her new master could be as bad or worse than the previous lecher.

Enforced Celibacy

A maidservant who had a child by anyone other than her master was in worse trouble. Marriages without special consent of the master (not very likely) were illegal. Her illegal pregnancy could be punished by 21 lashes, plus two or three years of extra servitude. If a manservant was involved, he'd have to put in whatever extra time the master deemed necessary to support the child.

In spite of such harsh restrictions, the indentured immigrants who were mostly virile young people, produced a sizable number of illegitimate offspring. Like their free brethren, they helped to populate the vast open spaces of America.

A Struggle for Freedom

Servants in bondage and even many of their descendants weren't citizens. The only men who could vote were those who owned a certain amount of land, or were worth an amount of money specified by the Colony's rules.

However, in America people had a chance to move up in society. Even though they'd paid a staggering price of years of labor in order to come to the New World, they might accomplish what was never possible in the Old Country.

Although the premise was that an indentured man-servant would eventually end up as a farmer, not many did. Only about one in ten became a substantial farmer; another ten percent became successful artisans; the other eighty percent either died before their terms were up or ended up as the "white trash" scrounging odd jobs.

Q: "What pay was given at the end of an indenture?
A: The paper an indentured servant signed (perhaps only with an X if he or she couldn't read) spelled out some sort of reward for service at the end of the term. The payoff would generally consist of a suit of clothes, a few dollars, often a couple of basic farming tools such as a hoe and an axe, along with 50 acres of land. That was a paltry reward for perhaps five years of hard labor, but it represented substantial wealth by Old Country standards.

Many accepted their 50 acres, where that was provided as the payoff for their indentured service, and immediately sold that scraggly land for whatever cash it would bring.

Q: What did female servants receive after their indenture?
A: No land, perhaps a few dollars, mostly clothes. The law in South Carolina specified that a female servant be given shoes, stockings, a waistcoat, petticoat, white linen undergarment, two white linen caps and one blue apron. She could enter her new free life properly decked out to get herself a husband and start working in her own household from dawn to dusk.

Keeping Welfare Costs Down
As just indicated, not all who served out their indentures and moved to a free status were equipped to take care of themselves in rough economic times. They were the most likely to end up jobless or homeless, needing public assistance.

But supporting anyone out of work was not at all popular with our ancestors of the 1700s. Reluctantly they paid out a few dollars to help the aged or those temporarily incapacitated by epidemics of disease. But neither paupers nor orphans received any sympathy.

All those who were considered "able bodied" were expected to earn their own bread..

Paupers were rounded up by the town marshall and auctioned off to the highest bidders, which could put former indentured servants right back where they'd been. Orphans, often less than five years old, faced almost a similar fate. They were indentured to a craftsman, merchant or householder who took over the responsibility of feeding, housing and training them in a useful occupation until they were old enough to take care of themselves, generally when they reached 16 years of age .

Obviously such farming out of paupers and orphans cut welfare costs to a bare-bones minimum. Even in the worst of times, those receiving any public assistance averaged less than five percent of the population. That included mostly the sick and the aged, with a few orphans coming next and the poor, if any, at the tail end.

Beating the Draft

The advent of the Revolutionary War brought some indentured servants an opportunity to speed their trudge to freedom.

Some Colonies, short of their quotas of recruits for the Continental Army, looked to the supply of indentured servants to fill the ranks. They paid their masters a generous sum to hire out their servants for a term in the Army. Of course, the servants didn't get any of that money, but often their military service carried a promise of freedom. If they didn't get killed in the War.

Sometimes no money was needed to separate a master from his able-bodied servant. Instead, it was a chance to avoid the draft that motivated him. In the unequal society of 1776, if you had money you didn't have to carry a rifle and march through the mud for your country, as poor draftees did. You could hire a substitute. Or, since you undoubtedly had a few indentured servants, you could simply designate one of them to take your place in the army.

That wasn't necessarily an ideal job for the indentured man. But he had no choice; he was merely property. And a stint in an army camp, though it might be hazardous, wasn't likely to be worse than what he'd been doing. Besides that, a chance to gain freedom from servitude in a few years was a handsome bonus to be coveted.

17
At Rock Bottom
Black Americans

Not until the plantations of our southern colonies demanded a bigger supply of field hands did the demand for Africans begin to escalate in North America. Until the 1700s, the Colonists were just about as likely to purchase white servants, either indentured or redemptioners, as they were to get a few blacks shipped up from the Caribbean.

According to the first census, detailed in *Historical Statistics of the United States,* all the Colonies together contained only 28,000 Negroes by 1700. Even that estimate is believed by many to be on the high side.

Q: How did slavery get started in the Colonies?
A: It started out almost as an accident. The first African slaves arrived in 1619 when a Dutch warship brought 20 to the English settlers at Jamestown. The warship got them from a Spanish slave ship it had sunk, and didn't know what to do with them. The Virginians felt no special need for slaves, but the price was cheap, and they paid the Dutch with tobacco. For the next 50 years, the colonists imported few African slaves.

By 1776, the negro population in America had increased to more than 400,000, mostly in the South. By that time, more than a third of the population in Virginia was slave. In South Carolina, there were twice as many blacks as whites. Much of this large gain in the negro population came from births in this country, rather than from importation from Africa.

The first Africans in Virginia were not called "slaves." There was no such thing in England where the Colonists had come from. Until 100 years before the Revolutionary War, court records in Virginia listed Negroes as "indentured servants", so it's presumed they were treated in much the same way as whites in that category. Some Negroes in early-day Virginia were recorded as landowners, which would indicate they could gain their freedom after a number of years, as white indentured servants did.

That situation changed, drastically, when the plantation system grew in the South and huge numbers of Africans were needed to work in the fields.

A Tough People

It wasn't just because they provided a low-cost source of muscle that African slaves became popular in the Americas. That's proven by the fact that relatively few were ever imported as servants by our Northern Colonists, who were as greedy for cheap labor as anyone.

The Africans were tough people able to work under a hot sun that floored European laborers. Demand for the Africans started in tropical Brazil and other parts of South America, and worked its way up to the West Indies and Florida.

Early Spanish settlers in those areas first tried working their plantations with the labor at hand, the native Indians they could easily enslave. But the easy-to-get native labor supply proved unreliable. The natives of South America succumbed easily to diseases the Europeans had imported. As many as 90 percent of the native field hands died from Smallpox, Measles and Typhus.

Dutch slavers offered an answer to this problem. Blacks they imported from Africa had been in some contact with Europeans for centuries, and as a result they'd developed a degree of immunity to the diseases of white people.

Dutch ships began the big import of black slaves to the West Indies and other areas south of our borders that grew sugar, cocoa, coffee and cotton, all much in demand in Europe. As planters in Virginia and nearby Colonies started to cultivate big acreages of tobacco, that too required large gangs of laborers. Demand for the tough Africans also sprang up in the Carolinas and Maryland where rice was planted in hot malarial fields.

Poster advertising a shipment of 250 African slaves for sale. Note emphasis on the fact that most of them have had small-pox, which rendered them immune to that dreaded disease.

TO BE SOLD, on board the Ship *Bance-Island*, on tuesday the 6th of *May* next, at *Ashley-Ferry*; a choice cargo of about 250 fine healthy

NEGROES, juft arrived from the Windward & Rice Coaft. —The utmoft care has already been taken, and fhall be continued, to keep them free from the leaft danger of being infected with the SMALL-POX, no boat having been on board, and all other communication with people from *Charles-Town* prevented.

Auftin, Laurens, & Appleby.

N. B. Full one Half of the above Negroes have had the SMALL-POX in their own Country.

A Shared Scandal

Don't think that only a relatively few Americans, and only in the South, participated in or condoned the practice of slavery. From North to South there was no great outcry against it.

Even in New England it was common. By the time of the War for Independence, one out of every five families in Boston owned an African slave. In Rhode Island, it's estimated that black slaves made up more than ten percent of the population. And the righteous preachers of New England raised no objections. On the contrary, in a sermon to Negroes, the most famous preacher of early Puritan days told them their lot was preordained.

"God has appointed you to the role of a slave."
Rev. Cotton Mather

Some religious groups, such as Mennonites and Quakers, professed to be against slavery. Yet that didn't stop many Quakers from owning a few African servants.

197

Yankee traders, always quick to smell money, moved in on the trade. Although at first the Dutch and then British ships brought most of the Africans to America, captains from Rhode Island, New York and Massachusetts converted their fleets for slaving too. Did they ever! By the mid-eighteenth century, some people in the South complained that Yankee traders were unloading more slaves in their ports than they could possibly use.

Hypocrites in Big Houses

Many a mansion of a respected wealthy family in Newport, Boston or New York was built on slave cargo. At the time of the Revolution, half the merchant fleet of Newport, the busiest slaving port, was engaged in the infamous trade.

American slave ships were among the worst in the business, because they tended to be much smaller than the big British ships that transported nine-tenths of the Africans. Built as cheaply as possible, the Yankee vessels were crowded hellholes and barely seaworthy.

There was so little headroom in some of the ships that the slaves couldn't even sit up during the voyage to America. They were packed tightly together, lying down and all facing in the same direction, so it was almost impossible to lie on one's back or roll to another side. No wonder so many died during the trip.

Un-Christian Christians

Early Spanish voyagers to settlements south of our borders professed a zeal for baptizing the natives they came to conquer and enslave. No such religious motives, real or pretended, were claimed by settlers in our 13 Colonies.

Usually they preferred to drive away the Indians they encountered. And when they imported black slaves from Africa, religious proselytizing was not the motive. It's true that some Africans tended to adopt church customs of their American masters, often blending them with their own native rites. But our Colonists were not anxious to enfold them into their religions. To do that would have been admitting that Blacks and Whites were both beloved children of the same God. Especially in Southern Colonies where slaves abounded, that was not a popular view.

Any thought of miscegenation was the ultimate taboo. For example, the laws of Virginia were designed to make certain that no Christian minister in any way sanctioned it. Any preacher who performed a mixed marriage faced a fine of 10,000 pounds of tobacco-- a fortune that would surely exceed his net worth. In addition to that financial penalty, he'd almost certainly have been run out of the state, if he managed to get away alive.

Only One Advantage
There was only one advantage that Africans had over the white men and women in our colonies. It was a dubious benefit.

Whites could be hanged for a wide variety of crimes, ranging from theft to adultery to murder. For similar sins, blacks could only be beaten, though almost to the point of death. Except for the most heinous crimes (against white people) they were exempted from the ultimate penalty.

Why? Because hanging a slave *wouldn't be fair to his master.* It would deprive an owner of a piece of valuable property.

The War Offers a Way to Freedom
The American Revolution didn't put an end to slavery, but it shook up the system. Early in the War, the British saw an opportunity to damage the rebel economy seriously throughout the South. Slave labor was the cornerstone of farming and industry there. So it was obvious that the slaves, if enticed to do so, could disrupt the whole economic system.

When shooting started, Lord Dunmore, King George's Royal Governor of Virginia, began the enticing. He knew exactly how to shake up his treasonous subjects. He spread the word among slaves of that state that any who fought with the British would be freed at War's end. That was good news to Africans not fond of masters and overseers who drove them with a whip.

The promises of the Royal Governor precipitated massive defections that stripped many plantations of their able-bodied laborers. Other Southern Colonies also suffered severe disruptions as the word spread, and thousands of their slaves also ran to Britain's forces and the promise of freedom held out to them.

A Quandary for the Continental Army

How to counter the mass defections of slaves posed a difficult dilemma for the Colonists. If the black laborers decided to sneak away from the plantations when British troops came nearby, it was hard to stop them.

It wasn't good to have thousands of Africans, traditionally tough warriors and knowledgeable about the terrain, going to help the Redcoats. It would be much better, some thought, to recruit some of the best of the Africans for the Colonial forces. That was a dangerous idea, however, many planters argued. Southern officers shuddered at the thought of handing weapons to black soldiers. They feared that guns in the hands of slaves could end up pointed at their masters.

A solution sometimes used was to enlist restless slaves as drummers, drivers or laborers in the Continental army. Or as sailors. There were exceptions to the "no guns" rule, however. And they worked out well. A number of former slaves fought valorously in the Continental ranks.

> **"James Lafayette, a freed slave, acquitted himself perfectly**
> **with important commissions I gave him. He appears**
> **entitled to every reward his situation can admit of."**
> The Marquis de Lafayette

Actually, James not only served as a trusted aide to Lafayette, but also volunteered to move back and forth from the enemy camp so he could gather information and act as a spy-- a hazardous role he performed with distinction.

A Slow Awakening

Importation of slaves halted in Virginia during the War. None could be brought in unless they belonged to a master who had just settled in the Colony. These restrictions were designed to cut down on potential runaways. There were already numerous slaves on the loose who were terrorizing many areas, since they'd discovered they could find refuge with British troops, if necessary.

That precautionary measure had an unforeseen side effect. The slight stoppage of the "infamous trade" awakened some of the planters to the fact that it wasn't so indispensable after all. The faint beginnings of an anti-slavery spirit began to grow, even in the South.

Q: Which northern city had the most slaves?

A: New York. At the time of the Revolution, about 15 percent of its diverse population was of African origin. Slaves made up a large part of the labor force at its busy docks and warehouses, and rich New York families flaunted their wealth by maintaining liveried black household servants. The relatively large share of slave labor in the city was due partly to its early history when Dutch ships dominated the slave trade.

Gradually, toward the end of the 18th Century, the laws regarding the freeing of slaves by their masters became somewhat easier. It became legal for a freed negro to stay in Virginia--something not permitted earlier.

That was still not a universally accepted situation. Those few slaves given an opportunity for freedom were generally better off to head North. For example, as you'll read in a chapter about Thomas Jefferson, several of his mixed-blood servants (who some speculate may have been his own children) disappeared quietly when they were old enough and settled in the North.

Like the white Patriots who rankled at British rule, the black slaves of America favored the Revolution. But not for the same reasons. Their ideas of freedom did not rest on battling King George's troops. Generally they welcomed the sight of Redcoats.

18
Thomas Jefferson Pens a Declaration

Not long after Paul Revere and his fellow horsemen rode to warn of the British troops advancing on Concord, a man from Virginia made a much longer trip to join in the battle for freedom. His warning to his countrymen was not a verbal one, but an historic document detailing the rights they must fight for.

In the summer of 1775, Thomas Jefferson journeyed to Philadelphia to serve in the Second Continental Congress. He was a reluctant delegate because his wife was sick, again, and he hated to leave her.

His diaries tell us that on the night of his arrival in Philadelphia after the tiring three-day journey, he dined with other Virginia delegates at the City Tavern. In convivial company at that very popular spot, Jefferson renewed his energies before presenting his credentials to Congress on the following morning.

Quiet, Shy Young Man

Jefferson was only 20 years old when appointed to his first role in the battle for freedom. That appointment was to the Committee of Correspondence which Virginia set up to communicate with leaders in other Colonies that were following the example of Samuel Adams and his Massachusetts rebels. It was just two years later, when he was still only 22, that Jefferson was sent to the Continental Congress where he'd make an indelible mark on world history.

Obviously, he was destined for great things-- a very young man who'd already gained the respect of the elder statesmen of Virginia. Unlike most of them, he hadn't come from great wealth. Nor was young Jefferson a flambouyant or pushy and self-promoting sort of person that we might expect a rising politician to be. Far fom it.

Always shy in public, he spoke little and in such a quiet voice it was often difficult to hear him. He usually dressed in sober black. Thomas was impressive not for his clothes, but for his unusual physique. Exceptionally tall for his time (about six foot three) he was slender but strong, with large feet and hands. He inherited his rugged physique from his father.

Q: How strong was Thomas Jefferson's father?
A: Peter Jefferson was noted for his feats of strength. It was claimed that he could stand between two half-ton hogsheads of tobacco that were lying on their sides, bend down to grab hold of them, and pull them both upright.

A red-head in his youth, "Tall Tom's" hair remained sandy in color. His eyes were hazel, sometimes described as blue. His fair pinkish complexion freckled easily.

Brought up in rural Virginia, Thomas always remained an outdoorsman. He was fond of hunting, and was an excellent horseman. Yet Jefferson was equally fond of intellectual and artistic pursuits. He loved books and music, was an accomplished violinist and also played the cello. He accumulated a large libraries which eventually became the major part of the Library of Congress.

Jefferson was a writer, a deamer, a visionary. *And also a tormented man.*

Life Was a Headache

Life for Thomas Jefferson was always a *headache.* Literally. Throughout most of his adult years, he suffered from excruciating migraine headaches that often kept him in bed for *weeks* at a time!

Biographies of Jefferson tend to mention this affliction only very briefly. Most don't say anything at all about this severe problem. Yet can you imagine how difficult it must have been for Jefferson to concentrate on his many brilliant achievements while undergoing the walloping pain of a migraine at frequent intervals?

Of course, nobody knows exactly what caused his chronic affliction. Many doctors today ascribe emotional stress as a frequent factor in migraines. This may well be a strong possibility, for if there's anything that was seldom missing in the life of this complex man, it was stress from churning emotions.

The haunted eyes in this portrait of Thomas Jefferson hint at a man who was a loner and an enigma. In both his personal and his public life, Jefferson encountered a whole series of heartbreaks.

Early Traumas of a Loner
If youthful hurts stay hidden in our psyches, Jefferson had far more than his share.

His father was a tall husky frontiersman, handsome and charming. Though he had almost no education, he worked hard, became a fairly prosperous farmer, though not a big plantation owner. In addition, he surprised everyone by marrying the daughter of one of Virginia's most prominent families.

Thomas admired him greatly. But when he was 14, his father died. Young Tom's reaction to this loss had a strange side to it. Ever after that, he felt that with the death of his father he'd lost his only dependable family connection. His writings show that he regarded himself as an *orphan*.

Teen-age Tom evidently felt that, with his father gone, he didn't have a relative or friend left in the world that he could count on.

> **"At fourteen years of age the whole care and direction**
> **of myself was thrown on myself entirely, without a**
> **relation or friend qualified to advise or guide me."**
> Jefferson's Autobiography

That seems like a strange attitude for several reasons. For one thing, *Tom's his mother was still alive.* In addition, the boy had many uncles, aunts and cousins on her side of the family, the aristocratic Randolphs. He also had seven living siblings -- six sisters and a younger brother who was mentally retarded. Furthermore, the guardians named in his father's will were all capable men and close friends of the family.

Obviously, young Tom didn't feel any great warmth of family ties. Dutifully though, the teen-ager took over supervision of his family's financial affairs, a task that was generally expected of the eldest male. Yet although he kept an eye on family affairs, he remained away from home most of the time. He continued to attend boarding school, and later went to William and Mary college.

What about Mother?
In his voluminous writings (more than 60,000 entries in the Princeton Library collection alone) Jefferson said almost nothing about his mother. Stranger still was Thomas's reaction when his mother died at the end of March, 1776, after having survived her husband by 19 years.

At her death, Thomas, the prolific writer who wrote voluminously about everything, made no written statement of that event, except for a bookeeping entry.

In fact, his recording of her death consisted of only *a single sentence* which was dropped into routine comments about other occurances on the farm.

Q: What did Jefferson write about his mother's death?
A: In his daily diary where he recorded every activity around the farm, Jefferson noted his mother's death in a single brief statement. With no comment added. It read, " My mother died about eight o'clock this morning in the 57th year of her age. "

Many believe this rather bizarre behavior shows merely that Jefferson, the quiet introvert, couldn't exress much about any female realtionship. That may be true. They point to the facts that he dutifully came home from Philadelphia when his mother was ill, and that he suffered one of his shattering month-long headaches when she died.

One of his biographers, Paige Smith, who delved much more deeply into the personal side of Jefferson than most others, has a different conclusion. Smith maintains that Thomas *hated* his mother. He interprets Thomas' illness after her death as the result of guilt feelings, rather than sadness. As with many historical accounts, you can believe whichever version you prefer.

Beloved Wife, Martha
Whether or not Jefferson felt any real affection for his mother, there's no doubt that he loved his wife. He celebrated a Happy New Year on January 1, 1772, the day he married Martha Wayles Skelton, and he was a devoted husband until her death.

Martha was a young widow. She had married at 18, born a child at 19 and lost her first husband before she was 20. She and her young son, John, lived at her father's home for a while thereafter. But she had many suitors as soon as the expected period of mourning was over.

No portraits of Martha Jefferson are known to exist. However, she's described as a beautiful woman. Though not nearly as tall as her lanky second husband, she was above average in height, had auburn hair, large hazel eyes and a pretty face and figure. Far better educated than most women of her day, Martha liked to read and play the harpsichord. Those were two activities that appealed to her literate and music-loving husband.

This was a good marriage financially, something always considered to be very important in our ancestors' days. Jefferson noted in his *Autobiography* that when Martha's father died, in the year following their marriage, she received a considerable amount of property.

> **"On her father's death, her inheritance
> doubled the ease of our circumstances."**
> Thomas Jefferson

Part of Martha's welcome inheritance from John Wayles was not land, but came in the form of black laborers to work the land.

Daddy the Slave Trader
Martha's rich planter father made most of his money not from tobacco or cotton, but from dealing in slaves. A large part of his legacy to her (and therefore to her husband Thomas) consisted of *more than a hundred slaves.*

This human treasure posed somewhat of a dilemma for son-in-law Thomas. He was always talking and writing against slavery, a peculiarity which his Virginia neighbors found aggravating. Yet he gratefully accepted the valuable Africans, and could never afford to turn them loose.

One evidence of the dichotomy Jefferson felt about opposing slavery yet owning slaves is the fact that he avoided calling his household staff by that name. He always referred to the Africans at Monticello as his "servants", not as "slaves".

Black and White Family Mixtures
Some of the slaves John Wayles turned over to his daughter and son-in-law were boys and girls he'd created himself. Like many of his fellow dealers in flesh, Wayles made a practice of sexually enjoying the prettiest of his female properties.

Wayles was a big, barrel-chested, bad-tempered man who had outlived three wives by the time he was fifty. Thereafter, it was common knowledge that he maintained a black concubine in his household. She was a lovely mulatto named Elizabeth Hemmings. It was widely agreed throughout the neighborhood that dusky Elizabeth was the mother of six of Daddy Wayles' children.

Those half-dozen mixed-blood offspring were, therefore, half-sisters and half-brothers to Wayles young white daughter, Martha.

After Martha's father died and she inherited these darker-skinned close relatives, they became slaves in the Jefferson family, but they were treated as favored house servants.

This household situation of Betty Hemmings and her brood, though strange to us, was not unknown in slave days. It led to some peculiarly embarrassing problems for Jefferson when he became a prominent politician. You'll read more about those problems in a later chapter.

A Common Malady and Tragedy

If Thomas had his migraines, wife Martha had her persistent problem too. She suffered from a common malady of women of her times-- almost constant pregnancy. During the ten years of their marriage, frail Martha had several miscarriages, and yet she managed to bear six children. Four of the six died; two daughters were the survivors.

Jefferson's attendance at the Continental Congresses was far from regular. Much of his absence was due to his concern about wife Martha's illnesses. For example, the Second Congress had already been in session for six weeks before delegate Jefferson got to Philadelphia. The following year, 1776, while he was laboring on the Declaration of Independence, Martha was ill again. Jefferson wanted to get home to his sick wife, but was persuaded to stay in Philadelphia until the important document was finished.

Duty before Personal Problems

That must have been a dismal period for Jefferson. He wanted above all to go back home to his wife. Yet he felt duty-bound to remain in Philadelphia to write a document which would be a cornerstone in the hard struggle for freedom.

Q: Was Jefferson supposed to write the whole Declaration?
A: No. It was supposed to be a five-man job. Congress
appointed a committee of John Adams, Benjamin Franklin,
Roger Sherman and Roger B. Livingston to tackle the task,
along with Jefferson as its chairman. However, the older
men all begged off for one reason or another and persuaded
young Thomas (as we now know, for the best) to tackle the
job by himself.

Far from his beloved wife and the comforts of a beautiful home in Virginia, Thomas sweltered and scribbled away for 17 days and nights in June of 1776 in a tiny upstairs sitting room on the second floor of a house near what is now called Independence Hall. He rented these quarters from a bricklayer named Graff (or Graaf) who'd built a large brick home on Market Street for himself and his new wife. Taking in boarders provided much-needed extra income for the ambitious tradesman. The rent Jefferson paid for a bedroom and the small sitting room across the hall from it was 35 shillings per week.

You may picture Jefferson composing his famous document as he sat at a spacious handsome desk stacked with reference materials and an imposing array of books. Not so. The young legislator worked hunched over a tiny folding table barely big enough to hold his sheet of paper and ink stand. He described the little table on which America's most precious document was written as follows:

"It is plain, neat, convenient and takes no more
room than a moderate quarto volume."

Of course, the author still couldn't leave for home when he'd completed his writing. Having penned a crucial political document, he had to watch as various delegates to the Congress chewed over his phrasings. Fortunately, their changes were few, and The Declaration was soon readied for approval.

Alone and Lonesome

Martha survived her sickness in 1776. However, it was only six years later, when she was but 33, that she faced her final illness. It resulted from frequent childbearing.

This was the sixth child she'd borne in ten years. Of the first five, only the eldest lived. She was daughter Patsy, who'd reached the age of ten. This sixth and last child, Lucy Elizabeth survived too. But Martha never recovered from the delivery. She died four months after presenting Thomas with his second daughter.

> **"I lost the cherished companion of my life, in whose**
> **affections, unabated on both sides, I had lived the**
> **last ten years in unchequered happiness."**
> Jefferson's Autobiography

Throughout his wife's last illness, Thomas had been at her side constantly. He was desolated when she died, and vowed never to marry again. He never did.

19
General Washington Takes Command

In 1776, all Americans suffered wrenching changes in their private lives due to the Revolutionary War that swirled around them. Everyone tried to figure out what would happen next, and no one knew. For the events at the start of the War were *a collosal mix up.* Not surprising in view of the unique complications that existed.

First, *the Patriots had no army!* That's certainly a disadvantage if you expect to fight a war. Before they could hope to accomplish anything against the mighty military forces of the British empire, the rebels had to pull together 13 different militias operating from 13 separate Colonies.

Second, *they had no money!* It's true that the Second Continental Congress authorized $2,000,000 in credit to pay soldiers and buy military supplies, but that did not represent funds actually in hand. The real money would have to be coaxed somehow from the coffers of separate Colonies reluctant to part with their cash.

Third, *they had no commander!* To pull together an inter-Colony army, some impressive military man would have to be found to head the operation. In addition, he'd need to persuade a whole bunch of cocky militia generals to subordinate their individual powers (and powerful egos) to a common cause.

Time to Decide
There was one other complication as well. It was the most crtical lack of all. Before the Patriots could make any significant progress toward freedom, they'd have to *make up their minds* that they really wanted to split from England. They didn't make such a clear decision until a whole year after the fighting started!

Figure it out. It was in May of 1775 that the Second Continental Congress authorized the three warlike steps listed above-- raising an army, raising funds for it and a commander for it. But it wasn't until the Fourth of July in 1776, *a whole year later,* that Congressional delegates signed their Declaration of Independence from England.

In other words, the war against Britain began a whole year before the Americans even got around to saying, clearly and irrevocably, that they were no longer British subjects.

That was the mess George Washington walked into-- a situation as screwed up as a soap opera.

Only a Compromise Candidate
The battles at Lexington and Concord occured less than three weeks before the delegates convened at the Second Continental Congress. That bloodshed made it clear that this Second Congress could not be just talk, as the first one had been.

The time had finally come for the Colonies to consolidate their individual militias and appoint someone to head a common army. The delegates looked around at their membership to determine who would best fit the requirements.

George Washington obviously considered himself in the running for the job. He never asked for it, but the Colonel from Virginia, who'd always yearned for a military career, was the only delgate who showed up in a uniform. The tall warrior in his tan and blue of the Virginia Militia was an imposing figure.

However, Washington wasn't the immediate choice. He emerged as the compromise candidate.

Politics Decides the Selection
Those who looked for someone with prestige and money preferred John Hancock, even though his military experience was practically nil. He was President of the Congress at the time. But Hancock came from New England, and it was advisable to woo Southern leaders, many of whom thought the war was mostly being started to benefit the North.

Washington came from influential Virginia, so the Southerners liked him. And the Northerners didn't object too much.

Those who sought the most experienced military man looked for one who'd held high rank in foreign armies. Someone like General Charles Lee who'd not only distinguished himself as a British officer, but had also been a soldier of fortune for Poland and Russia. Or General Horatio Gates, veteran of many battles in the British forces.

Washington had nowhere near their experience. But the others were ruled out because they were not native-born Americans. It didn't seem right to many convention delegates that our top military leader should be a foreigner.

It was John Adams, often a bitter critic of Washington in later years, who finally persuaded his colleagues to settle on a man who'd spent just a few years commanding a small force of Virginia militia. And whose first military encounter was a fiasco that sparked an international uproar.

A Young Major Braves the Wilderness

When he took over his first military command, as a major in the Virginia militia, George Washington had never spent a day in uniform. However, he'd always wanted to be a soldier, and you'll recall that he had connections with the prominent Fairfax family into which his older brother, Lawrence, had married.

The powers at Williamsburg needed to learn what the French were up to in the western territory where the Ohio Company of land speculators, including the Fairfaxes, had been granted half a million acres. They had a hard time finding anyone reckless enough to march out into that dangerous wilderness.

Eager young George Washington, who'd done a little surveying in the near western areas, told his influential friends he'd take a force out beyond the Alleghenies. They listened because they figured that if worst came to worst, they wouldn't have much to lose, except the likeable gung-ho giant of a kid and a few helpers.

His employers made young George a major, gave him a fancy uniform, a couple of interpreters, a fur-trader guide and four scruffy backwoodsmen to manage the pack horses and heavy work. He was instructed to enlist the aid of some friendly Indians if he needed more support.

Washington survived that first expedition, and came back with news about the French and their forts that alarmed the Virginians. They decided to send him out again, with a force of soldiers this time. He was instructed to talk sternly to the French about their trespassing on what the Virginians considered to be their land, because it had been deeded to them by the British parliament.

During this second venture into the wilderness, 21-year-old Washington, now promoted to Lieutenant Colonel, made a couple of whopping mistakes.

Famous Military Screw-Up

When Colonel Washington and his small force found themselves in the midst of a much larger scattering of French soldiers, plus a forest full of French-allied Indians, he panicked. George made the mistake of listening to his chief Indian ally, who advised they make a surprise attack at night.

With 40 soldiers and a posse of Indian helpers, George sneaked up on a group of 32 sleepy Frenchmen. His troop killed ten of the unsuspecting French and took the rest prisoners. George was elated at his first victory.

> **"I heard the bullets whistle, and believe me,
> there is something charming in the sound."**
> George Washington

Unfortunately, this small-scale military triumph caused large-scale diplomatic repercussions. *The British and French were not at war.* Though both nations had been growling at each other, neither one wanted to make the first move toward all-out hostilities. *Now it was done.* Colonel Washington, the amateur soldier, had fired the first shot in what was to become the French and Indian War. Actually it should have been called the French and British War, since the redskins were merely pawns in the battles and they served both sides.

Don't Sign That Paper!

To compound George's error, the captured French screamed that one of their casualties was Joseph Coulon, the Sieur de Jumonville, a diplomat who had come to warn the British to leave what they claimed was their territory.

Eager George had killed an ambassador leading a peaceful diplomatic mission.

A larger battle ensued in which the Virginians lost more than a hundred men. The French had more than a thousand men in the area and could easily have wiped out the rest of Washington's small force. Instead of making that obvious move, they parleyed and made a seemingly magnanimous offer that seemed too good to be true. Of course it was!

The French commander, who turned out to be the slain Joseph Coulon's brother, graciously agreed to let the Virginians return home alive. He asked only that George sign a joint document, stating the whole episode was a mistake and the two sides wanted peace and harmony.

Washington was delighted to sign. That was his second mistake. The document, written in French which Washington couldn't read, said the French had engaged in battle only to avenge the *assasination* of their diplomat.

The Talk of the Continent

Although Washington was received back in Williamsburg as a hero -- after all, he'd fought a much larger French force and returned alive-- his two faux pas were the talk of the Old World.

Kings and premiers throughout Europe all shook their heads at that dunderhead young colonel. "Whatever possessed the idiot", they asked, "to attack and kill another nation's soldiers in peacetime. And to make matters worse, sign a document admitting he'd assasinated a diplomat on a peaceful mission?"

War could not be far off, and gung-ho Colonel Washington looked forward to being a player in it. He anticipated that his Virginia regiment would be made part of the regular British army, with him as its colonel, naturally.

To his dismay, he was told that the Virginia forces would be broken up. Also that the British army would never give any rank above captain to any provincial officer. A bitterly disappointed Washington resigned and headed back to the farm.

Right Man at the Right Time

Despite his checkered career as an impetuous young officer, George Washington proved to be exactly what the Colonies needed in 1775. At 43 years of age, he'd matured into a careful, thoughtful man who'd learned from his past errors.

The recollection that he was one of the few American officers who'd seen action in the French and Indian Wars was a big advantage. All that people remembered about Washington's experience in that fracas was that he'd beaten a French force. And the fact that he was a rich man since his marriage was a very important plus in an era that was far more class-conscious than our present-day society is.

Above all, Washington had charisma. Tall and ramrod straight, he *looked* like a leader. Deliberate in speech, he *talked* like one. Unflappable in all situations, he *acted* like the confident leader that was so badly needed.

Delegates to the Congress sized up the Virginia colonel. and they liked what they saw. Actually they had a slim choice, for most of the candidates with any amount of military experience were either too old and feeble for the arduous job, or they'd been born overseas. The delegates felt they had to appoint an American as the top commander-- not someone who was foreign-born..

An Inspiring Commander

Whatever else it lacked, and the lacks were many, the newly-hatched Continental Army always had a commander it could rely on. Often that was about all it had.

Even in the most disastrous of times, General Washington stayed calm and confident... at least, on the outside. In many a scary battle, the rag-tag rebels facing superior numbers of better-armed and better-trained soldiers, would have little else but their confidence in cool General George. He never failed to come through by bolstering their fading morale.

Right from the start, Washington made it clear that his motives were the highest. He'd been offered a magnificent salary of $500 per month-- not a skimpy sum compared to the $6.66 per month paid a private soldier or the $20 a captain received, and far more than most prosperous civilians earned in a year. But he grandly waved that generous sum aside.

> **"As to pay, Sir, I beg leave to assure the Congress that as no**
> **pecuniary consideration could have tempted me to have**
> **accepted this Arduous employment (at the expense of my**
> **domesttic ease and happiness) I do not wish to make any proffit**
> **from it. I will keep an exact Account of my expenses. Those I**
> **doubt not they will discharge, and that is all I desire."**
> Washington's offer to Congress

To his strapped-for-money fellow congressmen, that seemed like a can't-lose deal. Later, when his expense accounts began to come in, many expressed second-thoughts about the arrangement they'd agreed to, and became critical of George's grand standard of living.

Expenses Add Up

Meticulous George Washington, accustomed to keeping records of every expenditure on his plantation, did the same when he joined the Army. The expenses he added up far exceeded the amount he turned down as a salary. If he'd accepted Congress's offer of $500 per month, that would have amounted to merely $48,000 over the eight years the War dragged on.

General Washington's expense accounts totalled far more-- nearly ten times as much! The bills he submitted added up to $447,220.92.

Before you conclude that this billing, an astronomical sum in 1776, was out of line, consider what it covered. The General's expenses were not for his personal needs alone.

He had to pay not only for his own food, uniforms, swords, horses, and travel costs, but also for "business" entertaining, salaries and food for household staff. He even had to hire undercover agents to spy on the enemy. So our First General's pay went partially to run an entire headquarters department along with a network of spies.

Washington's expenses are eye-openers, not only because of their size, but because they involve such strange purchases. Here's a very brief sampling of Washington's expense accounts, taken from the hand-written records which are still on file at the Register's Office of the United States Treasury Department.

1775 - June 22 $831.45
    To Cash paid for Sadlery, a Letter Case, Maps, Glasses, &c, &c,
    for the use of my Command.

1775 - July 15 $39
    To cash for recovering my Pistols which had been stolen, & for repairing
    them afterwards.

1775 - October 3 $1,248
    To Walton White, Esq. for a Riding Mare.

1776 - January 9 $390
    To the Relief of the distressed sad Wives & Children of the
    Soldiers from Marblehead.

1776 - April 1 $5,232
    To amount of Sundry Inst per Memorandum for Secret Services.

1776 - June 26 $14,653.60
    To Mrs. Smith the Ho. Keeper at different times, frm. Thos.
    Mifflin Esq., the Q.M. Gen.

1776 - October 25 $131.11
    To Barber at Sundry times. *(Note: This probably was not just for haircuts,
    but to repair Washington's false teeth, a service barbers provided.}*

1777 - January 1 $8,414
    To Secret Services since the Army left Cambridge in April, while
    it lay at new York and during its retreat as above.

1779 - February 6 $1,913
    To my Exps. in Phild. to which place I was called by Congress &
    remained from the 22nd of Dec. to this date.

1780 - October 10 $62.40
    To Col. Lewis - the Caughnawaga Indian - a Present.

1781 - March $19,848.50
    To the Expenditures on a journey to Rhode Island on a visit
    to the French Army, per Colo. Tilghman.

1781 - August 25 $910
    To cash paid Mrs. Thompson the Housekeeper, in part of
    her wages, viz - 25 Guineas.

1783 - July 1 $27,665.30
    To Mrs. Washington's travell Exps. in coming to & returning from
    my Winter Quarters per accts. rendered. The Money to defray which
    being taken from my private Purse & brought with her from Virginia.

Whatever he cost, the General was a bargain. Without his skill and unwavering persistence, the scrawny little rebel army could never have survived. Yet he was not beloved by everyone. There were many rabid Tories who'd have liked to see him dead.

Q: Who tried to poison General Washington?

A: A New York Tory, Thomas Hickey, enlisted in Washington's guard with the express purpose of killing him. Hickey planned to get George's housekeeper, Phoebe Fraunces, to feed him a plate of poisoned peas, but she tipped off the General. He tossed the peas out the window. Chickens in the yard gobbled them up and keeled over, verifying Phoebe's warning. Hickey received swift punishment. On June 28, 1776, just 11 days after his plot failed, he was hanged before a large crowd in New York City. If Phoebe hadn't foiled the would-be murderer, the course of history could have been much different.

Everyone knew that the fight with the British would be against long odds. For all his unwavering resolve after he took command, Washington acknowledged early on that he faced a very difficult job. But he couldn't really imagine just how bad it would be.

On the Third of July in 1775, after a 12-day ride from Philadelphia, General George Washington assumed command of 17,000 Continental soldiers at Concord, Massachusetts. That was a proud moment for him. But little did he know that he'd just signed on for eight years of hell!

Molly Pitcher took her husband's place at the Battle of Monmouth..

20
Women at War

At the time of the American Revolution, war was a *man's* business. With the one exception of nurses, women were not supposed to exist in the Continental Army... officially. When you read official battle-by-battle histories of the War, you'd think no women were anywhere near the action.

That's not true. Women were present in the army camps and at the battles, *in large numbers,* on both sides of the conflict.

Bring the Kids and Come to Camp
The term "camp followers" connotes women of low morals who'd hang around an army installation to peddle sex to the soldiers. There were plenty of those in 1776 and the years thereafter. But not all the woman around a camp were hookers. Many were wives, with their children, who simply had no place else to live.

When Daddy grabbed his musket and skedaddled off to the War, leaving Momma alone to manage the farm and the kids and fight the Indians, she might not be able to survive.

She was supposed to stay home and keep everything cooking until her man returned victorious. But a married soldier received no extra allowance for his family--only the standard $6.66 per month. Even when he was lucky enough to collect that piddling amount. there was little to send back home to his wife. It was up to her to struggle along as best she could.

If the harvest failed and the cow died, what was she to do? Daddy couldn't return until his enlistment was up, unless he took a chance on being shot for desertion, which many husbands did. There was only one other possible course of action.

Wives and children, lots of them, packed up what scant possessions they owned and trekked off to follow the soldiers. At camp, they at least would get a share of the provisions, lean as those were.

Women and children, in large numbers, tagged along with soldiers on both sides in 1776. They performed many useful chores but slowed the marches and drained supplies..

In addition to spouses, other poor women also came to the camps. Times were hard, and they searched for whatever work they could find. Often there was nothing available. When they came to a military camp,they received no pay, but at least they could eat. They shared the soldiers' scant rations.

The Numbers Grow

Often there were *hundreds* of women and children, as ragged and dirty as the men, milling around in a camp. That wasn't an unusual occurance. Up until modern times, armies always had women tagging along with them. The British army followed this ancient tradition, and the Americans followed suit.

As with any infusion of troops, the free-spending and lonesome invaders far from their homeland became popular with many local ladies. And when a British regiment moved on to new battlegrounds, their extensive entourage of female friends tagged along with them.

That was logical for several reasons. Some simply didn't want to lose a meal ticket. Some were pregnant, and decided they'd need child support. All of them feared the rough treatment they'd surely suffer from angry Patriots, once they lost the protection of their Redcoat friends.

By the middle of 1777, a British Army report listed 2,776 women and 1,901 children accompanying 23,101 soldiers in America. That's a ratio of almost one camp follower for every five soldiers. In some regiments, the ratio was even higher than 20 percent. At one time, General Burgoyne carried approximately 2,000 women along with a troop of 7,200 men. That meant that more than a quarter of the people he had to move on a march were women and children, along with all of their baggage.

Q: How did the British attempt to control camp-followers?
A: Official quotas were established. Each regiment that landed on our shores brought a standard number of women with them. That was 60 women for each regiment of 677 officers and men. However, once in America, British regiments accumulated more and more hangers on, so the percentages increased.

General Washington's Dilemma

General Washington didn't like to have hordes of women and children tailing along with his troops, but he couldn't avoid it.

He tried to discourage the women who followed their men to the American camps. They posed greater problems for him than they did for the British.

For one thing, Washington was desperately short of money and supplies. Lacking adequate food for his soldiers, he didn't want to add a bunch of hungry women and children. Women who joined their husbands drew a regular ration. Children received a half ration. Babies got nothing because it was presumed that suckling infants enjoyed the advantage of their own portable food supply.

Bad for Morale

Some of the camp followers were a disreputable lot, prone to stealing and stirring up fights. Even the wives caused friction, because their sufferings reminded the men that they ought to get out of the army as soon as possible, either by not reenlisting or by deserting.

Washington also worried about the speed of his marches as he ran constantly to evade the superior British forces. Women and kids slowed him down. As a result, he alternated between ordering the women to ride in the wagons in the interests of speed, and decreeing that they stay out of the wagons which were already overloaded with supplies.

Q: How many women followed the Continental Army?

A: Eventually, Washington in his General Orders decreed that the ratio of women to men in camps should not be more than one to 15. That was often exceeded, and it didn't include children. One study estimates that as many as 20,000 women, with their children, accompanied the American army at some time during the course of the War.

Eventually, Washington had to acknowledge the reality of the camp followers, but try to regulate their numbers. That wasn't easy to do. When the harried General couldn't even keep an accurate count of how many soldiers he had at any given time, his chances were slim for regulating the number of women moving in and out of his camps.

Women Provide the Support Troops

Despite the problems they brought with them, women provided valuable resources to 18th Century armies.

Present-day regiments contain support and supply companies. Often they have as many or more soldiers performing support functions as they have actually bearing arms. In the 1700s, however, it was female camp followers who provided the troop support.

In an age when more soldiers died from wounds and diseases than from direct hits, nursing was important. Doctors were scarce, and not good for much except purging and bleeding their patients. Nurses were few in the army too, although the military paid them $5.00 a month. Wives and mistresses in the camps filled the gaps. As in civilian life, these women who may have had no formal training knew how to bandage wounds and utilize basic home remedies for a variety of illnesses. Their ministrations proved to be a Godsend to many a sick or wounded soldier.

Leave the Dirty Jobs to the Women

Women took on many hard dirty jobs the soldiers were happy to avoid. For example, washing and mending clothes was a chore that many recruits shunned. It was regarded as "woman's work", so soldiers would keep wearing their filthy clothes, rather than launder them. Women camp followers improved camp sanitation somewhat by doing the laundering. And the cooking.

That doesn't mean they were able to really neaten up the camps. Or even themselves. Living outdoors in tents or in temporary hovels, they possessed practically no household equipment or supplies. All of the clothing, pots, pans or utensils they had was generally what they could carry on their backs. You can imagine what a major handicap that presented.

In additon, of course, they had to lug their babies, often born along the road. When you consider the kids they toted, along with heavy packs of clothing and cooking utensils, the camp followers were little better than beasts of burden.

Famous Camp Followers

Although most were unknown to history, you've heard the names of a few famous camp followers.

Martha Washington could be considered to be a camp follower, since she did join George at Valley Forge for several months. Other American officers' wives followed that custom too. And the wives of many British officers sailed along with them to their assignments to the New World. Perhaps those British ladies were motivated to accompany their men because so many of the King's top warriors were noted for their fondness for acquiring foreign mistresses.

Of course, Martha Washington and others of her class didn't follow their men to cook and wash clothes. She was a *lady*. It was her duty, which she performed admirably, to lightened the tedium of camp by entertaining George's officers.

This she did at dinners and small parties in the comfortable stone house he occupied at Valley Forge. Mrs. Washington proved to be an excellent hostess and a help to General George in maintaining the morale of his staff.

Q: Who was Washington's favorite dancing partner?
A: Lucy Knox, the plump jolly wife of General Knox. While huge 280-pound "Knox-the-Ox" and quiet Martha, sat out the minuets, George and Lucy skipped tirelessly around the floor. It's said that at one party they "danced down 20 other couples". After the War, Henry Knox served George as his Secretary of War. Lively, intelligent, out-spoken Lucy was probably Martha's best friend and an advisor who helped her greatly with her problems as first-lady of a new country. Lucy bore 12 children, but only three of them lived to maturity.

The Saga of Molly Pitcher

A much less fortunate woman than Martha Washington or Lucy Knox was a helpful wife named Molly Pitcher. Molly's real name was Mary Hays. Her husband, a barber in Carlisle, joined the First

Pennsylvania Artillery early in the war. With his shop closed, Mary (nicknamed Molly) followed her husband to do his cooking and laundry, as many other wives did.

While her husband labored as an infantryman assigned to a cannon crew, she also helped with a dangerous task. During battles, when the fighting was hot, Molly carried pitchers of refreshing water to the sweating soldiers in her husband's crew. As she scooted along the firing line, the thirsty soldiers began to call her Molly Pitcher. Evidently hustling water to the edges of a battlefield was a common duty. It's likely that, besides Mrs. Hayes, there were other Molly Pitchers, or Sara Pitchers, or Prudence Pitchers.

Molly was an outstanding example of her kind. She made history at the battle of Monmouth, New Jersey in 1778. When her husband fell from heat prostration, she grabbed up his ramrod and took his place to help the cannon crew keep firing until the battle ended.

Sometimes the story of Molly's bravery is embellished further. Supposedly while she was standing next to her cannon, feet wide apart, a cannon ball from the enemy blasted through her skirts. Indomitable Molly's had an earthy comment for that.

> **"Good thing that canoneer didn't aim a foot higher,**
> **or he'd have blown away more than my skirt."**

Molly survived her first husband and married another army veteran, but left that shiftless clod. When she became too old to work, the Pennsylvania legislature awarded the famous heroine a pension. It was $40 a year, or $3.33 per month.

On that generous sum, legendary Molly Pitcher was able to live until the age of 78.

21
Heroine Deborah Sampson
Breaks the Taboos

The only woman who fought as a soldier in the Revolutionary War had to *disguise herself as a man.* The eventual discovery that a woman had fought bravely in its ranks was an embarrassment to the army. Evidently to George Washington. Even to the heroine herself.

Deborah Sampson led a hard life, from begining to end. Abused as a child, Deborah was taken from her parents by the town fathers of Plympton, Massachusetts, and bound out to a farm family to work for her room and board. Completing her indentured service at 18, Deborah worked on another farm and attended school, for the first time. She studied so intensely and learned so well that in a few years the town made her the teacher in charge of the school.

Inspired by the struggle for independence, Deborah wanted desperately to join in the fight. But soldiering was strictly verboten to women. She had to figure out some way to get into the army.

A Successful Transformation
If you had to be a man to fight for your country, Deborah reasoned, then she'd try to pass as a man. Secretly she made herself a man's suit and shirt, and walked to Medway, a nearby town where nobody knew her. Deborah told the enlisting officer she was "Robert Shirtliffe."

Captain Nathan Thayer had not yet recruited his full company, so he invited new recruit Robert to live with his family until the roster was full. Robert/Deborah managed to get by with his/her masquerade, even though Mrs. Thayer was surprised to discover that a young man could be so adept in using needle and thread to reshape his new uniform.

Evidently Private Shirtliffe, with hair trimmed short, looked to be a handsome soldier. Deborah was tall for a woman, muscular from hard farm work, and not too pretty in appearance.

Fortunately for the deception, soldiers in those days didn't shower together (sometimes *never* bathed) and had no physical inspections. Even when wounded twice, Deborah's medical attention was so cursory that the doctor noticed nothing out of the ordinary.

A Brave Soldier

Deborah fought bravely and well. In hand-to-hand combat at Tarrytown, New York, she received a sabre slash on her head. At a later skirmish, a musket ball went through her shoulder. How the doctor got her shirt off and patched her shoulder without noticing any feminine contours is a mystery.

Deborah's secret might never have been discovered if a high fever hadn't put her in the hospital. Her attending physician, a Dr. Binney, was more observant than others had been. To help her in her shameful deceit, the good doctor removed Deborah from the hospital to his own home for recovery, on the pretext that she needed closer care.

Deborah had a close call at the doctor's house. His pretty young niece developed a crush on the handsome twice-wounded war hero. How Deborah handled this unwanted romance is not known.

Though Dr. Binney did not embarrass soldier Deborah by making her sex generally known, he must have passed the word to her commanding officer. Her colonel didn't know how to handle such an unprecedented situation, so like any cautious officer, he ran it up the chain of command. As a result, Deborah was handed sealed orders which she was instructed to take to General Washington himself.

Go Home, Deborah.

Again, Deborah's presumptious efforts to serve her country in uniform was treated as a scandal not to be discussed. Brave General Washington was not brave enough to commend a female soldier for valiant service. Instead, he handed Private Shirtliffe a discharge. Gave her a note containing a few words of advice. Gave her some money so she could go some place, far from the Army, to find a home.

Deborah, who felt ashamed of herself for masquerading as a man, was thankful for Washington's delicacy in the matter. Her comments illuminate the prevalent feeling that only military service should be reserved solely for men.

> **"How thankful I was to that great and good man, who so kindly spared my feelings. He saw me ready to sink with shame. One word from him would have crushed me to the earth. But he spoke no word, and I blessed him for it."**

What a shame! Deborah married after the war and bore three children. Eventually her story leaked out. Her unconventional conduct in assuming a man's role in the army was not applauded by everyone. Far from it.

The Baptist church to which she belonged expelled her from its membership!

However, other people were more understanding. The state of Massachusetts where she lived after the War gave her a small pension. And Paul Revere used his influence with Congress to get her an additional pension from the United States government as a disabled veteran. That amounted to four dollars a month initially, later raised to the magnificent sum of eight dollars.

Deborah Sampson, alias Private Robert Shirtliffe, died at the age of 67, one of America's most unsung heroines.

Other Unsung Heroines

Deborah Sampson and Molly Pitcher were far from the only women who struggled valiantly for their country during the Revolutionary War, and received little recognition for it.

While our history books are filled with the brave exploits of Continental soldiers, not much notice is given to the women they left at home. Although they weren't shot at, the dames of America had a rough time during that war that ripped a young country apart.

Life was hard enough with a man around. Nine out of ten families lived on farms, mostly poor farms of a few acres hacked out of the wilderness. With no tractors, no electricity, no indoor water, no source of heat in winter except from trees that had to be cut down and chopped for the fireplace.

When war came and Father went away, Mother had to take over everything. Plowing the ground, planting crops, tending the garden, chickens, pigs, cows, chopping trees, hauling water. Also carding and spinning wool, making clothing, boiling dirty clothes, cooking, canning, etc. Taking care of a passel of kids, too, with no family allowance from a soldier's pay.

Sometimes accomplishing all of that was impossible. However, thousands of women did accomplish those tasks, in perilous financial times when the price of everything skyrocketed, and inflation made the few dollars they had practically worthless.

Makes you wonder where life was hardest. On the battle front or at home?

22
Sir William Howe
Our Favorite British General

Sir William Howe was an Englishmen who sympathized with the complaints of the Colonists, and therefore had little enthusiasm for waging war against them. That was not unusual-- many of his countrymen, even in the military, shared his belief that a severe crackdown on the Americans was a mistake.

What made General Howe's attitude unusual was that he commanded all of the British troops stationed in America at the beginning of the Revolutionary War.

From our standpoint, that was an ideal situation. For the British army, as you can imagine, it failed to result in maximum military effectiveness. In fact, some historians even speculate that General Howe deliberately held back in fighting the weak Continental Army.

Q: How was Howe related to George III?

A: He was a "left-handed cousin" of the King. His mother was an illegitimate daughter of George I. This out-of-wedlock relationship, widely known, was no handicap; it helped Howe to rise rapidly in his military career. Not only was Sir William Howe the head honcho of the British army, but his elder brother, Sir Richard, held an even more prestigious post. Brother Richard, known to his sailors as "Black Dick" because of his dark complexion, was First Lord of the Admiralty. His power was so great he ignored Parliament and sometimes even the King. The Howe brothers ran the entire British military establishment.

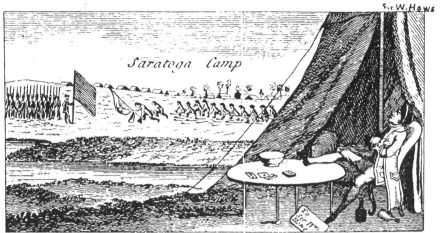

The Generals in America doing nothing, or worse than nothing.

A cartoonist in an English magazine illustrates what he, and most other Britons think about their defeat at Saratoga and the way General Howe preferred wine and gambling rather than fighting.

The Howe family were all Whigs, members of a political party which strongly opposed King George's repressive colonial policies. In fact, when Howe was notified he should take charge of all British forces in America, he at first refused to accept the command.

Luckily for us, Howe changed his mind and decided to obey orders. Without the unenthusiastic General in charge of Britain's efforts, our little Continental army wouldn't have survived the early years of the War.

Life of the Party

Like most of his noble colleagues, tall, husky, dark-complected Sir William Howe was a jolly, pleasure-loving fellow. It was claimed, both in England and America, that the General much preferred *"his glass, his lass and his game of cards"* to the dull tiresome task of waging war.

While Washington and his ragged troops froze at Valley Forge, Commander Howe and his fun-loving officers were too busy partying to go out and fight. Warmly ensconced in comfortable Philadelphia homes, they had a wonderful time. So did the cream of

Philadelphia society, most of them Loyalists, who wanted to end the revolutionary nonsense the nutty New England Patriots had gotten them into.

To the delight of the social set, General Howe's handsome officers concentrated on staging one glittering ball after another. Wherever they were quartered-- in Boston, New York or Philadelphia-- they squired the local ladies to lavish dinners, dances and theater parties.

Placating the Husband of His Mistress
He didn't care much for chasing Colonial troops, but Sir William enjoyed chasing American women. Although married for ten years (with no children) when he arrived here, the General quickly found joyous consolation in the company of a buxom blue-eyed blonde he met while he was supposed to be capturing Boston. The luscious lady, Mrs. Loring, not only shared his bed but became his constant companion. She appeared on Sir William's arm at the many parties where Loyalists entertained the King's officers who'd come to protect them from riff-raff such as the Sons of Liberty.

The idea of a top general publicly squiring a mistress was no scandalous novelty. After all, Sir William was far from home, and like other military men, not expected to remain lonesome. However, there was one inconvenience-- the lady he chose to romance had a husband. This presented only a slight problem, however, because she was married to Howe's commissary adjutant, a staff major with no inclination to cause trouble for his commanding general.

Despite the Major's calm attitude, Howe was a sensitive fellow who wanted no hard feelings. When he moved to sumptious quarters in New York, he rewarded Major Loring for his understanding. He made Loring his Commissioner of Prisons, a cushy post much sought after.

Joshua Loring considered this appointment to be a fair swap for his wife's services. Running the prisons was a very lucrative job. The Major gained control of all the food provided for thousands of Continental prisoners of war. Their rations were far from sumptuous. Mostly they were pork, rice, bread or biscuit, but such staples were quickly saleable in an inflationary economy.

Q: How much did Major Loring skim from his budget?
A: The Americans estimated that Loring peddled two-thirds of the prisoners' scant rations and pocketed the proceeds. This caused about 300 of the poor fellows to starve to death. Those who survived were so weak they could scarcely walk.

Such sordid details didn't bother Sir William or his merry companion. Mrs. Loring came to be called the "Sultana" because she became such a prominent figure in the social life of New York and later Philadelphia-- the first-lady who presided over the parties and was fawned on by all who valued the goodwill of the British commander. The cozy dawdling in the bedroom of the Sultana and her General, while he was supposed to be out chasing George Washington, even gave rise to a popular song.

> " Sir William, he, snug as a flea
> Lay all this time asnoring,
> Nor dreamed of harm as he stayed warm
> In bed with Mrs. Loring."

This ballad even reached the shores of England, and it did not go over well there. Especially as the War dragged on and became an increasing bother to the British. They had more than enough troubles at home without continually pouring money into troops and supplies for the American fiasco that was beginning to interest France, Spain and other longtime European enemies of the British.

A peevish parliament finally got fed up with Sir William. They were especially miffed to learn that he kept his 20,000 well-equipped and well-fed troops in Philadelphia while George Washington's 9,000 starving soldiers barely survived the winter at nearby Valley Forge. Why Howe never made a move to pulverize the Continentals huddled just about 20 miles away is a mystery that's never been solved.

Finally, a disgusted Parliament recalled Howe to England in May of 1778. They replaced him with General Clinton, who had strict instructions to get moving and put an end to the Colonial insurrection.

A Big Party and Tearful Farewells
Unhappy as the English Parliament was with Sir William's military efforts, or lack of them, his officers were even more distressed to see him leave them. They'd never dreamed of such a joyous time as they'd spent with jolly General Howe. Instead of sending his men out in the field to get shot, he allowed them to dine, drink, gamble and frolic in town. They liked that sort of military service.

To show their appreciation for the beloved warrior, they decided to stage a farewell bash beyond compare. The affair was planned and stage-managed by John Andre, a major always at the forefront of festive occasions. You'll read more about him in the next chapter on Benedict Arnold and Andre's dear friend, Mrs. Arnold.

Major Andre gave the big party an exotic foreign name. He called it the Michianza, which meant "the mixer" in Italian. For the last time in a really major event, it mixed the dashing British officers with the prettiest damsels of Philadelphia. Two of the officers imported their dates from New York City where they'd established cozy realtionships with Loyalist lassies there.

Talk of the Town
The spectacular Michianza was the talk of the town both before and after it took place. In setting the style for the big event, artistic Andre mixed together all the exotic themes he could think of. In keeping with the Michianza name, the mansion where much of the party took place was decked out to resemble an *Italian villa*. But one of the main events was a jousting tournament with knights in armor and a *Medieval* setting.

The costumes that maestro Andre selected introduced yet a third theme-- that of the *Arabian Nights*. He proposed that all the ladies should be garbed as *Turkish harem beauties*. Not all followed his suggestion. Their horrified fathers vetoed that idea.

Young lovelies lucky enough to receive invitations to the Michianza were requested to wear gauze turbans with plenty of sparkles and decorations, along with veils reminiscent of harem beauties. And they were to dress in white silk, with sashes to match the colors of the teams of knights they cheered.

Here's what one participant said about the elegant event.

> **"We never had, and never will have again,
> so elegant an entertainment in America."**

The Michianza was not just a dance or party. It combined a variety of spectacular entertainments that went on for hours. Here are some of the highlights of this many-splendored event.

- A river regatta opened the festivities at 2:00 in the afternoon of May 18th. Officers and their guests were rowed down the Delaware river on barges festooned with colorful ribbons and flags. They were accompanied by other decorated flatboats on which bands played music for the occasion. Crowds on the shore were able to enjoy this part of the festivities.
- When the boats reached the dock near the Wharton mansion, one of the most elegant homes in town, the passengers disembarked and strolled across the lawn between rows of British soldiers at parade rest in their scarlet uniforms.
- On the large lawn, the officers and their ladies were seated in canopied grandstands festooned with flags in two team colors-- orange and black for Knights of the Burning Mountain, pink and silver for those of the Blended Rose.
- The jousting tournament was next on the agenda. Charging each other at full gallop, the knights staged a mock battle with lances, swords and pistols. When they'd sufficiently worn themselves out and thrilled the ladies, a draw was declared.
- The crowd then entered the ballroom of the Wharton mansion. Andre had it decorated to simulate an Italian villa with walls of rose-colored simulated marble, blue and gold floors, a multitude of ribbons and flowers. Dancing lasted for hours.
- At 10:00 p.m. the dancers paused to go out on the lawn or peer out the open windows at a display of fireworks launched from riverside. A British engineers brigade had spent countless hours and countless kegs of His Majesty's powder to put together 20 spectacular fiery constructions.

- Supper was served at midnight by candle light-- hundreds of candles around the walls and on the tables. In keeping with the Arabian Nights theme, the waiters were soldiers decked out in Arabic costumes and with their faces blackened in imitation of Nubian slaves.

- After supper, guests could either resume dancing or try their luck at gambling. The dancefloor and the dice and faro tables stayed open until 4:00 the following morning.

A Sad Goodbye

It was only at the very end of the party that a sad note appeared. When Sir William's officers and his many American admirers said their goodbyes, they expressed regrets that an ungrateful government had not appreciated his heroic, though entirely unproductive, efforts. They all wished him success in whatever new assignment he'd receive when he got back to wife and home.

It's even said that some of Howe's stalwart officers shed a few tears as they bid their final farewells to the most congenial commander they'd ever served under.

America had its share of bumbling generals who handicapped the Patriot cause. But the British had their full quota of under-achievers as well. That long list has to be headed by Sir William Howe. The fun-loving and American-loving general managed to snafu the King's war effort for three years as he failed to nail General Washington and his troops time after time when they were most vulnerable.

We can thank the Lord for Sir William Howe. He was an unlikely but a Heaven-sent ally.

23
Paul Revere - Patriot Silversmith

In every town in America today the name of Paul Revere immediately conjures up his much-publicized ride to spread the alarm that British troops were on the march toward Concord where Patriots had stockpiled their main supply of arms and ammunition.

However, if you could have visited his hometown of Boston in 1775, you'd have discovered that Paul was not revered at all for any midnight ride. His neighbors in the old North End of town would have described him as a hard-working craftsman of no special fame, whose private life was not much different from that of many of his neighbors. If they knew about the ride at all, they'd have told you that Paul was one of a whole passel of horsemen (probably about three dozen) who covered the countryside that night to sound the alarm.

So where did Paul derive his fame? That didn't occur until 86 years later, long after his death.

Immortalized in a Poem
Paul Revere's great fame began when Henry Wadsworth Longfellow was inspired to write a poem about the historic night of April 18, 1775. Longfellow decided not to list 36 or so riders who made a midnight ride. He took poetic license and decided it would be better to focus his poem on just one hero.

He liked the euphony of the name "Paul Revere" because it rhymed with his opening line,"you shall hear". That's why Paul was selected and got all the accolades. Maybe you recall Longfellow's poem; perhaps you had to memorize it in school.

> **Listen my children and you shall hear**
> **Of the midnight ride of Paul Revere,**
> **On the nineteenth of April in Seventy Five;**
> **Hardly a man is now alive**
> **Who remembers that famous day and year...**
> **One if by land and two if by sea;**
> **And I on the opposite shore shall be,**
> **Ready to ride and spread the alarm**
> **Through every Middlesex village and farm.....**

Actually, Revere wasn't a very successful alarm carrier. He was captured along the way and never reached Concord. Dr. Samuel Prescott was the first horseman to arrive at that key spot, but you never hear of him. As often happens, *publicity* is the powerful searchlight that creates heroes.

Great hero or not, he's typical of thousands without whom the big movers and shakers like Adams, Hancock and Washington could never have won a war. Besides reading about those great leaders, it's just as important to understand craftsmen like Paul Revere whose hard work and ingenuity are what made America a land of achievement.

Following His Father's Trade

Paul was a second-generation American. As boys did in those days, he learned a trade from his father, French immigrant Apollos Rivoire. He became a silversmith. And like thousands of other decendants of immigrants, he Anglicized his family name.

Like most people who lived through the War, Paul never became rich. He lived in a small clapboard house near the busy waterfront.

As often happened in those days, Paul sired a flock of children-- *16 in all.* His first wife, Sara, bore eight of them before she died after a difficult childbirth. Just five months later, as was also a common custom, Paul acquired a second wife to care for his young brood. Second wife Rachel produced another eight little Reveres.

Paul was also prolific at his craft. Father Rivoire had taught him to be an expert silversmith. He not only became one of the very best in that field, but also expanded his skills to new fields.

Print Maker, Tooth Maker, Coppersmith, Etc.

Entrepreneur Revere saw three main related areas where his expertise could be useful. Skilled in engraving decorations or initials on silverware, Revere learned to apply his talents to engraving printing plates. Very profitably. His most famous engraving, a print of the Boston Massacre, sold thousands of copies.

His jewelers skills were also adaptable to the making of false teeth, a difficult process far beyond the abilities of most dentists of the time. One of his creations, carved of ivory and kept in place with metal springs, found its way into the famous jaws of George Washington.

Revere also became a premier coppersmith. His expanding firm was selected to copper sheath the dome of Massachusetts new State House. An even more prestigious commission came his way when Congress authorized the building of America's first war ships. One of those ships which you can still visit today, the USS Constitution, had its oak hull protected with copper, applied by Revere's craftsmen.

Q: How much was Revere paid for his work?
A: Paul received the immense sum of $3,820 for the job on the USS Constitution. That included not only sheathing the vast hull with sheets of metal, but also providing a variety of cast copper and bronze fittings.

His business card advertised that the versatile Revere could mend "umbrillos", make surgical instruments, fancy clock faces, sword hilts, baby's rattles and silverware for the table.

Revere's name still is a major one in the field of metalsmithing today. In fact, you may own a candlestick or Revere Ware pan made by a firm his descendants founded. It's known as the Revere Brass and Copper Company.

So you see, Paul Revere's fame may not truly be due to the midnight ride you've often heard about so often. But in spite of that, he really was one of our wonderful ancestors, a superb and inventive American craftsman.

Q: How famous was Paul Revere in his day?

A: *Before Longfellow wrote his poem in 1863 about the midnight ride, few American had heard of Paul Revere. He wasn't even mentioned in reference books that listed thousands of historical personages. That changed dramatically in less than a decade after the famous poem appeared. Revere became so revered that the D. A. R. in Boston bought his neglected house at 19 North Square and converted it into a popular museum.*

24
Benedict Arnold
Best General, Worst Traitor

No accounting of scoundrels of the Revolutionary War would be complete without delving into the turbulent multiple careers and the private life of Benedict Arnold.

Everybody knows that Arnold was the number-one traitor who tried to sell out his country. But do you know why? Or that he started out as an ardent patriot, and was considered by many Americans to be our *best* combat general?

Arnold loved to fight. And strut. He ran away at 14 to fight briefly in the French and Indian War. He grew up to be a short-of-stature but muscular and cocky banty rooster of a man. Despite his moderate height, he had an enormous head and shoulders. In fact, he was sometimes described as looking deformed.

Merchant, Adventurer, Smuggler
Shamed frequently by a drunken father, Benedict was quick with his fists as a lad. And quick to take offense throughout his life.

As a young man, he opened a shop on the New Haven waterfront as a druggist and bookseller. Business was good, but Arnold spent more than he took in.

To supplement his shop income, he bought a ship, and for the next ten years spent most of his time at sea in the West Indies trade. While he was away, his spinster sister ran the store.

A Troubled Marriage
Dashing Captain Arnold, always dressed to the hilt and a flashy big spender, was popular with the ladies of New Haven. When he was 25, Benedict seemed headed for a quieter life when he wooed and

wed the sheriff's daughter, Margaret (Peggy) Mansfield. Within a year of their marriage, Margaret bore him a son. Two more followed shortly after.

Unfortunately, Margaret learned that while her husband was away sailing the West Indies, he had lady friends there too. Some were evidently of the professional type.

Q: Why did Margaret refuse to sleep with her husband?
A: Margaret heard that Benedict had contracted a venereal disease from his West Indies escapades. When he returned home, she never let him touch her again. Whether or not Arnold was cured of his illness isn't known, but it didn't stop him from making new alliances.

Eventually Ship's Captain Arnold tired of sailing back and forth to the Bahamas. He arranged to run his business affairs from New Haven. He settled on shore and built the biggest house in the whole town, a mansion he couldn't afford.

Off to War
Perhaps to compensate for an unfriendly home life, the ebullient Arnold began to spend a lot of time with the boys. They were the young bloods who liked to parade around in military uniforms, and tell what they were going to do to the British if war came.

Even before the action started at Lexington and Concord, Arnold assembled a militia troop. The men he rounded up for the new military company naturally elected him captain of it.

As soon as the first shots in the Revolution were fired, Captain Arnold led his New Haven Company to the scene. From that day on, he was one of our most active and successful warriors.

When We Needed Victories
Captain, then Colonel, then General, Arnold was probably America's best field officer and strategist.

His daring exploits did much to buoy the American spirit at a time when our few rag-tag troops, arrayed against the mightiest army in the world, had little to smile about. He was always in the center of the action.

Along with Ethan Allen, he captured Fort Ticonderoga and its important supplies. Then the British fort at St. John's. Later he led a daring though unsuccessful attack on Britain's mighty fortress atop the steep cliffs of Quebec.

When the British developed plans to invade New England from Canada, former ship's captain Arnold gathered a fleet of boats on Lake Champlain that thwarted them.

Frustrated Hero

The hero so much admired by his countrymen fought one bitter skirmish after another with the politicians in Philadelphia. He suffered personal defeats as well.

When the Continental Congress promoted five junior officers over General Arnold, he was furious and threatened to resign, not for the first time. Even though General Washington himself protested on Arnold's behalf, there was no immediate redress.

Time after time, the impetuous Arnold had trouble in collecting money from Congress to pay bills. When he ran out of supplies, the impatient general would purchase them out of his own pocket, rather than waiting to go through the approved purchasing channels. Furthermore, he disdained the petty details of keeping the kind of accurate receipts that would satisfy the demands of the bookkeepers at army headquarters. As a consequence, his expense accounts were always challenged and often cut in half.

Each time this happened, Arnold exploded. He was highly insulted at any inference that he'd padded his accounts.

Personal Problems

The military hero suffered many personal defeats. At Quebec, Arnold was hit in the leg by a British bullet. In a later battle, this same leg was broken when Arnold was thrown from his horse. Doctors advised amputation, but Arnold said "Damned nonsense!" However, that leg became two inches shorter than the other, and he limped for the rest of his life.

Returning home from Quebec, he learned his wife had died just a week previously. Although his wife despised him for his venereal escapades, he entered a period of depression after her death. This was aggravated by a severe bout of gout.

His business, never too robust, was floundering. In addition, he never got over his fierce resentment against the politicians and bureaucrats back at headquarters. He felt they hampered the war effort, insulted him personally, did not appreciate his talents and many sacrifices.

Temptations at Philadelphia

General Washington admired and appreciated Arnold. He appointed him commander of Philadelphia after that capitol city was recaptured from the British in 1778.

Unfortunately, that move was like opening the cookie jar to high-living, free-spending, always-in-debt Arnold. The new commander traveled to the capitol city in a spectacular coach-and-four with liveried footmen. He bought the fanciest clothes and shoes by the trunkful, and attended all the glittering society parties.

Q: Was Arnold a good writer of love letters?

A: Evidently not. After his wife died, he wrote letters to several rich widows who might have solved the constant problems he faced because of his high living and low income. If he received any reponses, they were all negative. An interesting aspect of Arnold's amorous correspondence campaign is that all of the letters uncovered are almost identical, using the same phrases. Perhaps he should have tried a variety of approaches, instead of relying on a mass mailing.

The big-spender not only created gossip around town, but he also became involved in an official scandal. Arnold was accused of pocketing army funds. It was claimed that he was in cahoots with the army's clothier general in a scheme based on the fraudulent purchasing of uniforms.

A furious Arnold demanded a court martial, which cleared him of most of the charges. But not all of them.

Young Second Wife, More Trouble

At Philadelphia, the battered war hero became a drawing-room idol, a favorite as always with the ladies. This included many teen-age beauties, flattered by his attentions.

Popular 17-year-old Peggy Shippen, 20 years his junior, was especially enchanted. And he with her. As the middle-aged swain chased the young beauty, her family liked to call the stocky hero "Peggy's Little General."

When the veteran General married his second wife named Peggy, their union caused considerable buzzing among the scandal-savorers of the town. Partly because of the age difference. More because it was well-known that Peggy the Second was far from the avid revolutionary patriot that Arnold was still presumed to be.

Peggy's father was a prosperous Quaker merchant and therefore technically neutral about the war. However, his daughter seemed to tend strongly to the Tory side. That was not seemly for the bride of a colonial commander, some of the gossips thought.

During the previous year when the British held control of Philadelphia, debutante Peggy had been among the most enthusiastic partyers with the gallant young enemy officers. She was the belle of the many balls the wealthy Tories held for their British friends.

She still kept in contact with her good friend, Major Andre, who'd gone to New York as aide to the British commander in chief. One of Major Andre's major duties was to collect information about the American forces from his old friends back in Philadelphia.

In other words, her friend was the British Army's head spy.

Temptation and Treason

Both Peggy and Arnold loved to spend money, far more lavishly than their income afforded. Neither of them felt any warmth toward the administration at Independence Hall.

Peggy thought of a way out of their financial dilemma. She put Major Andre in touch with her disgruntled husband. Andre had access to a potful of British money that could be distributed to a corruptable person in the right place.

General Arnold was the perfect pigeon. For approximately five months, Arnold smuggled confidential information to the British

Major about General Washington's movements, usually in code. No one knows exactly how much he was paid for these tidbits of military information, but he needed big money to support his lavish style of living.

Building Up to the Big Deal

Arnold was soon talking to Andre about deserting from the American forces and joining the British. He promised to bring with him many other deserters, if he was made a high-ranking British general. Arnold also wanted 10,000 pounds sterling in advance, to compensate for the property he'd forfeit if he skipped to the enemy side. Expecting to have his offer accepted, he began converting his assets to cash so he could send the money to London and have it available when he deserted.

The British command preferred to keep informant Arnold where he was, at least for the time being. The General's desire to defect became stronger when his long-delayed court-martial came to trial. He'd demanded a trial so he could prove that claims of his improper actions were false.

To his dismay, the verdict of the military court was far from the complete exoneration he wanted. Among other breaches of his command, Arnold was found guilty of using army wagons to haul private goods in which he was trading. He got off with a slap on the wrist, a mere reprimand, but the verdict angered him.

Alleged shortages in his public financial accounts were also questioned again. However, the General's books were so scrambled no one could sort them out, so Congress came to no decision on them.

After the trial, Arnold figured out a way to earn a really big payoff from the British. *For 20,000 pounds, he'd give them West Point!* That was our important fort that controlled the Hudson river, the vital gateway to upper New York state.

To make the deal possible, Arnold had to talk General Washington into appointing him commander of the fort. This request puzzled George because West Point, despite its strategic importance, was not nearly as prestigious a post as the command of our capitol city. But Washington granted his friend's request. Of course, as you no doubt know, the outrageous plan to hand West Point over to the enemy fizzled.

Multiple Foul-ups

Traitor Arnold wrote a letter to Major Andre with his proposition. The head British general, Clinton, agreed to the terms. Go-between Major Andre met with Traitor Arnold again to finalize details. But when returning to his camp, although he was in disguise, the Major was caught behind American lines.

Andre had a wad of secret documents hidden in his boot. They included diagrams of the fort at West Point and advice on how to attack it. General Arnold had agreed that he would at first pretend to defend the fort, but then quickly surrender.When Arnold's perfidy was uncovered, his friend the Comander-in-Chief was appalled.

"Whom can we trust now?
General Washington

Unlucky Major Andre was convicted as a spy and hanged. Arnold fared better. He got wind of the Major's capture just in time. Without even going home to get wife Peggy, he high-tailed it to a British ship which carried him to New York.

Peggy Arnold's luck held out too. When questioned by old friend General Washington, distraut Peggy went into hysterics and claimed she knew nothing about her hubby's dastardly plot. (Later evidence shows that she did.) However, Washington believed the tearful lady, and chivalrously allowed the abandoned woman to join her husband.

Arnold thought he'd be highly regarded by his new allies. But he wasn't. Athough the renegade American got a commission as a British Brigadier General, he could persuade only 28 of his countrymen to join him. That didn't impress his new bosses.

They sent him to Virginia to raid the South. The wily turncoat general caused his old friend George Washington some sleepless nights. He burned his way through the countryside, and earned further contempt from his former colleagues.

No Hero in England
Arnold was sure that after the British victory-- he expected them to win, which seemed a reasonable bet-- that he'd be a hero in England. He expected to live there as a top General in the British Army, honored for his role in the triumph and living like a lord with the money he'd been promised for his sell-out.

That part of his plan didn't work out too well either. After the war ended, Arnold did eventually get paid, though not in his opinion what he'd been promised. His griping wasn't justified.

Q: How much did the British pay Arnold?

A: King George awarded him 6,525 pounds, a not inconsiderable sum. He also received a pension of 225 pounds annually as a British colonel. In addition, Peggy and his children got a pension about twice as large. He also received more than 13,000 acres of land in New Brunswick, Canada, where he lived for a few years, and engaged in some unsuccessful shipping ventures.

However, Arnold's ambition to culminate his military career as an active high officer for the British was a pipe dream. When he arrived in England, that was the end of his warrior career. There was no way the British high command would ever entrust him with any troops. *Once a double-crosser, always a double-crosser,* they reasoned.

Far from respecting him, everyone in Canada and England despised the traitor who lived among them. He died in London, a bitter outcast in a strange land. Sad end for a scoundrel who could have been one of America's greatest heroes.

25
Royal Rascals of Europe

Any account of our wierd, wonderful ancestors would have to include those who came from various parts of Europe to this melting-pot nation of ours.

In the early days of the Colonies, most immigrated from the British Isles. Along with the English, there were large pockets of Scots and Irish. But even as early as 1776, Philadelphia had its Germantown section, while Mennonite and other Germanic sects populated the farms of Western Pennsylvania. After the War, numbers of Hessian soldiers opted to stay in America, and were accepted with little rancor.

Of course, the Colonies were surrounded by other European nationals. Frenchmen formed a crescent curving from Canada to the north down along the Ohio, where Washington had fought them, to the lower Mississippi and New Orleans. There were Spaniards to the west of there and in Mexico, as well as along the Florida coasts and the islands of the Carribean. Dutch merchants came from the Southern Islands too, even after the War started, to trade with Americans and give the British blockaders fits.

Europe Was Where the Action Was
Even after 1776, the monarchs of Europe tended to view America as a loose conglomeration of colonies (which it was) that didn't amount to much except as places to sell some of their products. At first, those rulers paid little attention to the American rebellion because they were much more concerned with their local wars.

You could say that the continual European power grabs and seizures of somebody else's land were family fights. Because kings and queens could only marry others from a limited royal lineage, at least half of the major monarchs were blood relatives.

The Georges of England, you'll recall, came from Hanover. Catherine the Great of Russia was born in a part of Prussia that is now Poland. Her husband, briefly Czar Peter III, was another German. Marie Antoinette, about whom you'll also read, came from Austria to become Queen of France eventually. Spain, which aided the Colonies in their War for Independence, was ruled by Charles III, who was also the King of Naples and Sicily. The list of these convoluted inter-marriages and inter-regnums goes on and on.

Welcome Aid From a Nutty Bunch

Those cantankerous European monarchs played a major role in the American Revolution. In some cases, their fighting in Europe carried over into their colonies in the New World. In other instances, countries such as the Netherlands sent their trading vessels to the Americas, in defiance of British warships, with supplies the Colonists desperately needed.

When it became apparent that the meager American troops were miraculously going to survive for a while against British regiments, King George's enemies began to sneak both war supplies and money to the rebels. They didn't do this out of the goodness of their hearts. It was a calculated effort, designed to cause trouble for the powerful British Empire which was top-dog in the world and therefore the logical target for envious lesser pups in the pack.

Helpful as they were to our rebel ancestors, those European monarch were a strange bunch-- living proof of the geneticists' claims that interbreeding begets queer offspring.

Some of their shenanigans were stranger than a soap opera. Let's take a look at a few of them, starting with a couple who were on King George's side... when it suited them.

An Abused Boy Becomes a Bullying Man

Frederick the Great didn't enjoy a great childhood. He was actually the second Frederick of Prussia. His father, Frederick I, was a 275-pound sadist who acted as the drill sergeant of his nation and also of his family.

The First Frederick's greatest joy was in barking orders at his personal regiment, made up almost exclusively of extra-tall soldiers he'd gathered from across Europe. During his travels, he always kept an eye out for over-sized recruits. If they proved to be reluctant, it was claimed that on occasion he'd even kidnapped a few giants he coveted for his special forces.

His son Frederick didn't measure up to Big Daddy's dreams of future warrior material. Far from being a giant, the Prince was short in stature and delicate in build. Even worse, he preferred books and music to uniforms and guns. Big Frederick resolved to knock those tendencies out of him.

Q: How did Frederick I discipline his son?
A: He'd beat the boy, for no reason, and after knocking him down, he'd drag him around by the hair.

No Escape

By the time he was 18, Little Frederick decided he'd had enough of such treatment, and made plans to run off to England with his best friend. But they were caught. Daddy became so furious at this flouting of his authority as parent and commander-in-chief that he had both boys charged with desertion and *sentenced to death*. He meant it too!

Only pleading by horrified foreign ambassadors persuaded the stern father to reduce his son's sentence. Instead of a death sentence, Little Frederick got off with a stay in prison. But in addition, the teen-aged prince was forced to watch the executioner chop off his friend's head. That was a bloody scary sight that caused the young prince to faint.

If Daddy meant to teach his son an unforgettable lesson that would straighten him out, he evidently succeeded. During the following decade, Young Frederick obediently applied himself to learning how to drill soldiers, brow-beat the civilian population and scheme against all other countries. When he became king, he followed the path the old man had laid out for him.

Europe's Great Nightmare

Frederick II became a greater threat to the rest of Europe than his father had been. Scarcely was the old man buried, when new King Frederick marched his army without warning into Silesia, an Austrian province ruled by Empress Maria Theresa with whom Prussia had recently signed a pledge of peaceful coexistence.

Right off the bat, by that act Frederick II signaled to all of Europe that he cared nothing for treaties, and had enough military power to take on anyone who dared to cross him. Few ever did.

For the next 47 years, the gentle boy who became a true warrior king, dedicated all his energies and those of his subjects to building a powerful state. His small country became an efficient rigid bureaucracy that supported a military machine far greater than its size warranted. In the tradition of despots, he earned his title of Frederick the Great.

George III Liked Old Fritz

English kings liked Frederick the Great, not because he was a jolly fellow, but because he kept the rest of Europe scared. The more attention monarchs on the Continent had to focus on nasty Frederick in their midst, the less they could aim across the Channel.

Toward the end of his life, his obedient subjects gave him an affectionate-sounding name. Not really out of love for the warrior king who continued to drive them, but out of respect for the tired gray-haired battler, they called him "Old Fritz".

Only one lighter tendency from his boyhood did Old Fritz retain. He continued to love music, especially that of the flute. He wrote several concertos for that instrument, and frequently played it in concerts at his palace of Sans Souci in Potsdam.

A Great Woman in Russia

Like Frederick the Great, Catherine the Great started life as a long-shot ever to amount to much in the hierarchy of the Eighteenth Century. In fact, she looked even less likely to succeed to any position of power.

Catherine II of Russia, who earned the appellation of Catherine the Great, wasn't Russian. Her name wasn't Catherine either. She began life as Sophie Friederike Auguste Prinzessin (Princess) Von

Anhaly-Zerbst in Stetin, then a part of Prussia and now part of Poland. Sophie, more often called "Figgie" (or "Fikke") within her family, was the daughter of an obscure and nearly-penniless prince who owed his allegiance to Frederick the Great.

Her big break (or maybe it should be called her "bad break") came when Empress Elizabeth of Russia began scouting around for a wife for her nephew, the Grand Duke Peter. As heir to her throne, he was the most eligible bachelor in Europe.

Sophie Makes a Pretty Picture

Young Princess Sophie was the right age, a nubile 14. She was the right nationality, Prussian, for the Empress wanted to improve ties with Frederick the Great, hoping that an intermarriage might somewhat alleviate the hostilities between them.

The German teen-ager was not pretty, but a buxom healthy girl. She appeared to be well fitted for her most important job; she looked strong and built for child-bearing.

> **"Her health is known to be good. I want them
> to have a large family."** Empress Elizabeth

So 14-year-old Sophie dropped her German name and became the Grand Duchess Ekaterina (sometimes spelled Ykaterina) Alekseyevna. Off she went to her new country-- to a new language, new customs and a husband who was one of the all-time disasters.

Saddest of Marriages

Sophie, now Ekaterina to the Russians or Catherine to us, soon learned that her Grand Duke had a few flaws. Possibly because of royal inbreeding, he was mentally deficient. Also neurotic and obstinate. The fact that he drank heavily didn't help.

On her wedding night, Catherine discovered that Peter was impotent. Most authorities believe their marriage was never consummated, a constant source of gossip that humiliated the young bride.

Peter's limp performance in the bedchamber was unsatisfying not only to Catherine, but also to the Empress who'd envisioned an immediate production of little dukes and duchesses from the marriage. So miffed did Auntie Elizabeth become because the young couple was neglecting their primary job that she had them locked up for months in their suite of rooms. That was a threat that they'd better concentrate on some action if they ever expected to see the outdoors again.

Q: Did Catherine and Peter have anything in common?
A: They did at first. The two were related-- first cousins, in fact. Like Catherine, her young husband was not Russian. He'd started out as a Swedish prince with German ancestry. He was also the nephew of Russia's Empress Elizabeth, so she brought him to Russia to become her heir, because she was childless and needed to protect the succession from her enemies. Like his bride Catherine, Peter's favorite language was French (no, not Swedish or German) so they conversed in that tongue. Dull-witted Peter never did become fluent in his adopted country's language, but intelligent Catherine made a great effort to learn it and quickly became so proficient she could speak Russian without an accent.

A Hard Struggle for 18 Years

Contending with both her childish husband and unreasonable tyrant of an aunt, Catherine somehow managed to keep her sanity and also prepare herself to become an effective ruler of her adopted country. In her memoirs, she comments on the sad years.

> **"For 18 years, I lived a life that would have rendered ten other women mad, and 20 others in my place would have died of a broken heart."**

Peter's idea of a good time was to torture his pets when he was drunk. The idiot also dreamed of great military conquests. His hero was Frederick the Great, the enemy of Russia, a military genius he dreamed he might emulate some day. Therefore, his favorite playthings were armies of toy soldiers he manouvered around on the floor while imagining he was a second Frederick.

While witnessing this nonsense, Catherine read and studied extensively. She converted to the Orthodox faith of her adopted land, and changed herself into a dedicated patriot. She even managed to give Aunt Elizabeth what she desired from the marriage of her nephew, though not exactly in the way the Empress would have preferred. Catherine solved her pregnancy problems by bringing several lovers into her bed. During Peter's lifetime, she gave birth to three children whom everyone regarded as not being Peter's kids.

Q: Who said Catherine's children were sired by her lovers?
A: She did. Not at all shy about the parentage of her progeny, Catherine made remarks to the effect that none of them, including Paul the heir apparent, had been fathered by her doltish royal husband.

Life Changes Dramatically for Catherine

Empress Elizabeth's death in January of 1762 was good news to Catherine. She was free at last of that dominating woman. Her husband ascended the throne as Peter III and she sat beside him as the Czarina of Russia.

Almost immediately, simple-minded Peter infuriated his subjects by throwing away the gains the Russian armies had recently made against Frederick the Great, Peter's idol. On the verge of victory over Prussia in the Seven Year's War, Peter declared peace and gave back to Frederick all of the territory he'd lost to the Russian troops.

Besides making his subjects angry, Peter also infuriated his wife. That was an even dumber mistake that led to his downfall after a reign of only six months.

On taking power, stupid Peter gave Catherine several indications that he wanted to get rid of her. In front of a large crowd at a banquet, he'd shouted at her and humiliated her. He began flaunting his mistress in front of Catherine (who'd always been somewhat discreet with her lovers) and there was talk that he wanted to marry the ugly woman.

Of course, that would mean the end of Catherine. Her spies brought her rumors that Peter planned to arrest her, put her in a convent and disinherit her son, the Grand Duke Paul. There was no way Catherine was going to let such unpleasant events happen.

Catherine Takes Control

Unfortunately for Peter, he lacked the ability of his idol, Frederick the Great, to take quick action. Catherine had no such failing.

Since her current lover Gigori Orlov and his brother Aleksei were conveniently in command of the regiments at St. Petersburg, they were able to to lead a quick, bloodless takeover. Those two stalwart friends of hers presented Catherine to the troops, who greeted her with cheers. Jubilant crowds joined them. Even some soldiers from Peter's favorite regiment joined the triumphant procession acclaiming her as their sovereign.

After a brief but futile attempt to fight back, Peter surrendered. He was arrested, stripped of all his medals and ribbons-- even stripped of his military uniform. Then he was carted off under guard to be held at one of his estates briefly, on the way to a more secure permanent imprisonment.

Getting Rid of Competition

Outside observers predicted that Catherine wouldn't last long as the holder of power. After all, they reasoned, she was a German interloper not too popular with the Russian boyars. Also, not being a blood descendant of any Russian ruler, she had no legitimate claim to the throne.

If the noblemen of the court thought they'd soon snatch the power away from the new Czarina through some technicality, they didn't know Catherine.

One obstacle to her continued hold on the throne was removed quickly. Just a week after the takeover, the deposed Czar Peter, contracted a mysterious fatal malady. The official report stated that "hemorrhoidal colic" was the cause of his death. This caused snickers in foreign courts.

"Hemorrhoids can be a fatal disease in Russia."
Parisian writer D'Alembert

Non-official accounts of Peters death were less fanciful. One story bruited around the empire said his guards strangled him. Another account detailed how they pulled a featherbed on top of him and sat on it until he expired, a favorite method in such operations since it left no marks and therefore left open the possible explanation that it had been a natural death.

With Peter gone, there was still a possible contender for the throne. Decades earlier, before Peter's mother Elizabeth gained the crown, an infant named Ivan Antonovich was briefly designated the ruler as Ivan VI under the regency of his mother. However, as was the case with other Russian rulers, the crown didn't stay on Ivan's head for very long.

When tough Elizabeth had staged her coup to take over the throne, she shipped little Ivan off to imprisonment at the same fortress where Peter eventually ended up. There the poor kid had been languishing, all alone most of the time, *for 20 years!*

His bad luck persisted. After Peter's demise, some of the nobles conniving against Catherine's ascendency attempted to bring Ivan back to the capitol as the rightful heir. He had the blood lines Catherine lacked, and they figured they could set him up as a figure-head ruler under their control. But they were a bit late with their plans. When they attempted to snatch him from his prison, his guards killed him.

Whether or not Catherine gave the order for unlucky Ivan's murder, many concluded that she had been responsible for both his and her husband's deaths.

Q: Was this type of murder unusual?
A: Certainly not. Possible claimants to the Russian throne led hazardous lives. Both Ivan the Terrible and Peter the Great (Peter I) murdered their own sons to make sure they never usurped the throne.

A Powerful Ruler

The little German girl came to Russia as a teen-ager to wed a weak dolt of a grand duke, and struggled through nearly two decades of a horrible marriage. She was 33 years old when she finally grabbed the crown; was destined to reign for another 34 years. She became one of the greatest of all Russian rulers.

In contrast to her predecessor, Peter, who flaunted his German origins and ridiculed everything Russian, Catherine fervently followed the customs of her adopted land. She displayed devotion to the Orthodox church, which helped secure the backing of the powerful clergy and pleased the common people. She made her ambition the spread of Russian power, expanding her nation's control to both the west and south.

Encouraging culture in her backward land, Catherine created a dazzling royal court rivaling that of France. Her personal life, both before and after Peter's demise, was a lively one.

Lack of Beauty Poses No Handicap

Catherine was no beauty. Her best feature was her eyes--exceptionally big and blue, with long lashes. She had dark hair, a long chin and a long rather pointed nose.

As a young girl when she first appeared at the Russian court, her figure was shapely though even then on the full side. It expanded as she grew older. By the time she became empress, it was described as "stately". It became more than that in middle age. Royal gowns preserved in the Moscow museum indicate she couldn't have been much more than five feet tall, but amazingly chunky in her bust and bottom in her later years.

Lack of a beautiful face or figure didn't stop the Czarina from enjoying a steady procession of handsome, eager, strongly-endowed young lovers, right up until the time of her death. All of them were recruited from among the officers of her army.

More than one strapping lieutenant or captain who caught Catherine's eye catapulted instantly... well, after a busy night or two... to the rank of a colonel. More important, they served as her personal aide-de-camp. This important position required that they escort her to social affairs and also occupy an apartment at the palace conveniently near her bedroom.

Hard-Working Empresses Deserve a Bit of Fun

Ekaterina saw no reason why she shouldn't enjoy a satisfying amount of sexual relaxation after a hard day at the palace. When remarks reached her ears about the young lovers she snatched from obscurity and elevated to military and sometimes political power-- and she didn't miss any gossip-- the Czarina showed her indifference to criticism and also her sense of humor.

> **"I perform a service by educating young men."**
> Catherine II

Actually, Catherine's early liasons tended to be fairly long-term affairs. Her first lasted a couple of years. It was with Sergeii Saltykov who after two miscarriages fathered her first child, the Grand Duke Paul. Although the parentage of the little duke was no great secret, Peter didn't raise any fuss, nor did Empress Elizabeth who was willing to settle for a potential royal heir from any source.

True Love Arrives

The relationship with Saltykov could be considered just a warm-up. It ended rather abruptly when the new English ambassador brought along as part of his large staff a handsome suave young Polish nobleman. Count Stanislas Poniatowski set Catherine's heart apounding instantly.

When heart-throb Paniatowski entered the life of 26-year-old Catherine, she enjoyed a truly serious affair that percolated vigorously for more than six years. During those years, husband Peter looked the other way-- toward his own flirtations which are generally regarded as merely window dressing to hide his impotence, since none produced any children.

Poniatowski was truly a great love of Catherine's... at least one of her great loves. Early in her reign there were rumors she planned to marry him. That could have caused political problems, so she cancelled any such plans and never did remarry after Peter's death.

Eventually even her great affair with Paniatowski hit some bumps. He returned to his native Poland. But from time to time, he appeared again in Russia and Catherine's orbit-- though not to her bed, she claimed-- on strictly business matters.

Q: How did Catherine reward Poniatowski for his services?
A: *At the end of the Seven Year's War, in collusion with*
Frederick the Great, she set her lover Poniatowski up as
the King of Poland. He held that crown for 11 years and
tried valiantly to reorganize his battered country. But
eventually it was chopped up between Prussia, Russia and
Austria. The ex-King-- no longer safe in his native land--
returned to Russia where he died three years later.

Catherine's parting from Paniatowski may have been accelerated by the showing up of an even handsomer and younger stud. Grigorii Orlov was a youthful Guardsman Lieutenant (five years younger than Catherine) who'd already won fame for both his wild military and romantic exploits. The fact that he'd lost one eye in battle only seemed to increase his sexual appeal to women.

Another Love of Her Life
A boisterous burly bear of a man descibed as "gigantic" (supposedly in all his parts, the gossips said) this military hero became another of Catherine the Great's great loves. After about a year of tying up with Orlov, she bore a son by him. This boy, named Alexei Bobrinski, was made a count when he was five years old, and was semi-officially acknowledged as the Empress's son. This was possible because her husband was still alive when Alexei was born, so it could be presumed that Emperor Peter had fathered him... as it had been presumed that he'd fathered Prince Peter.

Eventually, Orlov sired two more sons with the Empress. This occured after Emperor Peter's death, so it posed some problems. It was not politic for the heir to the throne, Prince Peter, to have any brothers appear when Catherine was a widow. So although their royal parentage was common knowledge, Catherine had enough power to raise those last two boys with no princely titles or acknowledgement. Officially they were just another pair of kids of uncertain lineage, among others who lived at the palace.

Romance Ends But Business Continues

In addition to their romantic romping, Catherine discovered an invaluable political ally in the devil-may-care popular Orlov. It was he and his brothers who spearheaded her coup that made her Czarina in 1762.

Later he proposed marriage to her, but though tempted, she feared that union with an uneducated man who had no royal relatives would stir up a storm. As with Paniatowski before him, Catherine opted to remain a widow, though a merry one.

She and Gregorii remained lovers for 12 years, her longest laison. After their eventual splitting up, Grigorii also echoed Paniatowski by coming back to Catherine from time to time as a friend and trusted advisor. The Czarina changed lovers, but she didn't abandon them, nor they her.

No Pause in the Parade of Lovers

Orlov was followed by another Lieutenant from the Horse Guards, Alexander Vasilchikov, 15 years Catherine's junior. He lasted only 18 months to be succeeded by a more mature old friend of hers, General Gegorii Potemkin. This third Gegorii in her string of lovers had been one of her chief ministers for years, on a strictly business basis. He became another one of her serious loves.

Rumors even had it that they were secretly married. But the hot romance with Potemkin only kept steaming for about two years. After that he continued to be a major force in the government. In fact, as Prime Minister, he practically ran the country and was responsible for much of Catherine's success. He maintained a close friendhip with Ekaterina until his death.

So good a friend was General Potemkin that when his situation between the royal sheets began to cool, he good-naturedly looked around for a potential successor. That turned out to be a fellow officer, Colonel Peter Zavandovskii.

According to palace observers, who didn't miss anything at all, Potempkin and Zavandovskii for a time even shared the labors of keeping their Cazina satisfied. Perhaps this menage a trois was Potemkins method of on-the-job training. Or perhaps he was merely reluctant to lose his place in the private steambaths which he and Ekaterina were both so fond of.

A Search for Youth

Perhaps we should say "a search for youths". Never a raving beauty, Catherine became decidedly fat as she aged. *The fact that she lost most of her teeth didn't help her appearance either.* But that didn't stop her conquests of ambitious young officers who lusted after the power and great wealth she could give them.

Following liasons with Soltykov, Paniatowski, Orlov, Vasilchikov, Potemkin and Zavandovskii, which stretched over decades, middle-aged Catherine began an even faster turnover in her lovers. While not exactly one-night stands, many were one-year stands.

Hefty Catherine enjoyed an extremely active amorous life in her later years. No longer seeking true love, she settled for a steady procession of handsome men-- all under 25 years of age-- whom she kept for a couple of years each, and then sent off with good wishes and gobs of money.

In her mid-forties and fifties and sixties, she enjoyed *known* relationships with 13 young lovers, all between 22 and 25 years of age. They lasted as her "personal aides" for about a year and a half or two years apiece.

The first new lover in the fast-turnover string was Zorich, who bore the strange-to-us but appropriate first name of Semen. After Semen came Stakhiev, Strakhove, Rontsov, Levashev, Vysotskii, Mordinov, Lanskoi, Ermolov, Dmitriev-Mamonov, Stoianov, Miloradovich and finally Miklashevskii. Not necessarily all in that order, for there was some overlapping.

Q: How did Catherine line up her lovers?

A: Supposedly she had recruiting assistance from the always-helpful Potemkin. Then to make sure she wouldn't waste her time and be disapponted with below-average performance, it was rumored that her good friend Countess Bruce would road-test the young prospects for her. Stories about the Countess's screening procedures include speculation that Catherine would watch through a peep-hole so she could personally rate the vigor and durability of new recruits before they made the final jump to the royal matress.

Sour Grapes

Other important people of her time (mostly men) often decried Catherine's morals and bemoaned the example she set for other women. They called her a libertine. If that means she was unconventional, it's certainly true she ignored restrictions that bound ordinary folks. But remember, kings of her time routinely dallied with so many different bed partners they could scarcely keep track of them all.

Q: How promiscuous were other monarchs?

A: Very! It was generally conceded that a king's desires were always to be fulfilled. Nearly all of them developed a considerable appetite for female companionship, and were rarely rebuffed. One extreme example is a king of Poland who was said to have sired at least 350 bastard children. A Hessian ruler begat more than 100.

Catherine the Great has sometimes been called the most effective of all female monarchs. She certainly was a remarkable woman, a brilliant visionary dedicated to her job. Revelling in power, she was strong and lusty and charged ahead at what she wanted, both in politics and in her personal life, throughout her long reign.

She died unexpectedly from a stroke at the age of 67, leaving her current young lover disconsolate and unemployed.

Maria Theresa - Model of Morality

Lest you think that all monarchs of the Eighteenth Century led licentious lives, you should know about Maria Theresa of Austria. She was squeaky clean personally, though as clever a politician as any devious ruler around.

Like Catherine of Russia, Maria Theresa of Austria assumed power as a young inexperienced woman, married to an ineffectual husband. Maria Theresa ruled even longer than the Czarina; coming to her throne in 1740, she remained there for 40 years.

Unlike Catherine, Maria Theresa was a beautiful woman who depended more on charm than force to get her way. Yet while maintaining a happy marriage and raising a large family, she managed to stand off the threats of half of Europe.

Prolific Wife and Faithful Widow

Unlike her contemporary, Catherine, Maria Theresa enjoyed a happy marriage. Although the man she married, Emperor Francis I, was a weak ruler who left the running of the nation mostly to her, he was a strong husband. Maria and Francis conceived 16 children in their 20 years of marriage. Surprisingly for those days, 13 of their offspring lived to adulthood.

Besides his busy homelife, Francis also had strength enough to maintain a mistress. None the less, Maria Theresa understood that prerogative of emperors, and she adored Francis. In fact, when he died, in 1765, she shared her grief with the Emperor's mistress and graciously paid off the lady's debts.

So distraut was widow Maria that she sheared her hair off, removed all jewelry and adopted black mourning clothes for the rest of her life. She never remarried. She even talked going into a convent, but that never happened. Maria Theresa did retire for a while, appointing her son co-regent and Emperor. That didn't work out, however. She soon found fault with his liberal plans and took back most of the reins of power.

No Hanky-Panky at Schoenbrunn

Like her contemporaries, Maria Theresa wanted her palace to outshine that at Versailles, where French culture was considered to be the epitome of its time.

She added to the royal residence of Schoenbrunn until it had 1,441 rooms, plus a vast array of stables and out-buildings. There were 139 kitchens required to feed all of the residents and visitors. For music at the glorious balls and recitals at her palace, the boy genius, Mozart, demonstrated his virtuosity by playing sonatas he had composed especially for his royal patroness..

In one respect, life at Schoenbrunn differed sharply from that at Versailles or St. Petersburg. Sex outside marriage was verboten. The standards of sexual morals she insisted upon were undoubtedly the most rigid in all of Europe.

Chaste, devout Maria Theresa even set up a Chastity Commission. Its purpose was ferret out and punish any ladies in her court whose conduct was not impeccable.

Marry Off Those Kids as Political Pawns

Maria Theresa made good use of her flock of children in the political arena. Princesses were destined to become ambassadors that royal parents planted in other kingdoms. There, their purpose was to breed many more offspring so all the palaces in the area would be filled with a mixed-nationality melange of royal cousins, nephews, nieces, etc.

The Hapsburg clan, to which she belonged, had been very successful in spreading its influence in that way. With her 16 kids, Maria Theresa was amply supplied with bridal material to keep the process rolling.

When King Louis XV of France began looking around for a suitable wife for his grandson, that was an opportunity Maria Theresa couldn't pass up. Her 15th child, Maria Antonia, was a very beautiful girl who seemed like an ideal candidate to form a marriage alliance with the powerful Bourbon family of France.

So little Princess Maria Antonia went to France where her name changed to Marie Antoinette. When she traveled to Paris to begin a new life, Maria/Marie entered a fast-moving world and met several strange men named Louis.

Three famous French beauties.
Madame de Pompadour, at top
left, and Madame du Barry at
lower left, were paramours of
King Louis XV. Pictured at the
right, Marie Antoinette became
the Queen of his grandson, the
ill-fated Louis XVI.

26
French Kings, Queens and Mistresses

Perhaps you wonder why French queens and kings should be mentioned in a book that's primarily about the personalities of key people in America's War for Independence. There's a simple answer. America couldn't possibly have won that war without them. No way!

When young Colonel George Washington and his Virginia militia were walloped by French troops in the Ohio Valley wilderness (exactly 20 years to the day before the signing of the Declaration of Independence) little did he dream that the French would some day be his best friends. And ultimately his salvation against the British.

After the American Colonies finally split from England, it wasn't the ill-equipped and poorly-trained amateur colonial warriors that George III and his ministers were afraid of. What they really feared was that the King of France and other European monarchs would take advantage of their difficulties in the New World to cause them trouble. Their fears were justified.

The 15th Louis Put Play Before Work
Louis XV was known as "the well-beloved king" early in his reign, perhaps because he was much more affable than his predecessor had been. That previous monarch, Louis Number 14, became so unpopular that his subjects celebrated when he finally kicked off after a reign of six decades.

Louis XV became king when he was only five years old. His was a strange succession because he took over the throne from his *great-grand-father*. Practically an orphan, his mother and father, brothers and sisters had all perished in one horrible month when the entire family was hit by a severe measles epidemic, made much worse by the royal doctors who finished them all off with brutal bleedings and purgings.

Like great-grand-pa, the little 15th Louis grew up to become a big spender. Under his guidance, the royal court sopped up an incredible amount of the country's income. As much as one quarter of all the government's revenues was diverted to running his vast pleasure palace at Versailles.

Louis had a practical reason for making his palace so big. There he could keep as permanent "house guests" all the powerful noblemen in the country, more than 5,000 of them, so he could watch them and keep them away from their home power bases. But he had to entertain them lavishly, as well as provide mountains of food and rivers of wine, maintain thousands of servants, horses, carriages, etc.

No cheapskate with his girlfriends either, he gave them fabulous allowances for gowns and jewels, an extravagance which helped to keep the royal treasury in a constant state of over-draft..

Q: How did the kings manage to keep up with their bills?
A: They didn't pay them, or put off paying up year after year. Many a poor tradesman was caught in a trap-- he dare not refuse to supply merchandise, yet he had a devilish time trying to collect from the King, and from many other nobles at the court as well.

High-stakes gambling, however, helped the Louies to cover some of their deficits. Huge amounts of cash exchanged hands at the gaming tables, and the lucky Kings of France won more often than not.

Of course, there was a reason for this extraordinary luck. One courtier was bold enough to explain this phenomenon.

"A courtier must be careful to play gallantly in the King's presence. That is to say, he must be sure to lose."

Famous Mistress

Lonely at the death of his mistress, Madame de Chateauroux who expired suddenly of peritonitis at the age of 27, King Louis XV immediately sought another. There were plenty from which to choose; ambitious ladies of the court preened and paraded before His Majesty, hoping they could land an enviable position of wealth and prestige.

To their dismay, Louis was snared by the charms of a woman, who though rich by marriage had come from middle-class beginnings. Born Jeanne-Antoinette Poisson, this charming high-spirited little beauty was married to Monsieur Le Normant d'Etioles. She was a mother too. Her first-born, a boy had died in infancy, but her daughter Alexandrine survived. But, of course, none of that was an obstacle to a liaison with the King, if he wanted her. And he did.

Jeanne-Antoinette, Madame d'Etiolles, possessed a lucious figure, a round face with a lovely complexion, luxuriant light brown hair and sparkling eyes that danced with merriment.

> **"With her grace, the lightness of her figure, the beauty of her hair, she resembled a nymph."**
> Marquis de Valfons

> **"Not a man alive but would have had her for his mistress if he could. She absolutely extinguished all the other women at the court, although some were very beautiful."**
> Dufort de Cheverny

But beauty was not her only attraction; it was matched by a rare intelligence. Regarded as an accomplished singer and dancer, Madame deEtoilles was also recognized as one of the best amateur actresses in France.

She had other talents as well. Her playing on the clavichord was described as delightful. She painted and sketched with better-than-average skill. She designed her own dresses (as did other women of her day). And she was widely admired for designing and overseeing her beautiful flower gardens.

A Job with Unlimited Perks

Even before Louis latched onto her, Jeanne Antoinette had it all. But now she had the King and all the extraordinary perks that came with the job of absorbing his amorous energies.

Her rewards included fabulous clothes beyond counting, plus an outpouring of diamonds and other jewels that literally cost millions. In addition, when the King elevated a woman of ordinary birth to the extraordinary status of his official mistress, he felt obligated to raise her to a title of nobility.

She left her lovely home for the even lovelier premier palace in the world, and became the Marquise de Pompadour. We hear of her most often as Madame de Pompadour.

For the next 20 years, Madame de Pompadour remained not only the King's mistress, but the real power in the country. Bored with chores of state, Louis devoted himself to pleasure while he allowed Pompadour to take over more and more authority. As the person who had to be persuaded if you wanted any project approved, she was called, behind her back, *"the prime minister in petticoats"*.

Love Proves Stronger Than Sex

Charming and wily Madame de Pomapdour managed to maintain her hold over the King even after the sexual attraction between the two of them waned.

Actually, the gossip at Versailles (where courtiers kept informed about *all* aspects of the King's sex life) maintained for years that Pompadour had never been overly enthusiastic in bed. That's understandable because she suffered many miscarriages, and Louis never gave her more than two or three days to recover before starting to work on yet another pregnancy.

Finally, worn-out Pomapadour, encouraged by her doctor, said "enough!". According to snooping courtiers, that was the last of the physical liason between Louis and his beloved mistress. But not of their friendship or her influence.

A Harem of Teen-Agers

To avoid the advent of a new mistress, Pompadour engineered the recruitment of a constant supply of young companions for the randy King. It has even been maintained that she trained them in how to please him. In that way, she managed to keep him sexually satisfied, but still retained her control over him.

The King's young harem became well known to his subjects, as did all the hi-jinks of the ruler and his retinue of fun-loving nobles. The lechery of Louis, his mistress and their playmates were detailed in many scurrilous pornographic pamphlets that kept the printers prosperous and the reading public amused.

Q: What was the Parc-aux-Cerfs?

A: The name meant "Deer Park", but it came to designate specifically a small villa in that area. That unobtrusive house was the private brothel where aging Louis XV spent much of his time being entertained by young prostitutes who often did not even know who their famous visitor was. Louis preferred it that way. The pretty little girls there, often only ten or twelve years old, performed their duties without demanding jewels for themselves or titles for the children they bore. When replaced by new playmates, they received a retirement package of a modest dowry so they could marry a step up from their low-class beginnings.

Even after Pompadour died, the procurement service she set up continued to keep the randy king supplied with pre-teen playmates. Garnered from throughout the kingdom, they supposedly numbered in the thousands over the years.

As with all legends, more than one version exists about the recruiting of the King's child bed partners. There's little doubt that Louis became a pervert addicted to little girls. However, Nancy Mitford, one biographer of Pomapdour, maintains it was not the Marquise but the palace concierge, Lebel, who acted as the procurer for the King.

That may well be, but it was an arrangement that obviously suited Pompadour when she herself was no longer able to satisfy the King's constant sexual appetite. He still loved his mistress, but simply had to have additional services to keep him happy.

Another Flamboyant Mistress

If the French court had been miffed when the 15th Louis picked a middle-class woman, Pompadour, as his mistress, they were horrified at his choice of a replacement. When Pompadour died at the age of 41, of tuberculosis, Louis selected a new paramour who came from a considerably lower background.

The King chose as his new bed-partner a doxy endowed with professional skills in the boudoir department. She was Jeanne Becu, originally a girl of the streets, who had become a hostess at a gambling den which the titled libertines of Paris frequented for a variety of entertainments.

Middle-aged Louis was enchanted and rejuvenated by the erotic talents of the pretty courtesan. Like her predecessor, he bestowed a title of nobility on her. She became the Comtesse du Barry, better known as Madame du Barry.

Despite his early popularity, Louis had earned the hatred of his subjects after neglecting his responsibilities for decades while he and Madame de Pomadour squandered millions of livres on high living. In fact, he was stabbed once on the streets of Paris so neither he nor Pompadour dared travel through the capitol. A special road, circling far beyond the city, was built so they could by-pass Paris when they journeyed from Versailles. You'll still find this circular by-pass today. This street is named the *Avenue de la Revolte* in commemoration of the fact it was built because of fear of an impending uprising against the King and his royal government.

The King's unpopularity increased when he began flaunting his new mistress at every court gathering. By the time innocent Princess Maria Antonia from the prim prudish court of Austria came to France to marry a prince, ex-hooker Du Barry was the number-one female who dominated the French court at Versailles.

Young Queen in Training

Maria Antonia was only 12 years old when the 15th Louis and her mother, the Archduchess of Austria first entered negotiations about marrying her to the French heir. By the next Summer, a deal was agreed upon, and the young Austrian princess began a rigorous preparation for her forthcoming duties.

By the next Spring, the little princess, *accompanied by more than a thousand liveried bodyguards and servants,* rode halfway across the Continent in a awe-inspiring cavalcade of 48 gilded carriages and hundreds of horses. Her satin-lined bridal coach, emblazoned with the carved crowns of two empires, carried the nervous little girl from the center of Hapsburg power to the stronghold of the Bourbons, from whence she would never return.

After days of festivities and a magnificent wedding, the 14-year-old bride was ready to settle in at the work for which this whole rigmarole was arranged-- the production of an heir to tie two empires together. Unfortunately, her 15-year-old partner brought neither the requisite desire or ability to the task.

An Unsuitable Pair
Marie Antoinette was a lovely girl. Unlike most ladies at Versailles, she applied only a touch of powder to her lustrous blonde hair, and scarcely any rouge to enhance her youthful complexion, which was often described as smooth as porcelain. Sparkling blue eyes, pouting mouth, trim figure and bouncing walk drew admiring glances. She was a dish!

In contrast, her husband lacked any graces. Already putting on weight, he had a short thick neck, fat cheeks, pale heavy-lidded myopic eyes, the horsy extra-long Bourbon nose. Already developing some of the waddle that would accentuate as he grew older and still fatter, he was a clumsy kid.

Louis Auguste would never have become heir to the throne if his father, mother and elder brother had not all died within a short time of each other. With that, the 15th Louis had to move grandson Louis August up to Dauphin to perpetuate the Bourbon line. There's no doubt the old king had qualms early on about the lad's suitability for the procreative side of the job. (Other qualities, such as intelligence, were less essential to kingship.) Old Louis had once sadly remarked about his grandson:

"He is not as other men."

The old king's comment about the lad probably alluded to the fact that, unlike Grandpa, he showed no interest in sex. The young

Dauphin's only passion seemed to be for hunting. Every morning, he'd be up at dawn and off on his horse to chase and slaughter the denizens of the royal forests. Sadly for Marie Antoinette, by the time he returned in the evening, he was all pooped out. After a heavy dinner washed down with much wine, her hunter husband plopped down onto his side of the bed and was soon snoring.

When a year of marriage had still not produced any offspring, Marie Antoinette found herself in a precarious position. Old King Louis grew restive with the situation. His mistress Du Barry showed open dislike for the fresh young beauty at the palace. There was talk the King might have to arrange a marriage for some other prince whose wife was able to produce a child who could be made the Dauphin and successor to the throne.

A Public Search for Remedies
Heirs to a throne could expect no privacy at all, Marie Antoinette soon learned. The most intimate details of her marital difficulties were prime subjects for international discussion.

In 1774, they became even more newsworthy. It was then that old Louis XV engaged in a fatal dalliance. Not fully committed to Madame du Barry for all his sexual pleasures, he continued his depravities with his retinue of little girls at the *Parc-aux-Cerfs*. From one of those child concubines he picked up a highly virulent, and fatal, virus.

Some historians say it was the dreaded smallpox; others claim it was merely the juvenile disease of chicken-pox that played havoc with the old pervert's weak immune system-- a fitting retribution for his child molestations. Whatever the cause, one of his baby playmates was evidently the death of him.

That passed the crown to Louis Auguste, who at 16 years of age became King Louis XVI. Immediately, his lack of progeny became an even hotter issue than it had been.

Results at Last.
Various experts had made suggestions for correcting the lack of royal heirs. While Grandfather Louis was still alive, surgeons advised that an operation might loosen up young Louis. The boy shuddered at the thought of facing a scalpel. He managed to evade

that remedy for a while. But finally, after seven years of marriage, the 16th Louis agreed to let the surgeons work on his problem. They solved it and Louis began to get the hang of things. Very soon after that, Marie-Antoinette joyfully announced her pregnancy.

Not only did everyone rejoice in the news of the Queen's pregnancy, but it changed the personality of Louis Auguste. Now proud of his husbandly accomplishments, he began to appreciate his beautiful dutiful wife and to spend time with her.

Their first child was a girl. But even that disappointment in a royal family didn't dampen the King's spirits. Three years later, the Queen was pregnant again. In October of 1781, a Dauphin was born. He was christened Louis Joseph Xavier Francois. In 1785, Marie produced another heir. It was well for the succession that she bore another boy, because the first Dauphin died at the age of six.

Marie Faces Ugly Rumors
By the time Marie Antoinette and the 16th Louis reached their mid-twenties, the king's gorging and drinking had given him a vast protruding belly and multiple chins. His obesity renewed rumors that he couldn't be much of a lover.

Queen Marie Antoinette, though she'd acquired an ample bosom, remained a striking woman with a graceful bearing and her still-exquisite porcelain complexion, so rare in a time when pox marks disfigured many people severely. Among courtiers where extra-marital affairs were taken for granted, the contrast between the two inspired rumors that Marie must be looking afield for affection.

Some of the rumors suggested that numerous handsome men of the court were supplying what King Louis could not. Others insinuated that Marie had Lesbian tendencies. Envious that she spent much time with Madame de Polignac, courtiers whispered that the closeness arose because her friend procured young women for her pleasure.

Ignoring the back-biting, the Queen filled her days with a constant round of partying, dancing and gambling for very high stakes. So passionate was her gambling fever that observers reported she once stayed at the card table for 36 hours straight, though evidently she was not a very skillful player. *At the end of one year, which happened to be 1776, her gambling debts amounted to a hundred million francs.*

But all of Antoinette's time was not spent in enjoying pleasant diversions. Marie also took on some of the political duties her lethargic husband shirked.

Politics Can Be the Death of You

Oppressed citizens of France observed that people in America saw no need to support spendthrift kings, queens and their indolent relatives. They found that enlightening, and they too began to think about getting rid of royalty.

They had much more to gripe about than the American colonists did. In France, the thousands of dukes, marquises, counts and other titled members of the leisure class were excused from paying most taxes. So was the church, which owned huge chunks of the country. You can imagine who had to make up the difference at tax collecting time, which was continuous.

Marie Antoinette, following the tradition of queens, did her part to boost the deficit. In fact, because of her many extravagances and especially her ceaseless purchases of expensive jewels, Antoinette, whom many always referred to by the uncomplimentary title of *"the Austrian Woman"*, earned the added sobriquet of *"Madame Deficit"*. Those names of derision were shouted in the streets when the French revolutionary mobs began to realize their strength and to demonstrate in front of the luxurious palaces of royalty and nobility.

Q: Can you reside where Marie Antoinette did?
A: Yes, if you're willing to spend a bundle for a hotel room. Le Bristol hotel, located just down the street from the Presidential Palace on the Rue du Faubourg St. Honore, was once Marie's town house. At this cozy four-star hostelry furnished lushly with priceless antiques and museum-quality paintings, you and your spouse can be treated like royalty, sometimes at a special bargain rate of a trifle more than a thousand dollars for a weekend.

As France became more involved with the American War for Independence, diverting large sums to help the colonies against Britain, the financial pinch grew more severe. So did resentment against the extravagances of the court.

It's ironic that the rulers of France, by helping the Rebels in America, led to their own demise. Desire for freedom was contagious. And if a British king was expendable, so were the monarchs of France.

The course of the French Revolution is a long story extraneous to this book. You doubtless know that Marie Antoinette lost her head in the bloodbath after the Bastille fell. But did you know that it was the hero of the American Revolution, the Marquis de Lafayette who became part of the French revolt and escorted the Queen and her family to their final jail cell? You'll read more about him later.

Out With a Flourish

As she had lived, Marie Antoinette went out with a flourish. On October 16 in 1793, 30,000 soldiers marched in ranks to guard one unarmed woman on her way to the executioner's block.

The streets were packed solid with Parisiennes; more than 200,000 of them came to celebrate the end of the monarchy. Hawkers of wine and candies shouted their wares. Also for sale were pornographic folders detailing all the supposed wanton indecencies of the Queen. It was a sunshiny fine day for a holiday.

Yet when the cart trundled by carrying Marie Antoinette, a silence fell over the crowd. Her long hair shorn to expose her neck, hands trussed behind her, dressed in a coarse white gown, she didn't appear much like an evil temptress. She looked merely like a lonely woman who'd recently lost her husband and now faced a terrible ordeal.

When the cart halted at the guillotine, Marie Antoinette refused assistance in leaving it and ascending to the platform. No one said a word as she moved quickly up the stairs. There was only one slight hitch. As the Queen walked across the platform to the base of the awesome chopping mechanism, she accidentally stepped on the executioner's foot. The huge man in the black hood swore loudly at the little woman as her heel came down on his toes. Without flinching at his tirade, the Queen turned toward him for a moment with a wisp of a smile for a brief apology... or was it a mockery?

"Forgive me, Monsieur. I did not do it on purpose."

Then she knelt and calmly stretched her pretty neck onto the block in position for him. From beginning to end, Marie Antoinette, for all her regal excesses and extravagances, was a class act. She was a queen to be remembered.

27
Old Papa Franklin Charms the French

Of all Dr. Franklin's myriad achievements, the one that meant the most to our Patriot ancestors was his diplomatic success in Paris after the Revolutionary War got underway. He was the wily old ambassador that America depended upon to inveigle military and financial aid from the British-hating court of King Louis XVI and Queen Marie Antoinette.

Without Franklin's skillful manouvering at the French court, it's likely that the Patriots in the American Colonies would have been *defeated* in their battle for freedom.

America was pitifully short of everything-- money, amunition and supplies, ships (such as those provided for John Paul Jones) and trained soldiers. Our powerful allies, the French, helped us with all those essentials for war. They enabled us to survive, and eventually to win.

Dr. Franklin had served in London for a total of 15 years as a sort of lobbyist. He represented his colony of Massachusetts, and also at times other colonies as well, in their dealings with the British government. He'd spent much of his life in building friendships in London. Of course, after our Declaration of Independence and Ben's timely return to America before the English police could arrest him, his diplomatic skills had to be turned to an entirely new direction.

Now France, the country that had always been the common enemy of both Britain and its colonies, began to look like the best hope of salvation for the American rebels.

A Diplomatic Minuet

Turning relationships completely around between the French and the Americans was not something that could happen quickly. Or easily.

Remember, our Commander in Chief, George Washington, had fought against the French as a young officer in the French and Indian War. In fact, he'd fired the first shots that *started* that war. What's more, neither he nor his fellow Patriots could forget how the French armed and egged on the Indians to massacre American settlers during that conflict-- a tactic the British now began to adopt.

The French also had good reasons to hesitate about a new close friendship with the Americans.

Interested But Cautious

Although they hated the British, who'd bested them in a series of disastrous wars, the French were not anxious to get themselves involved in any new shooting. They'd suffered enough punishment from King George's navy and army, and were ostensibly now at peace with their old enemy. They wanted to keep things that way. So any aid they gave to America had to be done strictly on the quiet.

Another negative that cooled enthusiasm at Versailles was the anti-monarch attitude of American Patriots. After all, Louis XVI was a *king*. Therefore, it bothered him and his queen to see a plebeian rabble declare an uprising against their king, even if he was an English ruler. Such unseemly anti-royal insurrections against God-given authority might stir up similar revolutionary ideas in France, as it actually did in a few years.

Besides, nobody likes to bet on a loser. And the bookies wouldn't have taken a hundred to one odds on America back in 1776. No wonder negotiations between Philadelphia and Versailles moved slowly in an on-again, off-again manner.

Secret Negotiations With A Former Enemy

Secret negotiations for some sort of help from France started even before the Continental Congress signed its Declaration of Independence. King Louis XVI's foreign minister, the Comte de

Vergennes, agreed to supply some munitions and other supplies to the Colonies. But he stipulated that any aid must be given *clandestinely*-- not directly from the French government, but funneled through a dummy company.

A supposedly private firm, Rodrique Horaltez and Company, was set up in Paris to act as the source from which Americans could buy their supplies without paying for them. The new Hortalez' firm's organizer was Pierre Augustin Caron de Beaumarchais. He was an unusual character. Besides being an entrepreuner and hustler, Beaumarchais was the famous dramatist who wrote *The Marriage of Figaro* and *The Barber of Seville*.

Here's an excerpt from the instructions which the French Foreign Minister handed to Beaumarchais regarding the new private company he was to form.

> "The operation must have, essentially in the eyes of the British government, and even in the eyes of the Americans, the aspect of an individual speculation to which we are strangers... We will give you secretly a million livres. We will endeavor to persuade the Court of Spain to unite in giving you another. With these two millions, you shall found a great commercial establishment, and at your own risk and peril you shall furnish to America arms and everything else necessary to sustain war. Our arsenals will deliver to you arms and munitions, but you shall pay for them. You will not demand money from the Americans for they have none, but you can ask return in their staple products."   Comte de Vergennes

The Americans were equally cagey in this matter. The Continental Congress had set up a Secret Committee of Correspondence that could negotiate sensitive matters without public discussion. This Secret Committee asked Pennsylvania's agent in London, Arthur Lee, to handle the early negotiations with Beaumarchais and his Hortalez firm. (Remember that although Colonists were shooting at British soldiers, they were not yet officially at war, and still had diplomatic contacts in London.)

Call On Old Ben Again
So important was the job of obtaining help from France that the Continental Congress decided it required more than the borrowed

efforts of a Pennsylvania diplomat operating out of London. They wanted their own man located right in Paris. So they sent one of their own members, Congressman Silas Deane, to France to join in the negotiations.

Now America had two men assigned to tackle the same job, a type of confused situation that Congress was to repeat in other areas. Usually with poor results.

Lee in London and Deane in Paris didn't correspond clearly or coordinate their efforts. Congress ordered Lee to move to Paris so he could work closely with Deane, but that created no improvement because the two men had become jealous of each other.

As the Continental Congressmen pondered how to fix things, one name kept coming to the fore. Nobody had international contacts like Doctor Franklin. Or as good a reputation for getting results. They told old Ben there was no other choice; he simply had to brave another wearisome and dangerous Atlantic voyage that even young people shuddered to think about.

Ben was 70 years old at the time, and bothered by frequent attacks of gout which confined him to bed and sapped his strength. He'd been looking forward to retiring, not embarking for six-weeks of seasickness and terrible diet.

Q: What did a passenger need to take on a sea voyage?
A: Just about everything, if he or she didn't want to endure a miserable crossing. For example, when John Adams and his son, ten-year-old John Quincy, travelled to his ambassadorial post in France, the two of them took a mountain of supplies. This included two mattresses and bolsters, a barrel of apples to avoid the scurvy, a keg of rum (even though abstemious Adams was considered practically a teetotaler), a bushel of Indian meal, five bushels of corn, 14 dozen eggs, a miscellany of spices, tea. Also a supply of quill pens, ink, tobacco, clay pipes. Perhaps most surprising of all-- six chickens, to provide fresh eggs, and two live sheep. If you had enough money, your chances of surviving a six-weeks voyage could be improved considerably.

Even though he dreaded the prospect of another long voyage, to be followed by a nerve-fraying nightmare of a job, Franklin found it impossible to refuse. He couldn't say "No" when his country needed him. But he expressed reservations about his strength for such a task.

> "I am old and good for nothing. As the store keepers
> say of their remnants of cloth, I am but a fag end.
> You may have me for what you are pleased to give."

In addition to his physical infirmities, Franklin also faced the possiblity of capture by the British. His enemies in Parliament still wanted to arrest the old rebel for treason. Once he got on the high seas, British warships had a good chance of catching him. If they had, that could have been the end of Old Ben, for he was high on the list of Americans the British wanted to see in jail, or on a scaffold.

Off to France

Keeping secrets was not easy to accomplish during the Revolutionary War. Spies were everywhere, plying their lucrative trade. As happens today, some were even double agents, collecting from both sides.

The hush-hush voyage of arch-rebel Franklin didn't stay hushed. In fact, one of Britain's spies reported the proposed trip before it even got underway. Luckily for the good doctor, his ship, the *Reprisal,* made it out of port before it could be intercepted. A 16-gun sloop, the *Reprisal* was the first ship of the new American navy ever to land on the European continent.

Franklin made the trip, safely but far from comfortably. One of his letters spelled out the disastrous results suffered from of an extended diet of salt beef aboard ship.

> "Boils continue to vex me. The Scurf extending all
> the small of my back, on my sides, my legs and my
> arms, besides what continued under my hair."
> Benjamin Franklin, after his voyage

Besides the discomforts of a sea voyage, Franklin also faced a perennial problem of the Patriot efforts. No money. Even this didn't stop Dr. Franklin. In fact, he not only undertook his diplomatic mission with no clear picture of salary or financing, but he took more than 3,000 pounds from his personal bank account and gave it to Congress as a loan. The money would help to buy war supplies before he could get funds flowing from France.

Since Congress and its Secret Committee gave him no funds for any staff, Franklin supplied his own. He enlisted two of his young relatives to come to France with him.

Enlisting Young Relatives
One of his young staff assistants was his grandson, William Temple Franklin. Temple was the illegitimate child of Ben's son William, the Royal Governor of New Jersey who'd just been thrown into jail by Ben's Patriot friends. On much better terms with Ben than his father was, Temple was still a teen-ager, not yet 17.

The second member of Dr. Franklin's entourage was younger still. Benjamin Franklin Bache, only seven years old, was another grandson. He was the child of Benjamin's daughter Sally (Christened Sarah) and her husband Richard Bache.

Dr. Franklin no longer spoke to his Tory son William, whom he'd started on early political careers. But he was determined to continue training members of his family for government service-- the *right* government. Son William had defected to the British, but he'd try again with his two grandsons, lucky lads who'd benefit from the example of a diplomat and Patriot *par excellance.*

The Toast of Paris
The weary septuagenarian finally arrived in Paris to meet with one of his two fellow commissioners, Silas Deane, just before Christmas of 1776. Not only was Deane happy to greet him, but it seemed as if all of France was delighted to welcome *the wonder worker who harnessed the lightning.*

Commissioner Franklin quickly became the celebrity above all others. It was said that average French people knew more about the good Doctor than they did about their own famous countrymen. So great became his celebrity among the Gallic populace that it was remarked upon back home in America, even by some who were not always admirers of Ben.

**"Doctor Franklin seems to be better known
in Paris even than the famous Voltaire"**
John Adams

Franklin's appeal was due not only to his world-wide fame as a scientist. Besides his impressive accomplishments, the French were intrigued by the exotic character of the man they considered to be from the backwoods of America. So entirely different from their idea of a diplomat, they found him fascinating. And utterly charming.

While the courtiers of Europe dressed like peacocks and affected flamboyant manners to match their colorful silken and velvet garments, Old Ben showed up at court wearing an unadorned suit of plain cloth. Instead of a boufant powdered wig and yard-wide plumed hat that every second-rate Parisian nobleman affected, he topped his bald pate and scraggly gray hair with a funny little fur cap. A pudgy pixie with eyes twinkling through the strange bifocal spectacles he'd invented, the eminent Doctor looked less like a diplomat than a typical middle-class grandfather.

Q: Why was Franklin called the "noble savage"?
*A: At the time Franklin landed in France, the "in" author was
Rousseau, who theorized that simple primitive societies
exempified the noblest ideals. Then here came Benjamin, a
genius from the wilds of America, who looked and acted like
a peasant. He was the embodiment, they thought, of
Rousseau's noble savage.*

The newspapers couldn't write enough about him. Ladies of fashion demanded rustic fur caps, like Dr. Franklin's, from their coutouriers. Some had their hairdressers style their wigs in a similar silhouette

Envoy Franklin stimulated business for the purveyors of trinkets and memorabilia. Stacks of copperplate engravings limning the celebrated American were sold to his admirers. Medallions, small sculptures, snuff boxes, porcelain dishes, lockets and rings with his image filled the stores. There were even handkerchiefs decorated with the Franklin silhouette everyone recognized.

Q: How did King Louis react to Ben's huge popularity?
A: He didn't like the idea of anyone receiving more adulation
   than the monarch. It wasn't politic for him to say that his
   subjects had gone overboard for the likeable American
   ambassador, but Louis managed to put in a subtle dig. He
   had an artist take a porcelain chamber pot and paint old
   Ben's portrait on the bottom of it.

Franklin wrote to daughter Sally expressing amazement at the vogue for his images. He deprecated the strange craze. But the unprecedented wave of popularity was certainly a marvelous blessing for an envoy who had come hat in hand to a foreign land to seek favors.

Papa Wows the Ladies

One of the characteristics of Envoy Franklin that added to his admiration by the French was his ability to charm the ladies. Many a younger Parisian envied the appeal the old doctor obviously had for women of all ages. Even the youngest and prettiest seemed to flock to his company.

Ben was old enough to be the grandfather of many of the little darlings he flirted with, so presumably he was safe. But still they found him fun to be with.

The French ladies affectionately called him *Papa,* or even the more affectionate *Mon Cher Papa.* Papa was cute. A witty, interesting conversationalist with his sometimes slightly twisted French. Very famous, of course. Also a bonafide world-class genius, yet not at all highbrow or stuffy or condescending to a non-intellectual girl. On the contrary, he obviously appreciated their company, and complimented them generously on their charms.

Reciprocating, the young Parisian belles loved to fuss over their Papa. Since it was all in fun, they not only flirted outrageously with the old gentleman but vied with each other in hugging him and sitting on his lap. One of his favorite lap-sitters, Anne-Louise d'Hardancourt Brillon de Jouy, is often quoted for her teasing of Papa about this activity.

> **"Do you know, my dear Papa, that people have criticized the sweet habit I have taken of sitting on your lap, and your habit of soliciting from me what I always refuse?"**

Of course, this undecorous cavorting was big news when it reached the western shores of the Atlantic. It shocked some of the more straight-laced citizens of his homeland. When they heard that those loose-moraled Parisian coquettes were wont to sit on Ben's knee and kiss him, in public. *Well!*

Entertaining while soaking was a French custom which appealed to Franklin but horrified his countrymen. Versailles had more than 1200 bathtubs, perhaps as a means of keeping warm in a drafty palace.

Aware of the innuendoes about these supposed shennanigans, Franklin tried to assure his relatives back home that they were much overblown. He once explained that a friendly kiss was generally on the neck, so as not to disturb the paint on the ladies's faces. But he could never convince disapproving (or envious) Americans that such familiarity was merely a harmless foreign custom.

His compatriots were also horrified to learn that old Ben enjoyed the custom of chatting with a French lady while his hostess soaked in a bathtub. It seemed wierd enough to the Americans to hear that anyone would take baths more than once a month, but the idea of women making a daily solon of their bathroom and entertaining visitors while naked under the suds was mind-boggling.

Temple Maintains a Family Tradition

Suspecting Franklin of not-quite-nice amorous activities was a logical conclusion. After all, the males in his family had earned that reputation. You'll recall that Benjamin had sired an illegitimate son, William. And that William in turn had a bastard offspring, William Temple, who now accompanied Ben on his diplomatic mission.

> "Temple is just fit to be employed in a court, and to be the gallant of the French ladies. Nothing else."
> Polly Hewson

Old Ben's reputation as a Ladies Man had much to justify it. His grandson, Young Temple, now upheld the family tradition.

While in Paris with Grandpa, the youth became enamored of Blanchete Caillot, a well-known society woman several years older then he. Mrs. Caillot was the wife of the noted french actor, Joseph Caillot. Blanchette was open in her passion for the young man; she called him her "Little Excellency." Their affair quickly gained extensive coverage in the tabloids, and became the juicy gossip of two continents.

This tempestuous affair resulted, but did not end, with the birth of an illegitimate child. *Temple's son became the third such accident in the Franklin family.* Shocked Americans, such as Franklin's colleague John Adams and his wife Abigail, labeled the whole Franklin family a disgrace to his country. Both of them openly criticized their fellow American. Here are two examples of public statements they made about the Franklin clan.

"He (Franklin) is the founder of a dynasty of bastards!"
John Adams

"They are wicked, unprincipled wretches (Benjamin and Temple) from the old deceiver to the young Cocatrice."
Abigail Adams

Further Misadvenntures of Grandson Temple
Temple, as a young daddy, followed a tradition of negligent child-rearing that he'd experienced from his father. After the war ended, Temple said farewell to both Blanchette and their son, Theophile, and headed back to America with Ben.

Correspondence between Temple and Blanchette indicates he casually invited her and their son to join him in America, but she rejected any idea of living "in a wilderness." Temple never saw his son again. Theophile died as a child.

When that happened, Temple berated Blanchette, via letter, for not taking better care of the boy. That was the end of their relationship.

Temple's amorous escapades didn't end with the early fling in France. He remained a bachelor despite Grandfather Benjamin's efforts from time to time to get him safely married. More than a decade after he left Blanchette, and after Benjamin's death, Temple felt the urge to live overseas again. In England, he became involved in an unusual alliance.

A Complicated Affair in England
When he arrived in London, young Temple Franklin lost no time in establishing a friendship. This time his affair was with Ellen Johnson D'Evelin, the unmarried sister of *his father's wife*. (Who was not Temple's mother, for as you'll recall, William was not married when he sired Temple.) Temple and his sort-of aunt, Ellen, had a baby girl in 1798, whom they named Ellen Franklin.

This instance of Temple conferring the Franklin name on his child points to another strange situation in the clan. Temple himself had never been known by the surname of Franklin until after the

War. Neither his father nor grandfather had officially acknowledged him as a relative. Even though Ben was fond of the youth and brought him to France as his assistant, he was always known as William *Temple*. It wasn't until 1784 that Ben acknowledged Temple as truly his grandson, part of the Franklin clan.

Despite the use of the Franklin name for the baby, Daddy Temple and Mother Ellen didn't get married. On the contrary, in a few months Temple left mother and child in England, while he took off for France.

Again young Franklin never showed any interest in his llegitimate offspring. Fortunately, Temple's father did. William raised little Ellen, *who was both his neice and his grandchild.* A strange situation in a strange family. Assuming those convoluted latter-day escapades of Temple are all clear in your mind, let's get back to the war years and Grandfather Ben the Ambassador to France.

Finally, An End To Fighting

Not until the War wound down-- after the great American victory at Yorktown at the end of September in 1781-- could Envoy Franklin even begin to think about returning home.

By that time, he had wheedled a steadily growing flow of money, munitions and fighting men from Europe. At the climaxing battle of Yorktown, it was French warships that drove away the British fleet, and French soldiers who made up half the regiments that vanquished the Redcoats of Cornwallis.

After that humiliating defeat involving the surrender of 7,000 British troops, King George and his ministers no longer had any stomach for pushing the war in America. Peace overtures began the following April, but they moved slowly.

Four Peace Commissioners were appointed by the Continental Congress to represent the Colonies in the negotiations. They were John Adams, John Jay, Henry Laurens and Benjamin Franklin. However, Adams was in the Netherlands to get a loan and a treaty of commerce; Jay was on a mission in Spain; Laurens was still in the Tower of London as a prisoner of war following his capture by a British warship on his way to Europe. For several months, that left Franklin as the only one of the peace quartet on hand to get negotiations rolling.

It was not until November of 1782-- more than a year after Lord Cornwallis' surrender at Yorktown-- that a preliminary treaty was signed. This was not a treaty with a new nation, for none existed as yet, but with a loose confederation of 13 formerly-British Colonies. The important point was that Britain finally agreed to recognize American independence. That included agreement to clear out of the Colonies "with all convenient speed."

Home At Last
Not until July of 1785 did Benjamin Franklin finally return to America, eight and a half years after his arrival as a special envoy from the Continental Congress to the courts of Europe. Altogether, with his two earlier stints in England representing individual Colonies, he'd spent a total of about 24 years as a diplomat abroad.

In that nearly quarter of a century, Doctor Franklin had inevitably become closer to his many friends overseas than to the ones of long ago in America. He hated to leave them. Those he'd lived with so long in France begged him to finish out his days there. His friends in England wanted him to settle there.

France almost won out. It's believed that Ben proposed marriage to an elderly widow, Madame Helvetius, whom he'd admired for years. However, Madame Helvetius declined the offer. With that possibility gone, Franklin Benjamin was swayed by his desire to once again see his native land and especially Philadelphia, the city he'd always loved.

> **"The French are an amiable people to live with. They**
> **love me and I love them. Yet I do not feel myself**
> **at home, and I wish to die in my own country."**
> Benjamin Franklin

Dr. Franklin's departure from France was a memorable occasion throughout that country. There were numerous farewell parties hosted by famous friends. The whole little town of Passy, the Paris suburb where he'd lived for the past eight and a half years, turned out to see him off on his journey back home.

Even Queen Marie Antoinette expressed concern over the state of his health (his kidney stones were so painful they often kept him in bed) and the long fatiguing trip he faced. To ease the bumpy ride he faced from Paris to shipboard at Le Havre, the Queen provided the eminent diplomat with her own litter, an elegant canopied and curtained bed slung between two mules.

Traveling in such regal style and the ultimate in comfort then available, the pampered semi-invalid took five days to make the trip to the harbor. Every evening along the way, he dined with old friends and dignitaries who ranged from diplomats to cardinals. His entourage, including numerous coaches for friends accompanying him and for a mountain of luggage, truly resembled the convoy of a monarch. King Louis himself could scarcely have created more of a stir on that journey, and surely not nearly so much genuine affection.

Pudgy, homespun, plain-talking old Papa Franklin had come to France as a humble petitioner. He left it as a beloved conqueror.

End of a Long Career
After a brief stop in England, again to say farewell to friends, Franklin finally set sail for America. Six weeks later, his ship anchored in the familiar waters of Delaware Bay. The next morning, he was able to hobble down the gangplank to the Market Street Warf where a crowd gathered to cheer as Philadelphia's most famous citizen came home. The partiarch was 79 years old. It had been more than 60 years since he'd first settled in the Quaker City.

Franklin's last years were good. He was able to relax a bit, but that was difficult for him because so many organizations and societies he'd founded called on him to speak at their meetings. These included the university he'd founded, the fire company he'd started, and the American Philosophical Society.

He was elected President of Pennsylvania's state legislature. In 1787, he accepted his last important govenmental assignment. A Constitutional Convention was convened then at Philadelphia to design the rules and legal structure for a new nation that would replace a coalition of 13 separate governments. Benjamin Franklin, one of the most revered citizens of the land, served as a major influence in drafting the laws that still govern the United States of America.

Busy to the End
Even to his last days, Benjamin Franklin remained a prolific writer. He also kept busy in remodeling his house that had been long neglected, and in overseeing the planting of gardens and landscaping. He enjoyed playing cards and chess. Of course, he enjoyed music, sometimes performing for audiences on the melodious Armonica he'd invented.

Alert and inquisitive as always, Dr. Franklin never stopped thinking of new solutions to every-day problems. Now old and rather feeble physically, he aimed his intellect at easing chores he found difficult. One gadget he developed was a pole with a grip on the end that enabled him to reach up to top shelves in his library to bring down a book. Another was a fan, operated by a foot treadle, that he built onto his favorite chair-- a device that could be considered an early attempt at air conditioning.

One of Benjamin Franklin's last projects was his active participation in an anti-slavery campaign. Pennsylvania had long been ahead of other areas of the country in such efforts. In 1790, an anti-slavery group of which Franklin was a member, presented to the U.S. House of Representatives a petition to abolish slavery. That petition wasn't well received, but Franklin battled for it by writing newspaper articles in its support.

A Nation Mourns
By this time, Franklin was in very poor health and in constant pain which doctors tried to alleviate with opium. The final blow was an abcess on his lung. When that burst, Benjamin Franklin was finished. He died on April 17, 1790, just three months past the age of 84.

At his death, members of the U.S. House of Representatives agreed to wear mourning for a month. The Senate didn't go along with this idea. Neither did President Washington because he felt it would set a precedent that would cause controversy.

In France, however, the National Assembly voted unanimously to wear signs of mourning for three days. That was a hectic time in

France, just before the bloodbath at the Bastille erupted, yet a leader of the government took time to exress sorrow at the death of a man who'd come to be regarded almost as one of their own citizens.

> **"Franklin is dead. He has returned to the bosom of God, the genius who has liberated America and shed over Europe the torrents of his light."**
> Comte de Mirabeau

28
Not Worth a Continental

As this book is written, economists in the United States are concerned that our rate of inflation might rise from a comfortable level of about three percent annually to a dangerous four or five percent per year. At times during the Revolution, inflation zoomed five percent *each day!*

How'd you like to be a family of moderate means then, living on a fixed income? Or a soldier receiving no pay for months, with a family back home? No wonder our glorious Revolutionary War was an unpopular nightmare for many Americans, while a boon for profiteers who knew how to stuff their pockets.

What caused this economic disaster that so greatly affected the private lives of all the American men and women who are described in this book?

Who's in Charge?
As with many of the problems that plagued our country's first war effort, the rampant inflation started with a lack of responsibility. No one had control of the monetary system at the start of the war. In fact, there was no central financial or banking system-- not even a nation-wide currency.

Thirteen not-very-closely-bonded colonies had gotten together and agreed to start the revolt, some very reluctantly. They told George Washington and his troops to go win it, but they didn't set up any system to finance the effort. Then the delegates of the Continental Congress who signed the grand Declaration of Independence took off for home. By 1776, more than half of those who participated in the decisions that led to the Declaration had left the Congress in Philadelphia, never to return.

The individual colonies were supposed to come up with all the funds for the war, as needed. They didn't.

Start the Printing Presses

When it became obvious that contributions from the individual colonies would be sporadic-- which didn't take long to figure out-- the Congress agreed to create its own Continental currency. That was a step forward, but not a real solution.

A deluge of paper currency was printed. It's lack of value gave rise to the phrase "not worth a Continental."

For one thing, the central government didn't own anything. The only backing for the new currency was Congress' *promise* to pay, which wasn't worth much.

In 1776, there was reasonable doubt that the Continental Congress had many more months of life in it! General Washington had been driven out of Long Island, and the British were chasing him toward our capital, Philadelphia. Once they controlled that headquarters city, what good was our money? Nevertheless, Congress continued to print the Continental currency. By the end of 1776, the presses had churned out more than $25 million of it. Which depreciated rapidly.

The deluge of paper money continued. Congress printed $63 million. in 1778 and $140 million in 1779. This was not good for its value, and the phrase "not worth a Continental" was widely used, as the true worth of the notes went down and down.

A dollar was worth 33 cents in 1777...
12 cents in 1779...
2 cents in 1780...
less than 2 cents by 1790

Merchants, often forced to accept the questionable currency, papered their walls with it to show what they thought of its value. Debtors liked the almost-worthless scrip though. Legally, it was worth face value. Legally, they could pay off large debts with a handfull of scrip that actually had little true worth. The authorities would back them up if lenders objected. Unlucky George Washington was one who got thoroughly taken to the cleaners in this mess.

Q: How did Washington get stuck with scrip?
A: Those who bought produce from his farms often wanted to pay for it with debased currency. Righteous George felt that, in his position, he couldn't refuse the worthless legal tender, even though many of his neighbors did. Yet when he bought, sellers insisted on real coin from him. He was caught in the middle.

1,000 to One
The slogan of the day, followed by everyone who could enforce it, was *"plate, not scrip."* Plate was the common term for real gold or silver money, such as the highly-valued Spanish doubloons. If you had that, your purchasing power was greatly multiplied.

Specie was another term for money with real value. By the end of the war, most of the states were trying to finance their affairs with Bills of Credit or Notes, which promised repayment in specie. For example, even relatively prosperous Virginia printed Pound

Notes which supposedly could be redeemed in the future for specie. Virginia's promise was that $40 in its notes would be redeemed for $1 in hard coin. Maybe that doesn't sound like a very good ratio, but even that was overly optomistic.

Since nobody wanted to accept Virginia's notes at 40 to 1, the state officials were forced to get realistic. They revised the value ratio to $1,000 in notes for each dollar of real money.

Merchants Print Their Own Money

Virginia's monetary problems were no isolated example. Merchants in Philadelphia became so disgruntled by the lack of a dependable currency for conducting business that they decided to start their own bank. They raised a capital fund of more than a million dollars and opened the Bank of Philadelphia. It was bolstered by the reputations of that city's leading merchants and financiers, who were more solvent than the Continental government!

Certificates of indebtedness, much like our checks, drawn on the Bank of Philadelphia were widely accepted as a sound currency. Government officials, including George Washington, saw this bank operation as a wonderful solution to their problem of bastardized official currency. They urged merchants in other financial centers to set up similar banks, but none did.

Up Go the Price Tags

As both the Continental currency and State notes sank in value, the prices of everything rose proportionately. That made it harder and harder to finance the war, so more and more money was printed. It was a vicious circle.

Of course, not only the government felt the pinch of inflation. Everbody who bought anything got hurt by escalating prices.

Food became expensive. Anything imported was especially high in price. One report showed that a pair of woolen stockings cost more than a hundred dollars. Shoes became prohibitively costly. Even relatively wealthy Thomas Jefferson complained that necessities of life were getting beyond reach-- he paid $355 for three bottles of brandy.

George Washington's expense accounts, which you read about earlier, included proof of the trend of prices. Amounts he paid for basic supplies for himself and his staff seem terribly high, even to us accustomed to modern price levels.

The period during the war and shortly thereafter was a disastrous but fairly brief aberration in the economy. We think of prices as being very cheap in early days of our country. They were. Then they shot up incredibly as our brand-new little nation undertook a war against a rich country several times larger in population and assets. At war's end, after things got straightened away, prices settled down to the levels of a couple of pennies for a loaf of bread that persisted for several generations thereafter.

Mobs and Riots

One of the most bitter examples of resentment against inequities was a mob attack which occurred in Philadelphia late in 1779. This attack was directed against James Wilson, one of the signers of the Declaration of Independence, who had become a power in Pennsylvania politics.

Rich lawyer and land speculator Wilson had not endeared himself to patriots by acting as defense attorney for several Loyalists accused of aiding the Crown. He further infuriated people as leader of the aristocrats in the Pennsylvania legislature. He was among those who were determined to write strong conservative provisions into the new constitution for the Commonwealth. At a time when there was a great deal of financial distress and even actual hunger in the community, his autocratic views stirred up a considerable amount of anger.

It reached such a pitch that a riot ensued. A shouting mob of radical constitutionalists, including many militiamen, surrounded Wilson's house at Third and Walnut Streets in Philadelphia, while he and 35 political colleagues were meeting there. When the mob began hurling rocks, Wilson and his friends barricaded themselves in his house, which came to be known as *Fort Wilson*. The mob attack increased in violence.

Gradually the confrontation moved from throwing stones to firing muskets. Before the ruckus ended, several people were wounded and a few were killed. In the 1770s, a political battle could mean precisely that-- a real battle..

Beware of Counterfeit

A seldom-mentioned problem that plagued the financial health of our young nation was a flood of counterfeit currency. What made the influx of illegal money really sizeable and hurtful was that government was behind it. Not our government-- the British government.

Q: Why did the British print fake money?
A: Counterfeiting the enemy's money is a basic weapon of war. The Nazis did it to Britain during World War II; the British did it to America in 1776. It raises hell with the economy, and also provides free financing for undercover agents.

One busy counterfeiting press was conveniently located aboard a British ship, the Phoenix, anchored in New York harbor early in 1776. No danger of the cops raiding that operation! The notes from this nautical enterprise were sneaked out to receptive Tories in nearby areas, who were much in need of financial help and happy to receive bundles of currency.

There were also money-printing plants ashore, of course. Some must surely have been established by skilled and felonious tradesmen who saw a chance to profit hugely from an opportune situation. However, the King's officers gave all the help they could, and counterfeiters tended to claim they were merely loyal servants of the Crown. They said they were merely doing their patriotic duty to foil the rebellion against Britain and her administrators in the American Colonies.

Trouble for the States

Not only Continental currency, but also that of the states was easy and tempting for private or enemy printers to duplicate. Many states had death penalties against counterfeiting of their bills of credit.

Death to Counterfeit was a phrase that appeared on the bills of several states. South Carolina printed it *twice* on the back of each bill it issued, but there's no evidence that the double warning stopped the illegal practice.

Some of the counterfeiters did a volume business. Isaac Youngs and Henry Dawkins ran a thriving operation with a good engraving of Connecticut currency before they were caught. John Power of Massachusetts, an Irishman skilled in engraving, was supposed to have circulated millions in phoney paper bills. He claimed that he churned out all this funny money only to fulfill his patriotic duty as a loyal British subject, doing his best to serve his sovereign, King George, and his native land he loved.

Whatever the reasons, the fake money flowed freely. It added to the flow from the legal presses. Together, the two streams of cash floated the rate of inflation to ever greater crests.

Painful Reality for Veterans

Soldiers returning home after the War were the people hit hardest by inflation. Their separation pay, often for arrears that had accumulated for many months, was a handful of colorfully-printed Continental currency with almost no value.

When they offered those notes to merchants for the many things they needed to reestablish themselves in civilian life, the soldiers received a rude shock. Merchants told them to wake up to reality. Coins, plate, specie was needed to buy anything-- not Continental currency which was worthless.

As the returning veterans looked around, they saw those who had stayed away from the battlefields living a comfortable life. Shops were overflowing with imported luxury goods, which the veterans couldn't afford to buy.

Revolt After the Revolt

The bulk of the returning veterans couldn't even vote in the democracy they'd bled for! Not one of the states offered universal voting rights, even to men. Women, of course, were excluded.

To vote or hold office, you had to prove you owned property, which might be in the form of either land or cash. Or, if you paid taxes, that indicated that you were a person of means. A frequent standard set for voting rights was that you had to be worth $50, which was the price of a good-sized farm before the war. Few returning soldiers had that much cash or property.

Scandalous as the lack of universal suffrage many seem to us, it wasn't the main thorn that hurt the soldiers. The flaunted affluence of many men who'd evaded the fighting was what really bothered them.

The war had generated a host of loud nouveu riche who piled up wealth during the years when others struggled and starved. These profiteers dressed richly and lived ostentatiously. That really rankled as inflation reached its worst late in the War, when many veterans began to return home to actual food shortages.

There was great celebration throughout the Colonies when the War finally ended. Men could take off their uniforms, which some had worn for as long as *eight* years, and return to their families.

Yet for many veterans and civilians alike, the end of shooting didn't mean the end of uncertainty. The big question on everyone's mind was, "Now that we're free of England and on our own, *what do we do next?*

29
More Headaches for Thomas Jefferson

Like his friend Benjamin Franklin, whom he succeeded as Minister to France, Thomas Jefferson played a key role in the shaping of a new nation at the end of the Revolutionary War. Also like his friend from Philadelphia, the Virginian was a multi-faceted personality-- a genius in several fields, a complex individual, a dedicated public servant, a controversial character with a host of critics as well as a multitude of admirers.

One of our 20th Century presidents aptly summed up the brilliance of our third president. At a dinner to which he'd invited a group of Nobel Prize winners, he greeted his distinguised guests with this two-edged statement designed to both flatter them and keep their talents in perspective.

> **"I think this is the most extraordinary collection of talent and human knowledge, that has ever been gathered together at the White House...with the possible exception of when Thomas Jefferson dined here alone."**
> John F. Kennedy

By anyone's criteria, Jefferson rates as one of the all-time greatest of Americans. Here are some of his accomplishments.

1773... Member of Virginia Comittee of Correspondence
1775... Delegate to Second Continental Congress
1776... Wrote the Declaration of Independence
1776... Drafted a Constitution for Virginia
1777... Elected Governor of Virginia (at age 24)
1782... Appointed to Peace Commission

1785... Succeeded Franklin as Minister to France
1789... Proposed Bill of Rights to U.S. Constitution
1790... Became Washington's Secretary of State
1796... Elected Vice-President of the U.S.
1797... President of American Philosphical Society
1798... Acknowledged as leader of Republican Party
1801... Became the Third President of the U.S.
1803... Doubled size of U.S. with Louisiana Purchase
1804... Sold his library, to become Library of Congress
1815... Founded the University of Virginia

During all this demanding activity, Jefferson was also a farmer, innovative architect, musician, inventor and a prolific writer. You can read about Jefferson's myriad achievements in literally *hundreds* of histories and biographies, as well as in his Autobiography. There's no need to duplicate that voluminous well-known material here. Instead, let's take a look at some unusual aspects of this famous American's life that few people are aware of.

Not What You Imagine
If you read the history books, or visit our nation's capital city and view a giant marble figure seated so impressive and serene in a softly-lighted monument, it's easy to imagine the adulation Jefferson received from his grateful countrymen throughout his long public career.

Wrong!

If you visit lovely Monticello perched high on a Virginia hillside, you're likely to envy the rich country squire who resided there, obviously free from the financial worries that so often plague us ordinary folks.

Wrong again!

Jefferson suffered about as many personal and public travails as any famous figure you can imagine. He may have been the most battered president the United States has ever had. In addition, he suffered no end of financial problems. And like his friend Franklin, his relationships with women stirred up constant scrutiny and criticism.

An Old Scandal Ressurected

You might suppose that when Jefferson was young, the tall, good-looking, sports-loving lad who was fond of partying could take his pick from swarms of pretty Virginia belles. That's not the case. As a youth, shy, gangly "Tall Tom" Jefferson had little luck with the ladies of his community.

His earliest recorded attempts at romance were a flop. Stories of another very strange early romantic attempt surfaced many years later, after Jefferson had become president. The details and authenticity of it aren't at all clear, but when one becomes a leading political figure, the reality of old adventures aren't likely to stop a juicy story in the tabloids.

As the story goes, young Jefferson became obsessed with the wife of his good friend, Jack Walker. In fact, Jack was such a good friend that Jefferson selected Tom to be one of the groomsmen at his wedding.

Presumably, ardent Tom propositioned Betsy Walker on several occasions, but she never reciprocated and never told her husband about these advances. It was not until many years later, after Jefferson became famous, that Betsy couldn't resist telling some of her lady friends how much the President had desired her in his youth.

Of course, the rumors then spread until they reached husband Jack, who demanded a complete accounting. He talked about "getting satisfaction" (which meant a duel) to settle the old affronts to his wife. That never transpired. He did, however, make a public statement about the supposed affair. That became prime material for the gossip writers and a great embarrassment for the President.

Jefferson denied the accusations, and eventually they faded away.

Fun in France

In 1785, three years after his wife's death, Jefferson succeeded Benjamin Franklin as our Ambassador to France. Like Ben before him, Thomas enjoyed both the intellectual life of Paris and the charming women of that city.

Always basically a shy man, Thomas may not have been quite such an overwhelming success with the ladies. At least, Ben couldn't resist a joke in that regard. When the two old friends were reunited in Paris and the old ambassador packed up to leave, Jefferson observed with some envy how the ladies of all ages were smothering Mon Cher Papa with their farewell hugs and kisses. He said to Ben, "I hope you'll transfer those privileges to me as the new ambassador."

Ben's reply,"No, you are too *young* a man for that."

Although widower Jefferson never did achieve the nation-wide affection that was showered on Old Ben, he managed to brighten his stay in France with romances. For sure, he had one affair that raised eyebrows back in America, though fewer among the understanding Gauls.

He was also involved in a second romance, still widely discussed today, about which there was no certainty but a mountain of scandalous speculation.

Lucious Mrs. Cosway

The first lady to rekindle a romantic spark in widower Jefferson was an English woman. Maria Louisa Catherine Cecilia Hadfield Cosway was an enchanting blonde with big blue eyes and delicate features. A well-known artist like her husband, she had recently come to Paris with him because of a portrait commission.

Q: How did Richard Cosway get his money?

A: Maria's husband was a miniaturist painter who garnered a lot of cash from a special sideline for which he was famous. He charged extravagant prices for painting pornographic pictures on snuffboxes. His naughty snuffboxes were much in demand.

When tall distinguished Thomas was introduced to petite vivacious Maria, sparks flew at first glance. Not only was she pretty with a trim graceful figure and always fashionably-dressed, but Maria also possessed the intelligence and talents that appealed to intellectual Jefferson. She spoke several languages, read widely, and like the American diplomat was an accomplished musician and lover of music.

Her husband, Richard Cosway, was no hindrance to the romance. Her friends generally agreed that the beautiful Maria, encouraged by her ambitious mother, had married the little pipsqueak for his money and not for love. He was 17 years older than Maria-- a year older than Jefferson.

If Maria had ever felt any initial fondness for Richard, it faded quickly. After their marriage, she discovered that the pornographer was having numerous affairs with other women. And with quite a few handsome young men as well, it was rumored.

A Passionate Affair

Jefferson, the 43-year-old diplomat, and his lovely 27-year-old friend were reported to carry on like teen-agers. They cancelled business appointments, and spent many days and evenings together. If husband Richard noticed at all, he was too busy with his girlfriends and boyfriends to pay much attention.

Strictly laudatory biographers, who tend to see heroes like Jefferson as 100 percent virtuous, have trouble in reporting on Tom's sporting with married Maria, or other affairs mentioned earlier and later in this chapter. However, Jefferson himself made it difficult to ignore this affair. Secretive as he always was about personal matters, he preserved copies of correspondence to and from Maria. This is strange, since he burned all the love letters he wrote to his wife.

When Maria's husband took her back to England, Thomas travelled to Italy for a while. During this separation the lovers wrote to each other constantly.

> " Why were you not with me? Come then, my dear
> Madam, and we will breakfast every day a l'Anglois
> ... dine under the bowers of Marly, and forget
> that we are ever to part again."   Thomas

> "My heart is full, ready to burst. Your letter could
> employ me for some time, an hour to consider every
> word, to every sentence I could write a volume
> ... Your letters will never be long enough."   Maria

"The way will ever be wrong which leads us farther apart."
Thomas, urging Maria to sail to America with him

**"Pray write, pray write & don't go to America
without first coming to England."**   Maria

A Hopeless Affair

Gradually the hopelessness of their affair became apparent to both Thomas and Maria.

A devout Catholic, Mrs. Cosway was troubled by her adultery and not prepared to leave her husband (though she did so eventually, and founded a nunnery). Also, she was obsessed with fear of a pregnancy during her trysts with Jefferson.

For his part, Jefferson had too many responsibilities back in America to turn his back on them all. Gradually he cooled his ardor too, though he and Maria continued to correspond for a while. Eventually he moved along the political path to become Vice-President and then President of the United States, which made strange liasons unwise.

His affair with Maria was enjoyed thoroughly by the gossips in Paris. Some rumors of it reached the shores of America as well, but caused no great stir here. However, another romantic adventure of Jefferson's resulted in quite a ruckus.

Lovely Slave-Girl Sally

After Jefferson's wife Martha died, a striking reminder of her remained in his household. This was young Sally Hemmings, her vivacious half-sister, known to everyone at Monticello as Dashing Sally.

A product of the loose sexual habits of John Wayles, Thomas Jefferson's slave-dealer father-in-law, Sally was of mixed white and African blood. Even though she shared the parentage of Thomas's wife, under law she was a *slave girl* in the household.

When lecherous Daddy Wayles died, he'd willed his slaves to daughter Martha. Six of these were reputed to be children of his mulatto mistress, Elizabeth Hemmings. One boy, David Hemmings, became Thomas' personal servant. Dashing Sally became the governess to her white half-sister's young children.

After Jefferson had been in Paris for about four years, a violent whooping cough epidemic in Philadelphia killed one of his daughters. Terrified for the safety of his remaining child, Martha, he ordered that she come to Paris with slave-girl Sally as her escort.

By this time, little Sally had grown to be a strikingly beautiful young woman of 16. A light-skinned quadroon, she was intelligent, effervescent and easily mistaken for a Caucasian. She had a lovely olive complexion, long straight auburn hair, a classic profile, the manners and bearing of a refined lady.

There was said to be a considerable resemblance between dusky-skinned Sally and her half-sister, the beloved wife Thomas had lost.

Daughter Martha and Sally lived in Paris with Ambassador Thomas for about a year until he returned to America. While abroad, Sally tasted the freedom of living in a non-slave society. Reportedly she was treated as a family member and dressed in the latest Parisian fashions.

Were They Lovers, Or Not?

Abigail Adams, in Paris with her husband John, had always been critical of the morals of Ambassador Benjamin Franklin. Now she transfered her suspicions toward the affairs of the new ambassador, Thomas Jefferson, and was especially critical of his relationship with his daughter's pretty governess.

According to Abigail, the 46-year-old widower was entranced by the way pretty teen-ager Sally, 30 years younger than he, had blossomed to womanhood. She urged Ambassador Jefferson to send Sally back to America, but that was something which he refused to do.

When tales of too-close companionship within the Jefferson household began to circulate in America, both Abigail and John Adams stated publicly that the rumors were true.

When the entourage returned to Virginia, Sally stirred up some speculation. She was beautifully dressed-- not at all in accepted fashion for a slave girl-- and visibly pregnant. She bore a son named Tom. The boy grew to be a tall and lanky lad, so much like the master of the mansion that it's said people often mistook one for the other when they saw them at a distance.

Accusations and Denials

With his customary stoic reticence, Jefferson stayed silent and tried to ignore the gossip. That was impossible. Now that he'd become a leading political figure in the nation, he was fair game.

As the years went by, the rumors about Jefferson and his Dashing Sally only increased. They really escalated when the leading scandal-monger journalist, James Callendar, launched a vendetta against Jefferson. This muck-raker was a busy man who worked all sides. He averred that Jefferson had subsidized him and encouraged him to attack Washington and Adams in the press, after the three old friends split over party differences. (Does that sound like present-day shenanignas?)

However, the ties between Callendar and Jefferson soon unravelled. When Callendar got himself into legal trouble, his buddy President Jefferson made no attempt to help him out of it. So the journalist turned on him. He announced to the world that Jefferson had been his backer in attacks on other political figures.

Callendar also came out full blast in airing the Sally Hemmings Affair. Shortly thereafter, miffed Callendar also resurrected the old supposed affair between Thomas and his friend Jack Walker's wife.

Federalist newspapers throughout the country jumped on the Sally Hemmings Scandal. Poems and songs were even written to immortalize the affair. Here's an excerpt.

> **Of all the damsels on the green,**
> **On mountain or in valley,**
> **A lass so luscious ne'er was seen**
> **As Monticellan Sally.**
>
> **Yankee Doodle, who's the noodle?**
> **What life were half so handy?**
> **To breed a flock of slaves for stock,**
> **A blackamoor's the dandy.**
>
> **When pressed by load of state affairs,**
> **I seek to sport and dally.**
> **The sweetest solace of my care**
> **Is in the lap of Sally.**
> **Tucked up between a pair of sheets,**
> **There's no perfume like Sally.**

Jefferson refused to answer any questions about Sally Hemmings, even though their relationship became the talk of the nation. His daughter Maria (Christened Mary and often called Polly) gave reasons why no affair could have taken place. In addition, his grand-daughter, in a letter not made public until 1974, made the same claim. She maintained that Sally's children were sired by one of Jefferson's nephews-- either Peter Carr or his bother Samuel, both randy young men reputed to know intimately many pretty slave women in the area.

Eventually, other events pushed the nasty scandal out of the news. The Louisiana Purchase, addings millions of acres to the United States, became the big excitement. To Jefferson's relief, the heat about the Sally Hemmings scandal died down.

Never-Ending Questions
More than two centuries after the alleged Hemmings/Jefferson romance, questions continue to be raised about it. A theatrical play launched in 1995 headlined Sally Hemmings as its star.

Early biographers tended to accept daughter Maria's stories and ignore possibilities that their hero could have been a secret miscegenist. They back up her claim that one of Jefferson's nephews, known for such bi-racial adventures, sired Sally's several pale-skinned children. However, as other historians delve into old records, some of them conclude that Maria's version of events do not always jibe with reality.

Their view is that Thomas and Sally did in fact enjoy a 38-year intimate and happy relationship while she was ostensibly only the housekeeper who ran the household for the widower at Monticello. Some of the facts that have been uncovered over the years make for a confusing story.

Sally bore seven children. She had four sons and three daughters, two of whom died. All the survivors were given training in a useful trade. They also received some academic education, probably along with Jefferson's grandchildren. At a time and place when slaves were *forbidden by law* to learn to read, this was a very radical thing for a Virginia planter to do. Conversely, Jefferson held radical views about many things, including slavery.

A Coincidence of Timing

A recent author, Annette Gordon-Reed, has devoted an entire book, *Thomas Jefferson and Sally Hemmings,* to unravelling the mystery of their relationship. Her conclusion is that a long-lasting love affair undoubtedly existed.

Among many factors this researcher cites is her calculations of the very strange timing of Sally's several pregnancies. During Jefferson's frequent lengthy absences from Monticello, Sally *never* became pregnant. But when he returned, *and only during his brief returns*, the beginning of another nine-month incubation would occur. As Gordon-Reed points out, if one of the lecherous Carr brothers were doing all this repeated implanting, wouldn't he be chasing Sally at least sometimes while his Uncle Thomas was away -- not just when Uncle was around to perhaps be aware of the hanky-panky?

Sally's Son, Madison, Stirs Up the Scandal

Much of the continuing Jefferson-Hemmings gossip was based on allegations by Sally's son, Madison, who told an Ohio newspaper that he was Thomas' child. But Madison's stories are particularly suspect by those who doubt the scandal. They point out that Madison and one other of Sally's children were born in Jefferson's later years, *after* the charges first surfaced and *after* he became president. "Wouldn't it be strange," they ask, "for Thomas to continue such a controversial affair after it had been widely publicized and everyone would be on the alert for any further hanky-panky?"

Nevertheless, Madison and his descendents have stuck by their claims. They say that while in France, Sally delighted in the freedom from racial prejudice she discovered there, and refused to return home with her master/lover until he promised to manumit her children when they reached the age of 21. This raises the question, "If Jefferson truly loved Sally, did he follow through, as Madison claims, and free her children as they came of age?"

It's obvious that if dusky Sally really was Jefferson's mistress, he couldn't possibly acknowledge her as such. Not and remain in

Virginia or in politics. And not without subjecting Sally, her children, and even himself to physical harm.

Did Jefferson Keep His Promise?

There's evidence that Jefferson freed Sally's children as they reached maturity. Whether it was to keep the sort of promise that Madison Hemmings described, or only out of humanitarian principles, all her children eventually disappeared from Monticello.

Two of the mixed-blood children were listed as runaways, but the customary reward was not offered for their capture and return. Another simply vanished from the carefully-kept property records of the estate when he turned 21. Her two remaining children were freed at Jefferson's death. Madison wrote that one of his brothers and a sister moved to Washington D.C. and there passed as white.

What happened to Sally? In Jefferson's will, she was not freed as her remaining children were. Had she been, Virginia laws would have forced her to leave the State, as most of her children did. Legally bequeathed to Thomas' daughter, Sally stayed at Monticello for two years. Thereafter, she lived in a small house near Monticello for the last seven years of her life.

One biographer searched the old census rolls of Albemarle County where he found that, in the midst of slave country, home-owner Sally Hemmings was listed as white.

The questions and controvery about Thomas and Sally will never end. As with many historical accounts, you can choose from a variety of scenarios and believe what you prefer.

Another Personal Tragedy

Jefferson, the widower who never remarried, doted on his two daughters, Martha and Maria. Therefore, Maria's tragic death at the end of his first term as president was a blow he never completely got over.

Daughter Martha was the mother of six healthy children. But as with so many women in the 18th century, Maria Jefferson Eppes had trouble with child-bearing. And as often happened, having children proved to be the death of her.

Maria underwent three pregnancies in five years. The first child died. Her second, a daughter named Francis and the only one of her offspring who lived to adulthood, was two and a half years old when the young mother faced her third delivery.

A month after the birth of child number three, Maria became ill. The month after that, she died, at the age of 25. Jefferson was shattered, but after three weeks of mourning at Monticello, he dragged himself back to Washington to resume the onerous chores of leading his country.

Money Troubles Too

Jefferson, the innovative thinker, philosopher and idealist, was never clever with money. Even as a farmer, the vocation in which he took so much pride, he was a financial bust.

The Monticello estate, perched majestically atop a dry and rocky hill, never yielded the best of crops even though Thomas was far ahead of his time in experimenting with crop rotation. His other chief vocation, politics, didn't pay off financially either. In Jefferson's time, government service didn't make its leaders multi-millionaires.

That's putting it mildly. After decades of public service at the highest levels, Jefferson had no pension whatever. And he was broke. *Worse than broke; he was $100,000 in debt.* That was a huge amount a century and a half ago.

Jefferson engineered the most monumental land bargain in history-- the Louisiana Purchase of 828,000 square miles, that just about *doubled* the size of the United States-- for about three cents per acre! But he couldn't manage his own finances.

The High Cost of Hospitality

In fairness to Jefferson, it should be noted that Ex-presidents in his day faced unique expenses. With no pension, no allowance for an office and staff, no millions of dollars per year for a presidential library, they were expected to perform an extensive public relations job for their country *at their own expense.*

As popular George Washington had before him, Jefferson learned that every American who toured through Virginia expected to drop in at the Ex-President's house for a visit. And, of course, all these visitors expected to enjoy a good dinner. In fact, they might stay for several meals if their visit proved a pleasant one.

In addition, foreign notables visiting our shores all seemed to make a point of stopping at Monticello for lengthy stays. Sometimes they lasted for weeks! And of course, good host Thomas felt impelled to put on a good show with not just ample victuals but a constant flow of expensive vintage wines from his famous cellar.

Let's Try a Lottery

Jefferson's plight became so desperate that the Ex-President sought permission to offer some of his land as a prize in a lottery. Only organizations, not individuals, were permitted to organize lotteries. But sympathetic friends in Congress got him the go-ahead for this plan to pay off his debts.

Like his other financial ventures, the lottery was a failure.

After it was over, friends took up a collection to help out the bankrupt former chief executive of the United States. People throughout the country sent him money, but it wasn't nearly enough to get him back on his feet financially.

Monticello Sold to Pay Debts

Jefferson's finances continued to deteriorate. When he died, his heirs were forced to sell Monticello to pay off some of his debts. The beautiful home he'd designed himself and perfected during 40 years of remodeling and additions went for a bargain price. The spectacular 21-room mansion, along with 525 acres of land, was sold for *only $7,000.*

The first purchaser of the magnificent mansion used it as a place to raise silkworms. That scheme failed so that owner resold Monticello to Uriah Levy. The price dropped to only $2,500 this time.

Q: How badly did Monticello deteriorate?

A: At one time, while no one lived at Monticello, the stately mansion was used as a cow barn!

Uriah had a patriotic motive in mind when he bought the place. He deeded it to the people of the United States to serve as an historic shrine. Unfortunately, Uriah's relatives didn't share his altruistic vision. When he died, they broke his will and retained title to the mansion and grounds, though they had no special plans for it. For the next several years, Monticello stayed uninhabited and the farm and grounds grew up to weeds and pasture land.

Not until 1923 did the historic mansion come into its own. Inherited by a nephew of Uriah's it was sold to the Jefferson Foundation. Eventually the home the Ex-President's children relinquished for a mere $7,000 was repaired and refurbished to become the beautiful edifice it is today.

The Final Chapter
Toward the end of his days, Thomas Jefferson patched up his differences with another great patriot who'd become his enemy during years of political conflict. He and John Adam finally mellowed and remembered the good times when they labored together to make a new nation free and independent.

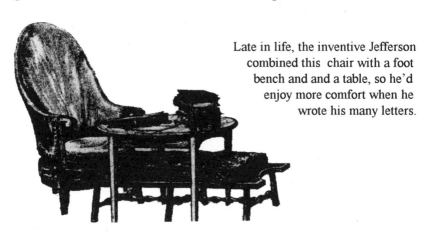

Late in life, the inventive Jefferson combined this chair with a foot bench and and a table, so he'd enjoy more comfort when he wrote his many letters.

The two old warriors were too ill by that time to get together personally. But they began to correspond. Both realized they were approaching the end of the road. Jefferson expressed this to his grandson, Jefferson Randolph, who stayed close to him in his final months.

**"I'm like an old watch, with a pinion worn here
and a wheel there, until it can go no longer."**

Both of the revered statesmen died on the same day. Thomas Jefferson was 83; John Adams was 90. Those two great patriots, the Second and Third Presidents of the United States, died on a highly significant date.

Their passing was on the *Fourth of July,* a date that meant so much to both of them. What's more, their deaths occurred in the ' year 1826, precisely on the 50th anniversary of the day when they both signed the Declaration of Independence.

30
The Roller-Coaster Life
of the Marquis de Lafayette

Most Americans are familiar with only a very brief snippet of Lafayette's life-- the period when he came here as a teen-ager to become a general and fight valiantly alongside George Washington for a few years. But after the Marquis returned to his native land, he lived for *another half-century* filled with turbulence. When he died, an old man of 76, he was one of the last survivors of the great war of '76.

His family life, love life and his two very different careers on two continents were filled with contradictions. That's why the Marquis, idolized in American annals as suave, brilliant, sophisticated and skilled, has also been depicted in French accounts as a clumsy young idiot from the back-woods who lucked out in the American Revolution. They claim that later in the French Revolution, the Marquis became a despicable traitor to his family and friends and a dupe of clever politicians.

He's also been called other contradictory names. He's been labelled a doting husband to his adoring wife, but also an adulterer and an uncaring absent spouse and father.

You could find some truth in all those paradoxical names. Many prominent people did. Marie Antoinette disliked the Marquis from the beginning and despised him at the end. On the other hand, George Washington came to love him like a son. Napoleon feared him. All with good reason.

Long on Name, Short on Money
The man we often identify simply as "Lafayette" (or La Fayette) began life with a much grander name than that. His christening

papers list him as the very great Lord, Monseigneur Maria Joseph Paul Yves Roch Gilbert du Motier, Marquis de Lafayette, Baron de Vissac, Seigneur de St Romain.

However, although little Maria Joseph Paul etc. (generally called Gilbert by family and friends) had an illustrious moniker, he possessed little else. Although part of one of the most prominent families of France, he came from a part that didn't count. His family branch was a sprout from a younger brother, and it was only the eldest of a noble line who got all the money, vast estates and a prestigious place at the royal court in Paris.

The little wrong-side-of-the-family marquis grew up in the poor and primitive region of the Auvergne on a small estate at the end of an unpaved road far from the power center of glittering Paris. In this isolated backwoods, he was raised mostly by his grandmother and an aunt. When the boy was still short of his second birthday, his father, a colonel in the Grenadiers *who had never seen his son,* was killed in a battle against the English. His mother had already left the family home and her baby to live with her father and grandfather in Paris where she might with luck gain some advantage for her boy's future.

Q: Wasn't it unusual for a parent to be away from a child?
A: Not for wealthy Europeans in the 18th Century. Babies were often farmed out to live with a wetnurse soon after birth. Even though they came back to the family home after a couple of years, a rich mother and father who had several homes and many business and social obligations in distant places might spend time with their children only occasionally. Until they approached maturity and could start to become assets, a passel of kids was regarded as a nuisance rather than as the center of the family universe as they tend to be today.

Swift Change of Fortune

When Lafayette was eleven, his mother, whom he'd seen only rarely in eight years, sent for him to join her in Paris. There he needed to learn the social graces of the court so he could someday be presented to the King from whom all favors flowed. Eventually his rich influential grandfather, on his mother's side of the family, would wheedle him an appointment as a lieutenant in the army. That would enable the lad to scrape out a living as a soldier as his father had before him.

Moving to the big city with the stranger who was his elegant mother was a scary move for the young country bumpkin. Enrolled at the College du Plessis, he was an oddball unaccustomed to fancy mannerisms, powdered wigs and silken clothes. He found no friends. He hated his life, but it was soon to change.

In 1770, when Lafayette was 12, his mother, though still a young woman of 32, became ill and died in a few days. In the same week, her father, the very rich Marquis de La Riviere, also died suddenly.

Ordinarily, all the rich old man's land and money would have gone not to his daughter or to Lafayette, but to a male of the Riviere family. But there were no living male heirs left in the Riviere line. So Lafayette metamorphosed overnight from poor relative to one of the richest young men in France.

At the age of twelve, he became lord of vast lands in Brittany and the Loire as well as numerous investments. His annual income amounted to about 150,000 livres, or more than $600,000. That's not peanuts even today; back then it gave Lafayette the kind of purchasing power only a *billionaire* would enjoy now. He became not just a wealthy young man; he was BIG rich!

Up the Military Ladder
After falling into the pot of gold, Lafayette no longer had to wait to get his foothold into the army. Still only 13 years old, his guardians bought him a commission as a lieutenant in the prestigious Royal Guard. The fact that he was still but a little boy put in charge of a group of grown soldiers was not unusual; even younger aristocrats were made officers, since they were not really expected to do any fighting.

With an exalted military career practically assured, the rich teen-age bachelor now needed to find a suitable wife, or have one selected for him by his guardian. Arrangements were made for a union with Adrienne Noailles, daughter of a very distinguished family, and a more than a million dollar dowry was agreed upon.

Adrienne was only 12 at the time and Lafayette but two years older, so Adriene's mother insisted that the pair should wait a couple of years to get acquainted before a wedding took place. That was an unusual request for the time, but Momma got her way. Lafayette came to live at the Noailles home, known only to Adrienne as a friend of the family.

Strangely, it was not until the marriage was imminent that Adrienne was finally told that the Marquis would be her husband. Long before that, however, the young girl had developed a crush on their permanent house guest.

Having It All, But Not Enough

Not only was Adrienne Noailles a beautiful girl from the top of the social register, bringing a huge dowry with her, but she was madly in love with her new husband. Such a novel situation was considered a charming novelty in French high society-- certainly not a requisite for marriage. For example, in that milieu, it was customary for wives and husbands to have separate bedrooms, and to attend social functions separately. It was okay to invite one's mistress or lover to a party, but not conducive to a good time to have one's spouse present.

For a wife and her husband both to have lovers was considered a natural state of affairs, so long as the liaisons were conducted discreetly. Only if an affair might cause embarrassment to the family did a spouse object. This attitude of "okay so long as no one else knows" was expressed by a husband who entered a room unexpectedly and surprised his wife being ecstatically impaled by a gentleman friend. Here's how hubby chided his indiscreet spouse:

> " Madame, how can you be so careless! What
> if someone else had discovered you here?"

Lucky Lafayette had no such problems with his Adrienne. Greeted with ardent love-making in his marriage bed, he responded with enthusiasm. His career was moving pleasantly too. He'd been promoted to a vacant captaincy, jumping a couple of notches upward, although there's no record he'd done anything spectacular (or anything at all) of a military nature.

Striving To Be a Gallant and Lover

Lafayette did his best to fit into the fast lane at Versailles. First of all, he recognized that to be accepted as one of the truly fashionable crowd at court, he must have a mistress. That seemed like an interesting requirement.

To step up to that obligation, the young man, married less than a year, picked out a gorgeous lady of the court as his target, and began a persistent pursuit. However, the Comtesse Hunolstein, whom he'd singled out, had more interesting amours underway. Much to his dismay, it became widely known that she abruptly brushed off the awkward lad.

Loving Adrienne, of course made no remonstrances to her new husband's little romantic foray, but she must have felt some embarrassment. Not because a bit of bed-hopping would be unexpected, but because this particular bit of skirt-chasing attracted considerable attention. The reluctant Comtesse whom Lafayette chose to pursue was already the girl-friend of the Comte d' Artois, and the two men nearly came to a duel over her.

His early clumsy attempts at extra-marital amours caused young Lafayette to pull back briefly from such endeavors, and to be regarded in sophisticated court circles as uninterested in such pursuits. However, his close friend, the Comte de Segur, knew from the start that this situation would change as soon as the Marquis learned how to get what he desired.

> " How I laughed to myself when I heard Lafayette described
> as a cold pedant, even by those who knew him. They were to
> learn later that ardour was the thing he lacked least of all!"
> Comte de Segur

Lafayette's forays onto the dance floor at royal fetes were equally disastrous. Tall, gawky Lafayette, who seemed to have two left feet, actually stumbled and fell during one of the royal dances. That brought a laugh from Marie Antoinette, an insult he never forgot and a faux pas that made him the butt of jokes.

Despite all the wonderful advantages he enjoyed, he was uncomfortable at the palace and wanted to get away.

A Chance for Glory in America

With the French army "downsizing" after the costly war with Britain, many officers found themselves unemployed or likely to be put on reserve. The only real action with chances for big promotions seemed to be in America. What's more, an entre into the American army was right in Paris in the person of ambassador Silas Deane. It was his job to butter up prominent aristocrats who might persuade King Louis XVI to help the Colonist's rebel cause.

Deane encountered slow going with Louis, who wasn't at all anxious to get into new battles with England or to delete his treasury for the sake of rabble rousers who didn't respect their monarchs. So when French aristocrats close to the King asked about Colonial commissions, Deane was quick to hand them out, just to get those influential Frenchmen on our side.

The upshot was that several of Lafayette's relatives and friends got themselves commissions in the Colonial army from ambassador Deane. What's more, they were all going to come in *as generals!*

Eager Lafayette couldn't resist such an opportunity. He still had no combat experience whatever, yet he might be able to catapult overnight from captain's bars all the way up to general's stars. What a deal! He joined the group.

Farewell Wife-- On to Glory

Without going into all the details, you should know that cautious King Louis forbade his officers to embark for America and stir up trouble with England. Going against the King's decrees was a dangerous offense. But Lafayette was not to be deterred. Since money was no object, the rich young man *bought his own ship* so he could sneak away to America without being apprehended.

A footnote to this adventure, rarely mentioned in accounts of the Marquis' exploits, is the fact that Adrienne was pregnant with their second child at the time he took off for the New World. In defying the King, Lafayette risked being thrown in jail, or worse, so *he didn't even tell his pregnant wife about his plans.* He told her and everyone else he was sailing to London and would soon be back.

It must have been quite a shock to Adrienne when she finally heard that daddy-to-be was headed west on the high seas. She knew that meant that her husband wouldn't be seeing her or his year-old daughter or the new child in the womb for a very, very long time. Here's how she expressed her confusion:

> " I was pregnant and loved my husband tenderly. My
> father and the rest of my family were all violently angry
> at the news. My mother tried to console me, both by
> preparing me to hear what had happened, and then
> by looking for ways to help M. de Lafayette."

After the Marquis arrived in America, he kept up a steady correspondence with his family back in France. But his loyal wife Adrienne waited patiently, without complaint, for years before she saw her husband again.

George Washington's Dilemma

General George was not at all pleased when Lafayette and his aristocratic pals arrived in the New World. He understood Silas Deane's motives, but these haughty Frenchies in their fancy uniforms acted as if they'd come to show the dumb Americans how to run an army. They couldn't speak English, yet all of them expected to command brigades of men who couldn't understand their orders.

Washington quickly became so fed up with these would-be generals that he ordered them all to sail back home, at their own expense. All except one. Such a monstrously rich lad as Lafayette, who could buy his own ship and whose family was close to the King, simply couldn't be insulted and turned away, Washington was advised.

General George sort of liked the quiet young man anyway. He wasn't as mouthy as his friends, and he offered to serve without pay, an important consideration in the money-strapped Colonial army. Reluctantly, Washington agreed to let Lafayette stay. And even call himself a general, if he insisted.

There had to be limit though, Washington decreed. No kid not yet 20 years old who'd never even seen a battle was going to command a brigade, or anything else. That disappointed Lafayette

A portait by Alonzo Chappel of Marie Joseph Paul Yves Roch
Gilbert du Motier, Marquis de Lafayette in his general's uniform.

who was primed to hear bullets whistle and become a hero. He had to settle for joining Washington's personal staff where he couldn't cause too much damage.

Hero of Two Worlds

The young glory hound got his wish for fame and honor fulfilled sooner than expected and in ample measure.

Wherever he traveled, the tall aristocrat received warm welcomes from the American people. Here was a symbol that the French were on their side and hopefully would soon be sending money, ammunition and other supplies to the desperate Colonial army. The rich Marquis gave personal evidence of this by handing out his own funds generously to buy uniforms for ragged troops he met.

The "boss", General Washington, also grew to like his young aide increasingly, for the eager boy who idolized him seemed almost like the son George never had.

All that was wonderful, but Lafayette kept yearning and hinting for a chance to see real action. He got it at the battle of the Brandywine when Washington and his aides noted with alarm that a large British force was about to flank them. When the Commander in Chief sent General Sullivan to meet this threat, Lafayette begged for a chance to help. General Washington agreed that he could.

Wounded for America

That was a day of glory for the Marquis. He showed extraordinary bravery in the battle, leaping from his horse to shove reluctant troops forward against a superior force. Wounded in the leg, he continued to fight until loss of blood made him stop to be bandaged, so he could go back into action and rally his troops again.

His wound was not severe, but that and his outstanding bravery gained Lafayette acclaim as the foreigner who'd sailed across the ocean to shed his blood for America and freedom. The Colonials lost the battle at Brandywine, as they did so many others, but they gained a colorful hero.

Newspapers throughout the Colonies played the Lafayette story big. They loved it in France too. Silas Deane was right when he predicted that French officers fighting alongside Americans would help to stir up crucial support in Paris for the War for Independence.

Lafayette proved to be a very good officer then and later. But far more important, he became a truly wonderful public relations star who helped greatly to win foreign support for America.

Triumphant Return

American history books are full of the further exploits of the Marquis de Lafayette in our War for Independence. But that was only one side of his varied career, for he led a long and hectic life after returning home.

As you'd guess, he was a big hero when he finally got back to Paris early in 1782. Persnickety courtiers who'd snubbed him as a hick years ago now fawned over him. King Louis XVI, delighted that his subject Lafayette had played a major role in the crushing British defeat at Yorktown, forgot he once wanted to toss him into jail and proudly proclaimed him a *Marechal de Camp* (a brigadier general).

Even Marie Antoinette invited the medal-bedecked hero to dance with her, though she still didn't like him and he still trod the quadrille clumsily. But he'd become too famous to ignore. Like Ben Franklin, his likeness was immortalized in statues and in innumerable plaster busts sold as souvenirs.

The Marquis was called the "Liberator of America" and "Washington's Savior." He now had the fame he coveted, plus always-loving wife Adrienne, plus an ample choice of the mistresses that he'd never been able to attract previous to his fame.

> **"When I arrived back in France, I had the honor**
> **of being consulted by all the ministers, and much**
> **better still, kissed by all the women."**
> Lafayette's Memoirs

Surprisingly, it was Aglae Hunolstein, the haughty Comtesse who had turned him down years earlier, who was the first to claim the honor of jumping into bed with the returning hero. Like everyone else at court, the Comtesse was impressed with celebrity.

Lafayette's Mistresses

It's speculated that Lafayette may have welcomed Hunolstein to his arms mostly as a vindication of her rejection of him in earlier days. However, their relationship developed into a lengthy affair.

Although that romantic success of the popular general was favorably noted at the royal court, another conquest stirred up a much greater approval. With horizons now unlimited for the conquering hero, he cast covetous eyes at the number-one belle of French society. She was the Comtesse de Simiane, known as the Beauty Queen of Versaille.

When the Liberator of America toppled the dazzling Simiane, newspapers throughout France faithfully reported all the details they could uncover, plus embellishments they made up. So intense was interest in the Lafayette-Simiane affair that the papers even interviewed experts for their opinions. The Duc de Richelieu and the Duc de Lavalle, two lotharios famed throughout the country for their countless liaisons, joined in publicly applauding Lafayette's newly-won success in the boudoir.

> **"In winning the favor of Madame de Simiane,**
> **he has accomplished a more glorious victory**
> **than in storming the proudest fortress."**
> The Ducs de Richelieu and de Lavalle

There was one unseemly consequence to this affair. The nation-wide publicity about the hanky-panky between France's number-one military hero and France's number-one beauty, reported in all its lurid details, evidently proved too much for her husband. The Comte de Simiene surprised everyone by committing suicide.

Although it was generally assumed that he must have lost his mind to get so upset, the count's demise caused Lafayette to withdraw from the limelight for a time. It didn't however, cause him to withdraw from the beautiful Simiene.

Nor did she attempt to knock off their relationship. Not having been especially fond of her husband anyway, and viewing Lafayette as a coming political power who'd probably be prime minister some day, Simiane settled in as a long-time mistress.

In fact, over the years the lovely Simiene became an accepted part of Lafayette's family.

Q: *How close did Madame de Simiene become to the family?*
A: *After the French Revolution shattered the lush lives of aristocrats like her, Lafyette's wife Adrienne invited his homeless mistress to come and live with them. She shared their food and their house. Now that's sharing!*

Liberte, Equalite and Lafayette

Hardly had the American Revolution ended when the French Revolution began to approach its boiling point. Lafayette, as the most famous man in France, got sucked into the midst of that cauldron. There's no reason, nor space, to talk much here about that complex mess that started in 1789, except to point out a few unusual happenings in it that involved the Marquis.

After the storming of the Bastille, frenzied drunken mobs running through the streets carrying bloody heads aloft led to complete chaos. At that point, the Marquis should have headed out of town as many of his friends did. Empress Catherine of Russia had invited the Hero of Two Worlds to visit her. Perhaps he could have joined her coterie of favorite generals.

At least he should have heeded the advice he received from wily Frederick the Great during a brief visit to the Prussian court. At that time, the crusty Prussian autocrat listened unbelievingly to the liberal ideas the young champion of freedom entertained about new constitutions, voting rights for all the people, etc. Their conversation ended something like this:

> **Frederick:** "I once knew a young man who spoke as you have done. Do you know what happened to him?"
> **Lafayette:** "No, Your Majesty."
> **Frederick:** "He was hanged."

However, Lafayette didn't listen to that warning he received at the Prussian court. Instead, he became involved with the revolutionary deputies who'd stirred up the mobs that now terrorized all of Paris and listened to no one. The deputies were looking for someone to set up a civic guard. They needed someone who had enough prestige and enough strength to halt the bloodshed and also fend off the King's troops that were surrounding and starving the capitol city. They could settle on no suitable candidate for this impossible job, and no one wanted it. They were stymied, until someone in the assembly hall, spotting a bust of France's most famous freedom-fighter shouted "Vive Lafayette!"

Others joined in, and the cry became a storm of approval. Even Lafayette was swept along by the emotion of the moment. The impassioned Marquis waved his sword aloft as he accepted the call, vowing to fight for the new liberties even if it should cost him his life. It very nearly did.

A Can't-Win Situation

Lafayette did a remarkable job. In defiance of his king, to whom he still claimed allegiance, he quickly set up a "Garde Nationale de Paris" of 50,000 men. Riding around the city on a white horse with squads of disciplined soldiers behind him, Lafayette's group was able to stop some of the excesses of the rampaging mobs. But soon found that his efforts to establish order were unappreciated.

> **"This furious drunken people will not listen to me."**
> Lafayette, Commander of the National Guard

When he managed to rescue a few people from the lynch mobs, the revolutionaries saw Lafayette as still an enemy aristocrat. When his former friends saw him command troops in a city still rife with bloodshed, they labeled him a traitor who was no better than the other riff-raff in the streets.

No matter what he did, he couldn't win. Eventually, his radical pals turned on him and Lafayette had no choice except to flee to Paris with his family.

Years in Exile

He went to Belgium, but royalist French emigres there stirred up such a storm against him that that the government there shipped him off to Austria. The Austrians wanted no revolutionary military man running around their country either, so they shunted him off to Prussia. There he was tossed into prison where he spent five miserable years in a squalid cell.

Q: What sacrifice did Adrienne make for her husband?
A: Still in Paris and spared from the Guillotine, she petitioned
the Prussians constantly to let her join Lafayette in prison.
Finally they allowed her and her two daughters, aged 13 and
18, to share his filthy cell and foul food. The terrible
conditions there broke Adrienne's health. When she
developed skin rashes and swollen feet, she asked to go to
Vienna for a week to see a doctor. Told she couldn't come
back if she left, Adrienne chose to stay with her man and
suffer with him.

Lafayette probably would have died behind bars if his old friend George Washington hadn't applied so much diplomatic pressure that the Prussians finally let him and his family go back to France. Actually, one member of the family escaped the French Revolution entirely. The son, christened George Washington Lafayette, had been shipped off to America when the mobs first began "the Terror" in Paris. There the boy stayed safely with his famous namesake as part of George and Martha's large household.

Out of Prison with Nowhere to Go
Lafayette was 40 years old when finally released from prison in 1797. Although still mentally feisty, his health was not good. He'd long suffered from a lung problem, probably because he had a touch of the prevalent disease, tuberculosis.

Napolean had grabbed control of France, and that dictator was not enthused about having a military hero with different ideas coming onto the scene. Although Lafayette never ceased to express his views about freedom and politics, often to the irritation of those in power at the time, he was always denied the chances he yearned for to hold important office. *For a long time, during Napoleon's regime, he was even denied the right to return to France.*

Lafayette survived many upheavals and new rulers in his homeland. Besides Napoleon, who became an emperor, there were a passel of Bourbon kings-- a 16th and a 17th Louis, plus Charles the 10th. When Charles was deposed, the old hero Lafayette was pulled again to center stage, briefly, to state his opinions.

His words still carried weight; he even swung the tide of public opinion in favor of making Louis-Phillipe the King of France. But he received little thanks for that help.

For one brief time, Lafayette was again given the honor of his old title, Commander of the National Guard. But after the new successors to power used the old hero to add luster to their plans, they always wanted him to get lost.

The Americans Remember
His American friends didn't forget the Frenchman who played such an important role in their fight for freedom. President Jefferson, offered to make Lafayette the Governor of Louisiana after that huge and undeveloped territory was purchased from the French. The Marquis declined.

He did spend a triumphant year in America, enjoying jubilant receptions wherever he went.

The United States Congress, usually miserly with money in those days, awarded the old soldier $200,000 because he'd never accepted any salary when he served with our army. Lafayette also received a land grant of 24,000 acres from the United States, a bonus to which he was entitled for his service and rank in the American Revolutionary Army. The money was a life-saver since the vast Lafayette family fortunes had pretty much evaporated.

No End of Problems
Late in life Lafayette endured many problems. He had fallen and broken his femur; then underwent a new stretching treatment for it that damaged muscles in his thigh and left him with a stiff hip and a permanent limp.

He felt lost without his faithful wife. Adrienne had died on Christmas Eve in 1807, with him at her side holding her hand. She was buried the following day at the site of a mass grave where scores of aristocrats had been executed and dumped during "the Terror" two decades earlier. She'd wanted to be laid to rest in that bloody spot near friends and relatives-- her grandmother, mother and sister-- who'd all been killed by the revolutionary mobs.

A poor manager of money without Adrienne to watch finances, the Marquis tried to keep up appearances and slipped increasingly into debt. Still a celebrity, he enjoyed the visits of friends and of his two living children, 11 grandchildren and 13 great-grandchildren. It's said he also never failed to notice any pretty women who came by, and if opportunity arose, to pat them where he shouldn't.

Disturber of Kings, Even in Death

At 76, the aged warrior caught a severe cold while standing in the chill January rain at the funeral of an old friend. Surviving until May 20, 1834, he died kissing a locket containing his wife's picture, and was buried next to her.

Mostly ignored by the powers of France, including Louis-Philippe whom he'd helped to obtain the throne, Lafayette in death attracted considerable interest. And anxiety. Although the burial of the famous fighter for freedom was marked with every conceivable honor-- pall bearers who were all marshals of France, escorts of ministers and other high dignitaries, tons of flowers, a parade of 3,000 guardsmen from Paris-- strange precautions were taken.

King Louis-Phillipe wanted no demonstrations against his regime stirred up by memories of the outspoken old rebel hero. He took extraordinary steps to make sure nothing happened.

Q: How did Louis-Phillipe assure an uneventful funeral?
A: The edgy King called out several garrisons of the national guard, fully armed, to make sure the funeral was a quiet one. He ordered that the entire route to the cemetery should be lined with soldiers, three deep, ready to fire on any demonstrators.

There was no national tribute to the deceased hero in France. The King was glad to see the end of him and his constant nagging about the need for freedom.

However, in his adopted country overseas that he loved and that never ceased to love him, an official period of mourning was decreed by Congress. And a handful of earth from America, gathered from the historic ground of Bunker Hill, was sprinkled on his tomb.

End of an Era

The long life of the Marquis de Lafayette stretched from the beginning to the end of an historic era. As an idealistic youth in his 20's, he'd played a prominent part in the early days of the American Revolution and become an international symbol of freedom. Back to France in his 30's, the Marquis participated in another historic revolution.

In his old age, although he was largely shunned by a succession of kings, Lafayette still retained enough popular appeal to be a king-maker. And to frighten kings and an emperor as an indestructible symbol of liberty.

By the time he finally died at the age of 76, the young warrior who'd fought alongside George Washington and his generals and become a respected friend of succeeding American presidents, had outlived almost all of his earlier companions of the conflict of 1776.

You might consider the Marquis de Lafayette to be an ultimate survivor of the American Revolution, one of the very last of the prominent participants to go. His final passing marked the end of an era that turned the world upside down.

*Their lives were truly
stranger than fiction--
those wonderful women and men
who struggled through the
chaotic era of 1776.*

Bibliography

The gathering of material for this book took place over several decades, as the author developed an increasing fascination with the strange lives and loves of our ancestors of 1776. As this interest grew, so did the accumulation of stories and personal data, from many sources over many years.

The author is grateful to those historians who painstakingly analyzed tons of correspondence and papers of the Revolutionary War era. The scholarly books they produced made possible this "light history" which focuses on the personal side of our famous ancestors. Most of those source books are listed here.

Akers, Charls W. *Abigail Adams, An American Woman.* Little Brown, Boston, 1980.

Alden, John R. *A History of the American Revolution.* Alfred A. Knopf, New York, 1969.

Alexander, John T. *Catherine the Great, Life and Legend.* Oxford University Press, New York, 1989.

Allen, Herbert Sanford. *John Hancock, Patriot in Purple.* Macmillan, New York, 1948.

Allen, W.B. *George Washington, A Collection.of Writings* Liberty Classics, Indianapolis, 1988.

Baily, Bernard. *Faces of Revolution.* Alfred A. Knopf, New York, 1990.

Bakeless, Katherine and John. *Signers of the Declaration.* Houghton Mifflin, Boston 1969.

Bernier, Olivier. *Lafayette, Hero of Two Worlds.* E.P. Dutton, New York, 1983.

Billias, George Athan. *George Washington's Generals and Opponents.* DaCapo Press, New York, 1994.

Bixby, W.K. *Letters and Recollections of George Washington.* Doubleday Doran. New York, 1932.

Block, Seymour Stanton. *Benjamin Franklin, His Wit, Wisdom and Women.* Random House, New York, 1975.

Boorstein, Daniel J. *The Americans: The Colonial Experience.* Vantage Books,New York, 1958.

Brandt, Clare. *The Man in the Mirror, A Life of Benedict Arnold.* Random House, New York, 1994.

Brooke, John, *King George III.* McGraw-Hill, New York, 1972.

Brookhiser, Richard. *Founding Fathers, Rediscovering George Washington.* Simon & Schuster, New York, 1996.

Brown, Wallace. *The Good American, the Loyalists in the American Revolution.* Morrow, New York, 1969.

Buehr, Wendy. *American Manners and Morals.* American Heritage, New York, 1969.

Burstein, Andrew. *The Inner Jefferson, Portrait of a Grieving Outcast.* University Press of Virginia, Charlottesville, 1995.

Bushman, Richard L. *The Refinement of America, Persons, Houses, Cities.* Alfred A. Knopf, New York, 1992.

Calhoun, Robert M. *The Loyalists in Revolutionary America.* Harcourt Brace Janovich, 1973.

Canning, John. *100 Great Kings, Queens and Rulers of the World.* Toplinger Publishing, New York, 1968.

Cannon, John and Griffiths, Ralph. *The Oxford Illustrated History of the British Monarchy.* Oxford University Press, Oxford, 1988.

Carp, E. Wayne. *To Serve at the Army's Pleasure.* University of North Carolina Press, Chapel Hill, 1984.

Cary, John H. and Weinberg, Julius. *The Social Fabric, American Life from 1607 to the Civil War.* Little Brown, Boston, 1981.

Clark, Harrison. *A Cloudless Glory, The Life of George Washington from Youth to Yorktown.* Regnery, Washington, D.C., 1995.

Clark, Ronald W. *Benjamin Franklin, A Biography.* Random House, New York, 1983.

Colley, Linda. *Britons.* Yale University Press, New Haven, 1992.

Conlin, Joseph R. *The Morrow Book of Quotations in American History.* William Morrow, New York, 1984.

Commanger, Henry Steele and Morris, Richard B. *The Spirit of 1776.* Bonanza Books, New York, 1983.

Dabney, Virginius. *The Jefferson Scandals, A Rebuttal.* Dodd Mead, New York, 191981.

Dann, John C. *The Revolution Remembered.* University of Chicago Press, Chicago, 1980.

Davidson, Marshall B. *The Horizon History of the Workd in 1776.* American Heritage, New York, 1975.

_____ *Life in America.* Houghton Mifflin, Boston, 1951.

Dunan, Marcel. *Larouse Encyclopedia of Modern History.* Crown, New York, 1964.

Ellis, Joseph J. *American Sphinx, The Character of Thomas Jefferson.* Alfred A.Knopf, New York, 1997.

Erickson, Carolly. *Catherine the Great.* Crown, New York, 1994.

Faulkner, Harold Underwood. *American Political and Social History.* Appleton-Century-Crofts, New York, 1952.

Fischer, David Hackett. *Paul Revere's Ride.* Oxford University Press, Oxford, 1994.

Flexner, James Thomas. *George Washington, the Indispensible Man.* Little Brown, Boston, 1974.

_____ *The Traitor and the Spy, Benedict Arnold and John Andre.* Little Brown, Boston, 1975.

Forbes, Esther. *Paul Revere and the World he Lived In.* Houghton Mifflin, Boston, 1988.

Franklin, Benjamin. *The Autobiography of Benjamin Franklin.* Many Versions Published.

_____ *Poor Richard's Almanac.* Many Versions Published.

Freeman, Douglas Southall. *George Washington, A Biography.* 7vols. Scribners, New York, 1948-1957.

Fry, Plantagenet Somerset. *Kings and Queens of England and Scotland.* Grove Press, New York, 1990.

Garraty, John A. and McCaughey, Robert A. *The American Nation.* Harper Collins, New York, 1987.

Gelb, Norman. *Less Than Glory, A Revisionist's View of the American Revolution.* Putnam, New York, 1984.

Gordon-Reed, Annette. *Thomas Jefferson and Sally Hemmings.* University Press of Virginia, Charlottesville, 1997.

Green, Vivian. *The Madness of Kings.* St. Martin's Press, New York, 1993.

Gruber, Ira D. *The Howe Brothers in the American Revolution.* Athenaeum, 1972.

Hall, Gordon Langley. *Mr. Jefferson's Ladies.* Beacon Press, New York, 1966.

Handlin, Oscar and Lillian. *A Restless People.* Doubleday, New York, 1982.

Haslip, Joan. *Marie Antoinette.* Weidenfeld and Nicholson, New York, 1987.

Hawke, David Freeman. *Everyday Life in America.* Harper & Row, New York, 1988.

Hecht, Marie B. *Odd Destiny, the Life of AlexanderHamilton.* Macmillan, New York, 1982.

Hibbert, Christopher. *Redcoats and Rebels, The American Revolution Through British Eyes.* W.W. Norton, New York, 1990.

Hughes, Rupert. *George Washington, The Human Being and the Hero.* William Morrow, New York, 1926.

Huisman, Phillipe and Jalut, Marguerite. *Marie Antoinette.* Viking, New York, 1971.

Kates, Gary. *Monsieur d'Eon is a Woman.* Harper Collins, New York, 1995.

Kitman, Marvin. *George Washington's Expense Accouint.* Simon & Schuster, New York, 1970.

Kelley, Robert. *The Shaping of the American Past.* Prentice Hall, New York, 1978.

Ketchum, Richard M. *The World of George Washington.* American Heritage, New York, 1974.

Langguth, A.J. *Patriots, the Men who Started the American Revolution.* Simon & Schuster, 1988.

Latzko, Andreas. *Lafayette, A Life.* Literary Guild, New York, 1936.

Levron, Jaques. *Daily Life at Versailles.* Macmillan, New York, 1968.

Loomis, Stanley. *DuBarry, A Biography.* J.B. Lippincott, 1959.

Longford, Elizabeth. *The Oxford Book of Royal Anecdotes.* Oxford University Press, Oxford, 1989.

Lopez, Claude-Anne. *The Private Franklin, the Man and His Family.* Norton, New York, 1975.

Malone, Dumas. *Jefferson, the Virginian.* Little Brown, Boston, 1948.

Maurois, Andre. *An Illustrated History of France.* Viking, New York, 1960.

McDonald, Forrest. *Alexander Hamilton, A Biography.* Norton, New York, 1979.

Meyer, Edith Patterson. *Petticoat Patriots of the American Revolution.* Gage, Publishing, Canada, 1976.

Mitford, nancy. *The Sun King., Louis XIV at Versailles.* Harper & Row, New York, 1960.

Moody, Sid. *The World Turned Upside Down.* Associated Press, New York, 1975.

Morgan, Edmund S. *The Genius of George Washington.* W.W. Norton,New York, 1977.

Morison, Samuel Eliot. *John Paul Jones.* Atlantic-Little Brown, New York, 1959.

Morris, Richard B. *Seven Who Shaped Our Destiny.* Harper & Row, New York, 1973.

Norton, Mary Beth. *Liberty's Daughters, The Revolutionary Experience of American Women.* Little Brown, Boston, 1980.

O'Toole, G.J.A. *Poor Richard's game.* Delacorte, New York, !982.

Petersen, Merrill D. *Visitors to Monticello.* University Press of Virginia, Charlottesville, 1989.

Quarles, Benjamin. *The Negro in the American Revolution.* University of North Carolina Press, Chapel Hill, 1961.

Randall, Willard Sterne. *Thomas Jefferson, A Life.* Henry Holt, New York, 1993.

———— *George Washington, A Life.* Henry Holt, New York, 1996.

———— *A Little revenge, Benjamin Franklin at War With His Son.* William Morrow, New York, 1984.

Randel, William Pierce. *The American Revolution, Mirror of a People.* Rutledge, New York, 1973.

Rhodehamel, John. *Washington, Writings.* Literary Classics, New York, 1997.

Reich, Jerome R. *Colonial America.* Prentice hall, Englewood Cliffs, 1994.

Royster, Charles. *A Revolutionary People at War.* University of North Carolina Press, Chapel Hill, 1979.

Rude, George. *The French Revolution.* Weidenfeld & Nicholson, New York, 1988.

Sachs, William S. and Hoogenboom, Ari. *The Enterprising Colonials.* Argonaut, Chicago, 1965.

Schlame, Simon. *Citizens, A Chronicle of the French Revolution.* Alfred A Knopf, New York, 1989.

Schouler, James. *American of 1776.* Corner House, Williamston, 1906.

Smith, Page. *Jefferson, A Revealing Biogrpahy.* American Heritage, new York, 1976.

_____ *A New Age Begins.* Penguin, New York, 1976.

Smith, Richard Norton. *Patriarch, George Washington and the New American Nation.* Houghton Mifflin, Boston, 1993.

Tebble, John. *Turning the World Upside Down.* Crown, New York, 1993.

Thane, Elswyth. *The Family Quarrel, A Journey Through the Years of the Revolution.* Duell Sloan & Pearce, New York, 1959.

_____ *Washington's Lady.* Dodd Mead, New York, 1960.

Thomas, Hugh. *The Slave Trade.* Simon & Schuster, New York, 1997.

Wallace, Willard M. *Traitorous Hero, The Life and Fortunes of Benedict Arnold.* Narper, New York, 1954.

Watson, Stephen. *The Reign of George III, 1760-1815.* Vol. XI of the Oxford History of England, Clarendon Press, Oxford, 1960.

Wilson, Susan. *Boston Sights and Insights.* Beacon Press, Boston, 1993.

Wolf, Edwin II. *Philadelphia, Portrait of an American City.* Stackpole, Harrisburg, 1975.

Wright, Louis B. *The Cultural Life of the American Colonies.* Harper & Row, New York, 1957.

Wright, Robert K. Jr. *The Continental Army.* U.S. Army Center of Military History, Washington, D.C., 1989.

Young, Alfred F. and Fife, Terry J. *We the People.* Temple University Press, Philadelphia, 1993.

Zinn, Howard. *A People's History of the United States.* Harper Collins, New York, 1990.

Index

Guillotine, 280, 333

Hamilton, Alexander, 68-79, 180
Hamilton, Betsy Schuyler, 70
Hamilton, James, 69
Hancock, Dorothy Quincy , 12, 17
Hancock, John , 12-24, 151, 212
Hancock, Lydia, 15
Hancock, Thomas, 15
Harrison, Benjamin, 20
Helvetius, Madame, 293
Harvard University, 15, 22, 144
Hemmings, Elizabeth (Betsy) 208,
  310
Hemmings, Madison, 314-15
Hemmings, Sally, 310-15
Henry, Patrick, 110
Henson, Polly, 290
Hickey, Thomas, 219
Hortalez & Cie, 283
Houses, Pest, 189
Howe:, Adm. Richard, 232
Howe, Gen. William, 232-38
Hunolstein, Aglae, Countess, 324
Hunting, Fox, 34
Hutchinson, Gov. Thomas, 147

Indentures (See Servants,
  Indentured)
Independence; Declaration of, 208
Independence, Hall, 209
Independence, War of (See
  Revolution)
Indians, 185
Inflation, Monetary, 299

James I, King, 47
James III, King, 55
Jamestown, 195
Jay, John, 292
Jefferson:, Martha, 120, 206-10
Jefferson, Peter, 203
Jefferson, Thomas, 34, 76, 83, 101,
  152, 157, 201-10, 300, 305-319
Jones, John Paul, 93-104, 281

Jumel, Eliza, 84

Kalm, Peter, 109
Kennedy, John F, 305
King's College (See Princeton)
King's Mountain, 181
Knox, Gen. Henry, 177, 226
Knox, Lucy, 177, 226
Konigsmark, Count, 56

Lafayette, Adrienne, 323-26,
  333, 335,
Lafayette, James, 200
Lafayette, Marquis de, 200, 320-
  336
Land Speculation, 85-92
Laudanum, 118
Laurens, Eleanor, 110
Laurens, Henry, 110, 292,
Lee, Gen. Charles, 213
Lear, Tobias, 116
Lennox, Lady Sarah, 61
Levy, Uriah, 317
Lexington, 212
Livingston, Roger B., 209
London, 127, 131
Longfellow, William Wadsworth,
  239-40
Loring, Maj. Joshua, 234
Loring, Mrs. Joshua, 235
Louis XIV, King, 269
Louis XV, King, 267, 269-71
Louis XVI, King, 99, 276-78, 282,
  288, 325, 329
Louisiana, Purchase, 313, 316
Louisiana, Territory, 81-2
Lotteries, 47, 53
Loyalists, 175-82

Madison, James, 157
Marriages (Weddings)
  106-08
Maria Antonia (See Marie
  Antoinette)
Maria Theresa, Empress, 266-68

Picture Credits

Listed below are the pages in this book which have illustrations, and the sources from which they were obtained. The author wishes to express his appreciation to those sources for their courtesy in making these pictures available.

Page 12 - Portrait by Edward Savage from the Corcoran Gallery of Art, bequest of Woodbury Blair. **21** - Dover Archives. **24** - Smithsonian Museum, Ferris Collection. **26** - Library of Congress. **35, 40, 47** - Smithsonian Museum, Ferris Collection. **49** - Detail from engraving by Hogarth. **51** - Smithsonian Museum, Ferris Collection. **60** - Dover Archives. **63** - Three-dimensional figure by Dennis Atkinson. **70** - Museum of the City of New York, Portrait by Ralph Earl, gift of Mrs. Alexander Hamilton and General Pierpont Morgan Hamilton. **71** - Dover Archives. **98, 100, 117** - Library of Congress. **119, 122** - Prints from an 18th-Century book on medical practices. **128, 146** - Dover Archives. **149** - Library of Congress. **160** - Original sketch by David Kellar. **162** - Winterthur Museum. **166** - Original sketch by David Kellar. **171** - London Magazine, September, 1777. **197** - Library of Congress. **204, 220, 222** - Dover Archives. **233** - British Magazine, 18th-Century. **264** - Library of Congress. **268, 289** - Computer and three-dimensional art by Dennis Atkinson. **298** - Dover Archives. **318** - Library of Congress. **327** - Dover Archives.

About the author
Donald Walton first began searching for true
stories of our famous ancestors of 1776 many
years ago when he lived near Philadelphia
midway between Valley Forge and the Battlefield of the Brandywine. He's the author of
three previous books. They include *A Rockwell
Portrait,* a best-selling biography of his friend,
Norman Rockwell, and *Are You Communicating?*
a business book that has been published in
several languages on four continents.